EAT WELL LIVE WELL

PAMELA M. SMITH, R.D.

CREATION
HOUSE
LAKE MARY, FL 32746

Creation House
Strang Communications Company
600 Rinehart Road
Lake Mary, FL 32746

Unless otherwise noted, all Scripture quotations are taken from
the Holy Bible, New International Version.
Copyright © 1973, 1978, 1984, International Bible Society.
Used by permission.

First printing, February 1992
Second printing, June 1992
Third printing, November 1992
Fourth printing, April 1993
Fifth printing, July 1993
Sixth printing, August 1993
Seventh printing, October 1993

ACKNOWLEDGMENTS

Special thanks to Carolyn Coats, who has opened her heart to me. She has gently encouraged me to grow by demonstrating powerful truths in a loving way and has played a significant role in shaping this book.

Special thanks to Debbie Cole, who through patient love and much work turned her vision for the publishing of this book into a reality.

Special thanks to Shelly Duff and Evelyn Bence for their countless hours in putting order, consistency and excellence into these pages.

Special thanks to Mark, Jerry and Murray for their patience with a very busy lady — and their dedication to getting this book out to impact lives.

And special thanks to Larry for believing in me, encouraging me, loving me — and being who you are, a marvelous husband and a terrific business partner!

CONTENTS

Recipe Sections

TABLES

INTRODUCTION

I started my practice as a registered dietitian working as a nutritionist for a hospital oncology unit — eighteen patients fighting cancer with every means available. My role as nutritionist was to provide them with high-nutrient, high-calorie feedings. The year I spent with these brave people and their families was both challenging and devastating, joyful and heartbreaking. As I worked with them, I refined my personal vision: to work with people *before* they become ill; to help them adopt an eating life-style that will prevent, not treat, disease.

This new vision led me into a private practice working with people seeking wellness, teaching that wellness is more than not being sick; it is a life-style of maintaining good health and preventing disease. Wellness education is for everyone — from a young couple just beginning a family to the senior citizen choosing to feel as good as possible.

For centuries medical care has looked at nutrition as one part of therapy for disease. After a person developed a medical problem, his or her diet was modified to work with other treatments. Was nutrition considered when the person was normal or healthy? Sadly, no. As the person grew less concerned and felt better, the diet ended up in the top drawer, unused. This is not nutrition for wellness!

Years of research tell us what we can eat and how we can exercise to feel better, concentrate better, manage stress better, *live* better! These foundational principles of wellness tell us what we can do today to prevent the diseases of tomorrow. Good health is part of our genetic heritage; healing and repair are scripted into every cell in our bodies. The secret is to live so as to promote rather than hinder that healing and repair

process.

You may not realize how much control you can have over your energy level, health and well-being. You can direct your own health by deliberately choosing to eat foods known to have positive health effects, giving your body the ability to ward off acute and chronic maladies. By meeting your body's natural need for food in an appropriate way, you can take charge of your wellness!

Let me invite you to read through this book and learn how proper balance is fundamental to this kind of well-being. In these pages you'll find vital information about making choices that can help you stay healthier, feel better and live longer. You can learn *what* to eat, *when* to eat and *how much* to eat for peak stamina and performance.

The right perspective will put you on the path to healthy eating. Eating well is not denying yourself. It is giving yourself a precious gift. Instead of focusing on foods to avoid, think about adding wonderful, new foods. You are not "going on a diet"; instead you are choosing a *live-it!*

I have tried to break down a complex subject into simple principles. These principles are expressed in the Ten Commandments of Great Nutrition. They will equip you to plan your own proper balance of nutrients for each meal, according to the foods you like. As you begin to eat the right things at the right time, you'll feel satisfied, not deprived, and you'll be so full of the best foods that you won't desire the ones that drag you down! These principles are not a magic formula to follow. They are simply timeless truths about how your body was designed to work and how you can get it working optimally. *Eat well* to *live well!*

CHAPTER ONE
RIGHT EATING AT THE RIGHT TIME

The typical American eats no breakfast, little or no lunch, and not much of anything till that unmanageable time of day between 3:30 and 5:30 P.M. Then, no matter how much energy they've had or how unhungry they've been, it all falls apart. During this "arsenic hour" the self-control, self-discipline and willpower fade away. The calories start rolling in. Statistics show that for most Americans 80 to 85 percent of a day's calories are consumed in just a few concentrated hours.

Regardless of the calories consumed, the human body is able to use only a small amount of energy, protein and nutrients at one time. The rest is thrown off as waste or stored as fat. Eating in this lopsided way robs your body of vital nutrients for all the preceding and remaining twenty-four hours. We don't go wrong only in how much or in what we eat; the big problem is that we eat too much at the wrong time.

A Better Way

Faced with the challenge of developing a lifestyle of wellness in the junk-food world, many Americans start singing the song "It's Impossible." The challenge, though daunting, is not as complicated as we have come to believe. Much of the information you learned in fifth-grade health class still applies today. But new information provides more specific guidelines to follow. My Ten Commandments of Great Nutrition cut through the controversies of nutrition, providing a foundation for putting all your good intentions to work. These foundational ten commandments, like the original "big ten," promise abundant life. These, however, aim toward *physical* abundance.

Unlike the diet books you may have read in the past, I put more emphasis on *what* you should eat (rather than what to avoid), *when* you should eat and *why* you should be eating it. The goal is education on *how your body can work for you rather than against you.* You will get to know food in a new way. Calories certainly do count, but how and when you eat those calories and where they come from is most important. Remember, you don't need to learn how to diet; you need to learn how to eat!

The first three commandments of great nutrition (see page 10) are vital for understanding and stabilizing your metabolism and well-being. They focus on breakfast, healthy snacking, wisely chosen meals and right balance: eating the right thing at the right time.

COMMANDMENT I
THOU SHALT NEVER SKIP BREAKFAST

Mom was right, though she may not have known why. Breakfast will make you feel better; it helps you start your day with your metabolism in high gear and your appetite in control. Mounting evidence indicates that proper meal timing is vital for optimal functioning of the body.

Think of your body as a campfire that dies down during the night. If it isn't stoked up with wood in the morning the spark turns to ash. There's nothing left. Your body awakens in a slowed-down state. If you don't break the fast with breakfast to meet the body's demand for energy and boost the metabolic system, the body turns to its own muscle mass (not fat!) for energy and slows down even more, conserving itself for a potentially long starved state. Then when the evening gorge begins, most of that food will be stored as fat because the body isn't burning energy at a fast rate; the fire has gone out. The food you eat is like dumping an armload of firewood on a dead fire. Many of us walk around with a lot of dead wood sitting on top of our fires!

While a calorie is indeed a calorie, your metabolism (the chemical process that converts food to energy) can increase or decrease depending on your eating patterns. Breakfast is one of the best ways to increase your metabolism. Don't think for a minute that you are saving calories by skipping breakfast; those calories would be burned by the higher metabolic state that eating breakfast allows. By skipping breakfast you are starving your body of valuable carbohydrates for energy and proteins that build the new you!

I bet you've said this: If I skip breakfast, I don't feel hungry till much later in the day. If I eat breakfast, I feel hungry every few hours. If you've noticed this happening, your body is working properly. When you starve in the morning, waste products are released into your system, temporarily depressing your appetite and allowing you to continue to starve without feeling hungry for many hours. Unfortunately *you are setting yourself up for overeating.* As soon as you begin to eat, your appetite is really turned on. Because you've allowed your blood sugar level to drop so low, your physical body overrides your willpower, prompting you to overeat. You may not realize that your energy, your appetite — even your mood! — are controlled by the level of your blood sugars. Eating breakfast begins your day by stabilizing these blood sugars, which in turn gives you more energy, an in-

THE TEN COMMANDMENTS OF GREAT NUTRITION

    I.   Thou shalt never skip breakfast.

   II.   Thou shalt eat every three to four hours and have your healthy snack handy.

  III.   Thou shalt always eat a carbohydrate with a protein.

  IV.   Thou shalt double your fiber.

    V.   Thou shalt trim the fat from your diet.

  VI.   Thou shalt believe your mother was right: Eat your fruits and vegetables.

 VII.   Thou shalt get your vitamins and minerals from food, not pills.

VIII.   Thou shalt drink at least eight glasses of water a day.

  IX.   Thou shalt consume a minimum of sugar, salt, caffeine and alcohol.

    X.   Thou shalt never, never go on a fad diet!

creased ability to concentrate and an appetite that is in control.

Most people skip breakfast because they don't have — or take — time to fix and eat it. The good news is that breakfast doesn't have to be a time-robber! It can be fixed quickly and eaten on the run if necessary. Try one of the quick and easy breakfasts on pages 85-99. Remember, breakfast is the "stick" that stokes your metabolic fire. You need more than a piece of toast and coffee to give your day a sunny beginning.

Healthy tip: Start your day with a boundless energy level, your metabolism in high gear and proteins actively healing and building new cells. Thou shalt never skip breakfast.

COMMANDMENT II
THOU SHALT EAT EVERY THREE TO FOUR HOURS AND HAVE YOUR HEALTHY SNACK HANDY

Once you've begun your day with breakfast, stabilizing your body first thing in the morning, the goal is to keep the system working for you. To prevent your blood sugar level from dropping and to keep the metabolic rate high, you need food distributed evenly throughout the day. The blood sugar will normally crest and fall every three to four hours. As it begins to fall, so will your energy, along with your mood, your concentration and your ability to handle stress. Going many hours between meals causes the body to slow metabolically. That means the next meal (balanced and healthy or not) will be perceived as an overload, the nutrients will not be used optimally, and the lowered blood sugar will leave you sleepy and craving sweets. Snacking on the right foods is much more fun and healthy!

When you eat frequent, small meals, your body has a chance to metabolize those calories efficiently, burning them for energy instead of storing them as fat. Yes, smaller, more frequent meals result in better weight control (and better cholesterol and triglyceride levels). Several small meals a day deposit less fat than one or two large meals. Remember the campfire comparison. Healthy snacking is like throwing wood on a fire all through the day to keep it burning well.

Your body, created to survive, interprets long hours without food as potential starvation. To prepare for the long haul it slows down dramatically so as not to burn much valuable muscle mass. Contrary to what you may think, in a starvation state when no carbohydrate is available, your body turns first to muscle mass for energy and later to your fat stores. You must

keep your body fed the right thing at the right time for it to metabolize calories efficiently.

We've grown up with a three-square-meals mentality that sees snacking as nutritional enemy number one. Granted, when most people think of snacks, they aren't thinking of healthy snacks but of potato chips, ice cream, candy bars and sodas. This type of snacking can be disastrous, providing high amounts of fat, sugars and salt and little or no nutritional value. It's best to realize right away that high-sugar foods can cause such a swing in your blood sugars that your appetite will increase not only for more sugar but also for more food of any kind. Most high-sugar foods are also high-fat foods. If these foods are a big problem for you, go to pages 39-40 for help in curbing your sweet tooth.

Remember, food through the day keeps a ravenous appetite away! Your blood sugar level controls your physical well-being and appetite. Initially I have most of my patients begin to stabilize their blood sugar by eating every two and a half to three hours. A body that is never too hungry is satisfied quickly with little food. Prevent your own "sinking syndrome" in the late afternoon and early evening by eating frequently throughout the day. If your physiological needs are met by feeding your body properly, *your desires for food will change*. When there is no physical need, you have more control over desire.

I develop my meal-plan strategies to achieve consistent eating throughout the day — three meals and at least one snack. Generally my plans give 25 percent of the day's calories at breakfast, 25 percent at lunch, 25 percent at dinner and the remaining 25 percent as healthy snacks throughout the day. It's important, however, to have those healthy snacks handy! When you don't have good choices available, you're likely to reach for an unhealthy snack or not eat at all, with either alternative setting you up for disaster later on. Many "power snacks" do not require refrigeration. Keep them available in your car, in your desk drawer, in your briefcase — wherever you may find yourself at those critical times.

Healthy tip: You may enjoy healthy snacks, and you can actually put snacking to work for you. Use snacks to keep your blood sugar up and even, giving maximum stamina all day. Begin to think of "power snacking," using snacks to arm you with a high-burning metabolism.

Power Snacks

Here are some suggestions for quick "power

TABLE 1

SIMPLE CARBOHYDRATES: FRUITS AND NONSTARCHY VEGETABLES

• All fruits and fruit juices.

Generally one serving of simple carbohydrate is obtained from 1/2 cup fruit, 1/2 cup fruit juice or 1/8 cup dried fruit.

• Nonstarchy vegetables include: asparagus, beets, broccoli, Brussels sprouts, cabbage, carrots, cauliflower, celery, green beans, green leafies, kale, mushrooms, okra, onions, snow peas, summer squash, tomatoes and zucchini.

Generally one serving of simple carbohydrate is obtained from 1/2 cup cooked vegetable or 1 cup raw vegetable or juice.

snacks." Recipes for additional snacks begin on page 111.

- whole grain crackers and low-fat cheese
- fresh fruit and cheese
- half a lean turkey sandwich
- nonfat plain yogurt blended with fruit or all-fruit jam
- whole grain cereal with skim milk
- black beans with rice
- Wasa bread or rice cakes with light cream cheese and all-fruit jam
- popcorn sprinkled with Parmesan cheese
- oat bran muffin with skim milk
- small pop-top can of water-packed tuna with whole grain crackers
- skim milk blended with frozen fruit and vanilla
- trail mix (recipe on page 111)

COMMANDMENT III
THOU SHALT ALWAYS EAT A CARBOHYDRATE WITH A PROTEIN

Eating evenly throughout the day is not the only important factor in keeping your metabolism burning high and your body working well. Every meal (and snack) should include both carbohydrates and pro-

teins. Understand that carbohydrates are *100 percent pure energy* — fuel for the body to burn. Proteins are the building blocks for the body; but if no carbohydrates are available, the body will burn proteins. A carbohydrate should be eaten with protein to protect it from being wasted as a less efficient fuel source. You need that protein for vital building functions: boosting the metabolism; building body muscle; keeping body fluids in balance; healing and fighting infection; and making beautiful skin, hair and nails. Protein is the new you!

You cannot be healthy without eating protein properly. But, frankly, it is so potent that you don't need much of it. A 6 1/2-ounce can of chicken provides all the protein you need in an entire day. "A little dab will do you" certainly applies to protein! The typical American diet provides two to three times the daily amount recommended. But because many of us don't eat evenly throughout the day, we do not use it effectively.

The body does not store protein, so it must be replenished frequently throughout the day, every day of your life. Without it, your body isn't building itself up. And without carbohydrates your body is burning protein as fuel. Never believe anybody who tells you not to eat carbohydrates, not to eat protein or not to eat them together. You'll be robbing your body of carbohydrate's energy and protein's building power all day long.

Remember, *carbohydrates burn, and proteins build!*

What's What?

The easiest way to categorize what's what is to consider its source. Anything that comes from a plant is carbohydrate. Anything that comes from an animal is protein. An exception to this is the *legume* family. Legumes (dried beans and peanuts), although a plant food, are grown in the ground in such a way that they absorb nitrogen from the soil, becoming excellent sources of high-fiber, low-fat protein.

A Closer Look at Carbohydrates

Remember that plants provide energy-giving carbohydrates — stored up energy from the sun. Simple carbohydrates (fruits and nonstarchy vegetables — see Table 1) contain a wealth of fiber, vitamins and minerals and are digested and released into the system as energy much more quickly than the complex type.

Complex carbohydrates (found primarily in grains and starchy vegetables — see Table 2) require a longer time to be digested and taken into the system as energy. In their unrefined form these foods are a source of much-needed fiber; they contain high quantities of vital nutrients for our well-being. An eating plan high in fiber and complex carbohydrates is your best bet for living long and well.

Contrary to what you've heard, carbohydrates are low in calories. One ounce of carbohydrate contains half the calories of one ounce of fat. It's not the potato or bread that makes us unhealthy or causes weight gain. It's the heavy sauce or the butter we spread on top. Don't throw out the pastas or potatoes. Your body needs them and will even thrive with them!

A Closer Look at Proteins

Remember that animal foods supply us with complete proteins. A complete protein is one that supplies all the essential amino acids (those the body can't make and doesn't store). Legumes, although a plant food and incomplete in essential amino acids, can be an excellent protein source if combined properly with a grain or a seed.

Unfortunately most of the popular protein foods are high in fat. And, as much as we need carbohydrates to burn and protein to build, it's fat that makes us fat! Fat also sets us up for a myriad of killer diseases. By choosing low-fat versions of protein foods, you will get all of protein's building power without the risks of fat.

TABLE 2

COMPLEX CARBOHYDRATES: GRAINS AND STARCHY VEGETABLES

Grains

The following amounts provide one serving of complex carbohydrate:

barley	1/2 cup cooked
bread	1 slice
bulgur	1/2 cup cooked
cereals	1 ounce (usually 1/4 cup of a concentrated cereal such as grape-nuts or granola, 1/2 to 3/4 cup of flaked cereals and 1 cup of puffed cereals)
crackers	5
crispbread	2
grits	1/2 cup cooked
kasha	1/2 cup cooked
millet	1/2 cup cooked
oats	1/3 cup uncooked
pasta	1/2 cup cooked
rice (brown and wild)	1/2 cup cooked
wheat germ	1/4 cup

Starchy Vegetables

black-eyed peas, corn, green peas, lima beans, parsnips, potatoes (white and sweet), rutabaga, turnips and winter squash

Generally one serving of complex carbohydrate is obtained from 1/2 cup cooked starchy vegetable.

TABLE 3

IDEAL PROTEIN SOURCES

Serving to equal 1 ounce of protein

- nonfat milk or nonfat plain yogurt .... 4 ounces
- low-fat cheeses (less than 5 grams of fat per ounce) .... 1 ounce
    farmer's, Laughing Cow reduced calorie wedges, light
    cream cheese, part-skim mozzarella, string cheese,
    Jarlsberg Lite, Weight Watchers, Kraft Light Naturals
- 1 percent low-fat or nonfat cottage cheese or part-skim ricotta ..... 1/4 cup
- eggs (particularly use the egg whites) 1
- fish .... 1 ounce or 1/4 cup flaked
- seafood (crab, lobster) .... 1/4 cup
- seafood (clams, shrimp, oysters, scallops) 5
- turkey, Cornish hens .... 1 ounce or 1/4 cup chopped
- chicken .... 1 ounce or 1/4 cup chopped (generally,
    1 leg cooked = 1 ounce protein, 1 thigh
    cooked = 1-1/2 ounces protein, 1 split
    breast cooked = 2 ounces protein)
- beef, pork, lamb, veal (lean, trimmed) .... 1 ounce
- legumes: black beans, garbanzo beans, Great Northern beans,
    kidney beans, lentils, natural peanut butter, navy beans,
    peanuts, red beans, split peas, soybeans and soy products such
    as tofu and soy milk. Note: Although a plant food, legumes
    contain valuable protein if eaten with a grain (corn, wheat,
    rice, oats) or a seed (pumpkin, sunflower, sesame) .... 1/4 cup cooked beans or 2 tablespoons
    peanut butter gives approximately one
    ounce of protein

To give your body the best proteins, shift the major source of it from meat and dairy foods to fish, soy products and the other legumes, which are low in calories and fat. (See Table 3 for protein source suggestions.)

Review the power snacks listed on page 12. Note that each is a carbohydrate-protein combination. When you eat one, eat the other.

The first three commandments call for right eating at the right time to achieve a nutritional balance: a breakfast that supplies adequate carbohydrate and protein; and meals evenly spaced every three hours or so throughout the day, not allowing long time periods without food — both carbohydrate and protein. Remember, carbohydrates burn, and proteins build!

CHAPTER TWO

FIBER AND FAT: MORE OF THE BEST, LESS OF THE REST

he next four commandments focus on eating the foods and nutrients that allow our bodies to work optimally and trimming away the foods that rob our health. The goal here is to *have more of the best and less of the rest!*

COMMANDMENT IV
THOU SHALT DOUBLE YOUR FIBER

Grandma used to say, "Eat your roughage." Now, years later, the surgeon general says, "Double your fiber." This can be done rather easily, not with fiber pills but with wholesome foods prepared in a wholesome way! Whole grain breads and cereals, unprocessed oat and wheat bran, legumes, fresh fruits and vegetables are wonderful foods loaded with fiber.

The part of plants not digested by the body is fiber. There are two types of fiber: *soluble* and *insoluble*. The soluble fibers, found in the gum and pectin of oats, barley, brown rice, legumes and some fruits, have been found to lower cholesterol levels and help control blood sugar levels. The water-insoluble fibers, found in whole wheat and grains (wheat bran is a concentrated source) and fresh fruits and vegetables, are vital for controlling bowel problems like constipation, diarrhea, hemorrhoids and diverticulosis. Though fiber seems unspeakably dull, there are numerous benefits from eating it.

A sufficient intake of fiber is linked to the prevention of our killer diseases: heart disease, obesity, cancer and diabetes. The time has surely come to return to the high-fiber diet humans have thrived on for thousands of years. But this is difficult, because so many supermarket foods have been refined, stripped of their fibers and most of their nutrients.

Refinement and Enrichment:
A Robbery That's Legal

Consider this story: A man walking down the street was approached by a robber who forced the man at gunpoint to turn over his valuables, including all he was wearing. After the man stripped, the thief said, "I have just refined you!" Then he returned only four items: the man's watch, one shoe, his undershirt and necktie. The thief proclaimed, "I have just enriched you!"

Returning four nutrients and leaving out twenty-one is what this enrichment caper is all about. When a whole wheat berry is refined, every nutrient is affected (twenty-one are completely lost), and all of its protective fiber is stripped away. In the enrichment process only four are added back. Don't be fooled by advertisements! White, refined carbohydrate, even though it's enriched, is never nutritionally as good as whole grain.

Whole grains make a big difference in maintaining appetite control and energy level. This is because the fiber acts like a time-release capsule, slowly and evenly releasing food sugars into your system. By preventing a rapid rise and dramatic downfall of the blood sugar level, by providing more bulk and staying in the stomach longer, whole grain foods will keep you full and satisfied longer than refined grains.

Population groups with high-fiber intakes have a low incidence of many types of cancers, particularly colon cancer. Thirty-two out of forty epidemiological studies worldwide show that eating high fiber foods, particularly wheat fiber, is linked to lower rates of human colon cancer. This may be due to the dilution effect of fiber; it pulls so much fluid toward it and produces such a bulky mass that cancer-causing agents in foods have less impact on the bowel wall. Such a high-fiber mass then exits the body more quickly, decreasing the amount of time the carcinogen stays in the body.

It is important to choose whole grain foods at home to fill the void of what is missing in restaurants.

How to Double Your Fiber

Shop and eat using the following guidelines:
• Use whole grains rather than the white, refined types. When purchasing, look for labels such as 100 percent whole wheat, with the word *whole* first in the ingredient list. Many manufacturers call products whole grain even if they contain minimal amounts of bran. Brown dye and caramel coloring do wonders in making foods *look* healthy!
• Eat vegetables and fruits with well-washed skins. Peel only those that have been waxed.
• Choose more raw or lightly cooked vegetables in as nonprocessed a form as possible. As food is processed, ground, mashed, puréed or juiced, its fiber effectiveness decreases. This is why fiber pills are ineffective; the concentrated fiber doesn't work nearly as well as the food itself.
• Add a variety of legumes to your diet.
• Add unprocessed bran to your foods. (See Table 4 on page 18.) How much bran do you add? The ideal is 3 tablespoons each day. Try eating it as a hot cereal, sprinkling it uncooked on your dry cereal or making homemade bran muffins. (Store-bought muffins have more hydrogenated oils, sugar and eggs than you

TABLE 4

UNPROCESSED BRAN

Wheat Bran	Oat Bran
• maintains a healthy, regular GI tract	• reduces blood cholesterol
• prevents diverticulosis and hemorrhoids	• stabilizes blood sugars
• is linked to lower rates of colon cancer	• is linked to cancer prevention
• relieves constipation	• may lower blood pressure

need.) Be careful to add bran to your diet gradually; begin with 1 teaspoon and gradually increase as your body adjusts to more fiber. Too much too quickly can result in a stomach ache or diarrhea. Wheat and oat bran can be found in the cereal section of your grocery store.

For a list of high-fiber foods, see Table 5.

COMMANDMENT V
THOU SHALT TRIM THE FAT FROM YOUR DIET

Fat is a nutrient that the body needs in very limited amounts for lubrication and for transporting fat-soluble vitamins (A, D, E and K). But it is also a very concentrated way of getting calories and disease! Never think that thinness gives you the freedom to eat excess fat. Look at these vital facts about fat:

• Excess fat intake increases your cholesterol level and your risk of heart disease and stroke.

• Excess fat intake increases your risk of cancer, particularly of the colon and breast.

• Excess fat intake increases your risk of gall bladder disease.

• Excess fat, particularly saturated fat, has been shown to elevate blood pressure, regardless of your weight.

• Excess fat fed to animals with a genetic susceptibility to diabetes has made them far more likely to develop the disease. People with a family history of diabetes can cut down the percentage of fat in their diets as one step toward prevention of this disease.

• Excess fat makes you fat!

As much as we need to eat carbohydrates and proteins at each meal, we *don't* need fat in the quantities we consume. Yes, carbohydrates burn and proteins build, but *it's fat that makes us fat!* One ounce of fat

supplies twice the number of calories as one ounce of carbohydrate or protein, and research shows that fats in food are stored as fat on the body much more readily than are carbohydrates or proteins. On the average, too much of our calorie intake is from fat — 40 to 45 percent rather than the recommended 20 to 25 percent. A typical adult eats the fat equivalent of one stick of butter a day! Even if you don't eat that much fat, chances are you are eating a lot more than you realize. Less fat in your diet means less fat on your body and less cholesterol in your blood.

Cholesterol: The Good, the Bad and the Very Confusing

Cholesterol is a fatty, wax-like substance present in all animal cells and all animal products. (No plant food contains cholesterol.) Cholesterol is necessary for hormone production, for digestion and to form cell membranes. But since the body makes all the cholesterol it needs, it isn't an essential nutrient. To stay healthy you don't need to consume any cholesterol. And too much cholesterol can build up in the bloodstream and deposit in the walls of blood vessels, especially in the heart. This condition, called atherosclerosis, limits blood flow and favors the formation of blood clots. When blood flow is cut off in the coronary arteries, it can lead to a heart attack; in the cerebral arteries, a stroke. For each 1 percent rise in bloodstream cholesterol, there may be as much as a 3 percent increase in coronary risk.

The liver produces cholesterol in three forms: HDL (high-density lipoproteins), LDL (low-density lipoproteins) and VLDL (very low density lipoproteins). HDL cholesterol is believed to protect the body from heart disease in two ways: (1) by dissolving fatty deposits from the blood-vessel walls and (2) by coating the inside of the walls to prevent the fatty deposits from initially building up. LDL cholesterol is the primary culprit in increasing the risk of heart disease. It is the very substance that builds up as plaque in the arteries.

Those with a genetic tendency toward atherosclerosis have liver cells that produce especially high levels of LDL cholesterol and liver cells with few or poorly formed receptors for "sucking" the bad LDL cholesterol out of the blood.

In addition, the average American consumes 400 to 500 milligrams of dietary cholesterol in food daily. Liver, eggs, beef and crab are foods especially high. Crustaceous seafood, such as crab, shrimp and lobster, is also high in cholesterol but is very low in fat

TABLE 5

HIGH-FIBER FOODS

Whole Grains
barley
brown rice
oats
whole grain cereals
whole wheat bread
whole wheat pasta

Fruits
apples
apricots, dried
bananas
citrus fruits
grapes
peaches
pears
pineapples
plums
prunes
raisins

Vegetables
broccoli
carrots
corn
peas
potatoes with skins
romaine lettuce
spinach

Legumes and Seeds
dried beans
peanuts
sunflower and pumpkin seeds

Before we discuss the merits and demerits of specific foods, let me give you one more definition and explanation that might help you understand another *why* behind several of these Ten Commandments of Great Nutrition.

One type of fat called a triglyceride transports nutrients through the bloodstream. A percentage of your triglycerides (20 percent) convert to the very undesirable VLDL cholesterol. High blood levels of triglycerides and this corresponding VLDL cholesterol cause a lower production of the desired HDL cholesterol, stripping the body of its protection. Triglycerides are elevated by excess sugar, refined carbohydrates and/or excessive alcohol intake. Most commonly they elevate as a result of *nutrient overload* — taking in most of a day's calories in one concentrated time.

The most effective method of reducing high triglyceride levels is to eat smaller amounts of whole grain complex carbohydrates and low-fat proteins more evenly distributed throughout the day — in short, following the Ten Commandments of Great Nutrition!

All About Oil

We eat four kinds of oil: saturated, polyunsaturated, monounsaturated and omega-3 fatty acids. Each has the same fat content and number of calories: 5 grams of fat and 45 calories per teaspoon. But these oils vary in the effects they have on our bodies.

Saturated Oils

Saturated oils increase bad LDL cholesterol and the risk of disease.

Visible sources: bacon, butter, coconut oil, palm oil
Hidden sources: marbling in meats, cream, cream cheese, dairy fats, salt pork, poultry skin, sausage, fried foods, cold cuts, hot dogs, coconut, nondairy creamers and toppings

Another hidden source of saturated fat is hydrogenated oils. In a manufacturing process called hydrogenation (used to make creamy products such as commercial peanut butter, nondairy toppings and margarine) a polyunsaturated or monounsaturated oil is converted into a saturated oil. When buying a product, be sure that hydrogenated oil is not listed as one of the first three ingredients, as it is heart-unhealthy.

Polyunsaturated Oils

Polyunsaturated oils decrease bad LDL *and* good

and is a good source of healthy EPA oils. The goal is not to take in any cholesterol-laden food with saturated fat; the cholesterol found in food is not the main problem in building up cholesterol in the body. Even with a low cholesterol diet, your body can convert saturated fats to LDL cholesterol. So if you desire to control your blood cholesterol, you must limit not only the amount of cholesterol you eat, but also your intake of saturated fat, which stimulates the body's production of cholesterol. Actually, saturated fat will raise your blood cholesterol level four times more quickly than dietary cholesterol itself.

HDL cholesterol.

Visible sources: safflower oil, sunflower oil, sesame oil, cottonseed oil, corn oil

Hidden sources: avocado, sunflower kernels, sesame seeds, almonds, walnuts, pecans

Monounsaturated Oils

Monounsaturated oils increase good HDL cholesterol and decrease bad LDL cholesterol and risk of disease.

Visible sources: olive oil, peanut oil, canola oil

Hidden sources: peanuts, natural peanut butter, olives

Omega-3 Fatty Acids (EPA and DHA)

Omega-3 fatty acids decrease total and bad LDL cholesterol, increase good HDL cholesterol, reduce tendency of blood to form clots and decrease triglycerides.

Sources: all fish and seafood, especially cold-water fish (salmon, albacore tuna, swordfish, sardines, mackerel, hard shellfish)

Eating Patterns and Life-Styles That Affect Cholesterol Levels

• Eat high-fiber foods, such as oat bran, barley, brown rice and legumes, as well as fruits high in pectin, such as strawberries and bananas. These slow the absorption of cholesterol into the bloodstream. The more evenly spaced your meals, the more exposure the fiber has to the cholesterol produced by your own liver — another reason why healthy snacking is important!

• Eat very little fat, and consume it in the form of monounsaturated (olive and canola) oils. Avoid saturated animal fats as well as highly saturated coconut and palm oils.

• Eat more fish, less poultry and meat. Fish contains wonderfully healthy oils that lower total cholesterol while increasing your level of the good HDL cholesterol. They reduce the tendency of the blood to clot and protect the arteries from damage. It appears from research that it is the fish itself that carries the most complete protection, not the oil in capsule form. Dutch investigators, headed by Daan Kromhout, Ph.D., at the University of Leiden, The Netherlands, identified fish's protective oils; they suggest that the oils may interact with other substances in fish, making the fish itself the therapeutic champion rather than the oil alone.

• Eat onions and garlic, as they appear to raise good

HDL cholesterol levels dramatically. Research done by Dr. Victor Gurewich, a professor of medicine at Tufts University, has found that half a raw onion a day can raise HDLs an average of thirty percent in about three out of four of his heart disease patients over a two month time period. Research by Indian Arun K. Bordia and separately by Dr. Benjamin Lau at California's Loma Linda University has shown large intakes of garlic to lower cholesterol, particularly the LDL form, and reduce the tendency of the blood to clot. So, if your breath and social life allow, eating at least half a medium raw onion a day and garlic whenever possible will have a beneficial effect on cholesterol levels.

• Lose excess body fat. This lowers your blood cholesterol.

• Be consistent with aerobic exercise. The best results in lowering bad LDL cholesterol and raising good HDL cholesterol are seen when you do an hour of aerobic exercise every other day.

• If you smoke, stop. Each cigarette smoked raises your cholesterol.

How Fat Is Your Diet?

Now that you know what fat is and how it is processed in the body, let's see where it's found in your diet. The first line of defense in fighting fat is identifying your enemies. The main sources of dietary fat are meat, poultry, dairy products and nut foods, along with butter and oil toppings. Fruits, vegetables and grains have little, if any, fat. Eat them guilt-free. Just be sure not to fatten up these beauties with butters and sauces! See Tables 6 through 9 on pages 21 and 22 for the fat ratings on dairy foods, protein sources, sauces, toppings and soups.

Reducing your fat intake requires commitment and effort — to learn new ways of cooking, to order more healthfully at restaurants, to remind yourself to go light on the fats added to your foods. Be assured that the benefits far exceed the effort! If motivation to cut back on the fat in your diet comes hard, consider this mental picture: Imagine white hamburger grease after it cools and hardens. Then imagine that grease trying to circulate through your bloodstream!

Small Steps That Make a Big Fat Difference (A Guide to Lighten Your Diet)

• Use skim milk, nonfat plain yogurt, skim-milk cheese, low-fat cottage cheese and "light" cream cheese instead of any higher-fat dairy product.

• Eat more fish and white meats and fewer red

TABLE 6

RATING THE FATS:
DAIRY FOODS

High Fat (8 or more grams of fat per serving)	Medium Fat (4 to 7 grams of fat per serving)	Low-fat (3 or fewer grams of fat per serving)
cheese: American blue Brie Camembert cheddar brick Swiss cream: whipping half-and-half commercial sour whole milk whole milk yogurt	cheese: farmer's feta mozzarella Light Philadelphia part-skim cheddar part-skim ricotta string cheese creamed cottage cheese 2 percent milk	cheese: low-fat cottage cheese Laughing Cow nonfat cheese nonfat ricotta 1 percent or skim milk nonfat plain yogurt

TABLE 7

RATING THE FATS:
MEATS, FISH, POULTRY AND LEGUMES

High Fat (8 or more grams of fat per ounce)	Medium Fat (4 to 7 grams of fat per ounce)	Low-fat (3 or fewer grams of fat per ounce)
bacon commercial peanut butter corned beef duck frankfurters goose ground meat lunch meats pepperoni sausage spareribs tuna, packed in oil	beef (rib roast, steak) eggs ham lamb chops pork chops liver veal cutlet	chicken clams crab fish lean beef (flank, round) legumes oysters scallops shrimp tuna, packed in water

TABLE 8

RATING THE FATS: SAUCES AND TOPPINGS

High Fat (8 or more grams of fat per serving)	Medium Fat (4 to 7 grams of fat per serving)	Low-fat (3 or fewer grams of fat per serving)
avocado butter coconut mayonnaise margarine olives oils shortening nuts: almonds pecans cashews walnuts	salad dressings nuts: Brazil peanuts	light sour cream light mayonnaise no-oil salad dressings

TABLE 9

RATING THE FATS: SOUPS

High Fat (8 or more grams of fat per serving)	Medium Fat (4 to 7 grams of fat per serving)	Low-fat (3 or fewer grams of fat per serving)
all creamed soups all chunky soups pea with ham	beef noodle black bean chicken noodle chicken vegetable	low-sodium chicken bouillon lentil vegetable vegetable bean gazpacho onion

Note: In commercial soups, even low-fat ones, notice the sodium content, as it is probably high.

TABLE 10

FACTS ABOUT FAT

Less than 25 percent of a day's calories should come from fat.

1 gram of fat = 9 calories (5 grams of fat = 1 teaspoon of fat)
1 gram of carbohydrate or protein = 4 calories

(It's fat that makes you fat!)

Most women should take in 20 to 30 grams of fat per day. Most men should take in 30 to 40 grams of fat per day.

Calculating Fat Percentages

fat grams x 9 = calories from fat
Calories from fat divided by total calories = percent of calories from fat

Example: A product containing 5 grams of fat per serving contains 45 calories from fat
(5 grams x 9 calories per gram). If there were 90 calories per serving of the product,
50 percent of its calories would come from fat (45 calories divided by 90 calories = 50 percent).

---

meats. If you eat red meats, buy lean and trim well, before and after cooking — and cook in a way that diminishes fat, such as grilling or broiling on a rack.

• Remove skin from poultry before cooking; you will cut the fat by 50 percent!

• Use nonstick cooking sprays and skillets that enable you to brown meats without grease. Sauté ingredients in stocks and broths rather than fats and oils.

• Adapt a recipe that says to baste with butter by basting with tomato or lemon juice or stock.

• Use monounsaturated oils such as canola or olive oil for salads or cooking. You can cut the amount called for in a recipe by two-thirds without sacrificing quality. For example, a recipe calling for 3 tablespoons of oil may be cut to 1 tablespoon and, depending on the recipe, may be cut out altogether if nonstick cooking spray is used. Ideally no more than 1 teaspoon of oil per serving should be used.

• Substitute nonfat plain yogurt or blended-till-smooth low-fat cottage cheese or part-skim ricotta in recipes calling for sour cream or mayonnaise. These products also make a great topping for baked potatoes, especially sprinkled with chives or grated Parmesan!

• Purchase tuna packed in water rather than oil.

• Use avocados and olives sparingly. Although vegetables, they are concentrated sources of fat. For example, five olives contain 50 calories of fat, and half of an avocado gives you 180 calories of fat.

• Use legumes (dried beans and peas) as a main dish or a meat substitute for a high-nutrition, low-fat meal.

• Use egg whites in place of whole eggs (2 egg whites = 1 egg). Egg whites are pure protein, and egg yolks are pure fat and cholesterol.

• Skim the fat from soup stocks, meat drippings and sauces. Refrigerate and remove the hardened surface layer of fat before reheating.

• Rarely, if ever, eat organ meats such as liver, sweetbreads and brains. They are loaded with cholesterol.

• Use only natural peanut butter and even this in small amounts. Avoid commercial peanut butter at all costs. Commercial peanut butter is not much more than shortening and sugar. Fresh-ground natural peanut butter still contains fat, but it is a good source of protein. If you have trouble switching from the commercial type, begin by mixing it half and half with natural. Gradually increase the proportion of the natural until you have abandoned the commercial.

• Order fats "to the side" in restaurant meals, and choose to apply them in small quantities. The typical restaurant meal contains the fat equivalent of 12 to 14 pats of butter — in the sauces, dressings, toppings and spreads.

• Use small amounts of added fats. If you use margarine, the soft, squeeze-type corn oil is best, then tub margarine, then stick. The firmer the margarine, the more saturated it is because of the hydrogenation process.

See Table 10 for facts about fat.

CHAPTER THREE
FRUITS AND VEGETABLES: A DYNAMIC DUO

COMMANDMENT VI
THOU SHALT BELIEVE YOUR MOTHER WAS RIGHT: EAT YOUR FRUITS AND VEGETABLES

Vegetables and fruits are simple carbohydrates that provide a storehouse of vitamins, minerals and other substances that are protectors against disease. They are also valuable, no-fat, no-cholesterol sources of fiber and fluid. The fiber serves as a time-release capsule, slowly and evenly releasing the carbohydrate energy into the bloodstream. All in all, they are satisfying munchies that make up an enormously healthy part of the healthy diet.

Color Power

You may not be able to tell a book by its cover, but you can sure choose a fruit or vegetable by its color! Generally the more vivid the coloring, the more essential nutrients it holds. That deep orange or red coloring in carrots, sweet potatoes, cantaloupes, apricots, peaches and strawberries signals their vitamin A content. Dark green leafy vegetables such as greens, spinach, romaine lettuce, brussels sprouts and broccoli are loaded with vitamin A as well as folic acid. Vitamin C is found in more than just citrus; it is also power-packed into strawberries, cantaloupes, tomatoes, green peppers and broccoli. If they're loaded with color, they're loaded with nutrition!

Vegetables and Fruits: Great Cancer Fighters

Research is providing a very persuasive message: People who eat more vegetables and fruits are less apt to develop cancer. There are several factors involved. Some food compounds, serving as antioxidants, suppress cancer promoters, preventing the spread of cancer. Then many vegetables and fruits contain substances that appear to halt cancer at its cellular conception.

The cruciferous family. The very substance that makes broccoli, broccoli or cauliflower, cauliflower has been found to have cancer-preventative properties, counteracting destruction coming from cancer-causing chemicals. These compounds, called indoles, are found in all vegetables in the cruciferous family, so named because all have flowers with four petals resembling a crucifix or cross, alluding to their protective power over death and disease.

Lee Wattenberg, M.D., a professor of pathology at the University of Minnesota Medical School, has been doing anti-cancer research since the 1960s. In meticulous experiments, complex metabolic processes are being identified that identify the wondrous ways food substances can fight cancer at the cellular stage. His chemical studies have been enhanced in human research by Saxon Graham at the State University of New York at Buffalo and in six out of seven major epidemiological studies done before 1987, finding that people who eat more cruciferous vegetables have less chance of cancer, particularly colon cancer.

You should eat one of the vegetables from Table 11 on page 26 cooked or raw every day. You'll even get an extra bonus in their vitamin C content. Studies show that vitamin C blocks the action of certain chemicals leading to cancer and heart disease.

Beta-carotene. One of the substances responsible for the vivid coloring in fruits and vegetables appears to be a powerful cancer fighter, blocking the process by which a normal cell turns malignant and cancerous. See Table 12 on page 26 for a list of champion cancer-fighting foods.

Particularly promising research shows carotene's protection against lung cancer, even among those who have smoked cigarettes for many years. Beginning in 1957, noted epidemiologist Richard Shekelle, Ph.D., now at the University of Texas, tracked two thousand men — how much they ate of 195 specific foods and who got lung cancer. Shekelle and his research team found that men eating the least carotene-containing foods were seven times more likely to get lung cancer than men with the diet richest in carotene. The grim connection between a low beta-carotene in the blood and the appearance of lung cancer was confirmed with findings from a dramatic 1987 study by Marilyn Menkes, Ph.D., of the Johns Hopkins University School of Hygiene and Public Health. This wonder substance is found in fruits and vegetables with a deep yellow-orange and even a dark green color (green chlorophyll covers up the orange or red hue). In the digestive system the body converts this pigment to vitamin A, though never in toxic amounts. Beta-carotene is also an antioxidant, giving it an even stronger protective quality.

It may not be only the carotene that makes these power vegetables and fruits such champion cancer fighters. They contain hundreds of other carotenoids, which is why the whole carrot, the whole broccoli floret and the whole spinach leaf are our protection, not just an isolated chemical.

Although scientists are making efforts to pinpoint the beneficial aspects of vegetables and fruits right down to their most minuscule components, the most practical advice about eating them hasn't changed:

TABLE 11

THE ANTI-CANCER CRUCIFEROUS VEGETABLES

broccoli
Brussels sprouts
cabbage
cauliflower
cress
horseradish
kale
kohlrabi
mustard greens
radish
rutabaga
turnip

Eat a wide variety of fruits and vegetables daily (at least five servings a day). Depend on fresh fruit and vegetables, rather than supplements, to meet your recommended daily allowance for vitamins and minerals. Why? Despite all the laboratory wizardry, science cannot begin to uncover all of the disease-fighting substances created for us in food. The only way to benefit from these is to eat the foods themselves.

Choose Variety

Eat at least one vitamin A-rich (dark green, orange) selection a day.

Eat at least one vitamin C-rich (citrus, broccoli, green pepper) selection with meals each day.

Eat at least two high-fiber selections each day (prunes, legumes).

Eat a cruciferous vegetable every day.

Tips for Buying Well, Cooking Well

One of the top-rated food concerns of today's consumers is the safety of our foods. We want assurances that the food we buy is pure and safe to eat. Unfortunately, with little regulation over organically grown foods and minimal consistency in state standards, those assurances are hard to get. With the lack of legislation, smart shopping techniques are your best bet to reduce risks and bring home the best for you and your family. Of course, bringing nutritious foods home from the market is just the start. The way you store and cook them matters too. Cooking affects not only the taste and appearance of the food, but also the nutritional value. Consider these tips:

Buy locally grown foods. Local producers may be less likely to use pesticides than producers who must ship their foods long distances.

Buy in-season fruits and vegetables. Out-of-season produce is often imported and may be only spot-checked for pesticide residues.

Buy vegetables as fresh as possible. When not possible, frozen is the best choice. (Avoid those frozen with butter or sauces.) Ask your grocer or farmer's market about freshest buying days and where the vegetables are grown.

Use well-washed peelings and outer leaves of vegetables whenever possible. That's where the highest concentration of nutrients is found. Thoroughly rinse and scrub vegetables in water. Peel your vegetables and fruits if appropriate, particularly if the food is waxed.

Store vegetables in airtight containers in the refrigerator. The most destructive force against many of the vitamins is exposure to air.

Do not store vegetables in water. Too many vitamins are lost.

Steam, microwave, stir-fry or pressure-cook your vegetables. Follow three rules for cooking a vegetable to retain its nutritive value: (1) Cook in little to no water. (2) Cook with very high heat. (3) Cook

TABLE 12

CHAMPION CANCER FIGHTERS

apricots
broccoli
cabbage, green
carrots
garlic, onions and scallions
grapes
kale
oranges and lemons
romaine lettuce
soybeans and soy products
spinach
sweet potatoes
strawberries
tomatoes
winter squash and pumpkin

quickly, *only* till crisp tender. Be sure to try the recipes beginning on page 186.

Let Fruit Satisfy Your Sweet Tooth

We are born with a natural sweet preference. Let fruit satisfy this inborn craving! It provides the sweetness in a form the body can handle easily and completely. It's even pleasing to the eye as well as to the palate; a hollowed melon or pineapple overflowing with fresh fruit is difficult to beat in taste or appearance. Fresh fruits are also an excellent source of fiber for digestion and carbohydrate for energy. Cantaloupes and watermelon are among the most nutritious and least caloric fruits. Oranges, grapefruits, honeydews, strawberries and pineapple are all high in vitamin C, a vitamin that helps maintain strong, healthy tissue, fight infection and heal cuts. Bright orange fruits such as cantaloupe and apricots are wonderful sources of potassium and beta-carotene, that powerful chemo-protector. And apples, prunes and plums are some of the best sources of fiber.

To get the most nutrition from fruit and to get the full benefit of its fiber, choose the fruit itself, rather than the fruit juice. The fiber in fruit serves as a "time-release capsule," slowly and evenly releasing the fruit's sugar into your bloodstream. Fruit juice has had all of this beneficial fiber removed, so the fruit sugar is absorbed instantly, causing a rapid rise and then a dramatic drop of the blood sugar level. In addition, much of the vitamin and mineral content is lost in the juicing process and the storage time that often follows. Fruit, however, is created with perfect protective packaging; enjoy it! (See Table 13 on pages 28-29 for a guide to sweet and wonderful fruit.)

Refrigerate fruit as soon as it is ripe and eat it as soon as possible. Remember, an apple (or a peach or an apricot or strawberries...) a day does help to keep the doctor away!

Dried Fruits

Dried fruits are wonderful little packages of sweetness *and* calories! When fruits are dried, they become very concentrated sources of nutrients. (Only vitamin C is lost when fruits are dried.) Calories aren't lost, however, so it's very easy to overdo dried fruits. As easy as it is to eat eight prunes, it's hard to imagine you are really eating eight plums! So use them with wisdom and moderation. See Table 14 on page 29 for dried fruit serving equivalents.

TABLE 13
A Guide to Sweet and Wonderful Fruit

Fruit	Description	Serving Equivalent
Apples	Should be firm and crisp without a watery, soft give. *Excellent for eating:* Red and Golden Delicious, Granny Smith, McIntosh, Jonathan, Winesap *Excellent for cooking:* Golden Delicious, Rome Beauty, Cortland, Granny Smith, McIntosh (never Red Delicious as they are too dry) *Hint:* Drizzling cut apples with lemon juice will prevent browning.	1 small apple = 1 simple carbohydrate
Apricots	Should be fat and golden. Easiest to find in dried form. Very high in potassium and vitamin A.	2 fresh or 4 dried halves = 1 simple carbohydrate
Avocados	Use sparingly as avocados are a source of fat. Are ripe when soft to the touch.	1/8 whole or 2 tablespoons mashed avocado = 1 serving of added fat
Bananas	Are considered ripe when covered with brown specks. Once ripe, refrigeration will keep them in excellent eating condition for another three to five days. (Skin may brown completely.) Bananas are very high in potassium. They are best for use as a sweetener when very brown and ripe. *Hint:* If using in fruit salad, top the salad with sliced bananas just before serving and sprinkle with lemon juice to prevent browning.	1/2 large or 1 small (6-inch) banana = 1 simple carbohydrate
Berries	Sweet packages of nutritional power! Berries should be firm when purchased; avoid stained containers.	1/2 cup = 1 simple carbohydrate
Cantaloupe	Very high in vitamins A and C, also potassium. Its color should be dull, creamy yellow when purchased, and the blossom end should be slightly soft when ripe. Look for pronounced lacy netting.	1/4 cantaloupe or 3/4 cup cubed = 1 simple carbohydrate
Coconut	Use sparingly as it is a source of fat. Most natural-food stores have unsweetened flaked coconut. For fresher flavor, soak in small amount of milk before cooking.	2 tablespoons unsweetened flaked coconut = 1 serving of added fat
Figs	Should be ripe (soft when squeezed) and plump; should smell sweet, not sour. Refrigerate.	1 whole medium-sized fig = 1 simple carbohydrate
Grapefruit and oranges	Should be round, heavy for their size and thin-skinned.	1/2 grapefruit = 1 simple carbohydrate 1 medium orange = 1 simple carbohydrate 1/2 cup sections = 1 simple carbohydrate
Grapes	Do not ripen off the vine. You must choose a ripe bunch. The point where the grape attaches to stem should be strong and fresh, and grapes should have a full color.	12 grapes = 1 simple carbohydrate

Fruit	Description	Serving Equivalent
Honeydew	Should have a soft blossom end; skin should be slightly sticky.	1/8 honeydew = 1 simple carbohydrate
Kiwi	Should "give" slightly to the touch.	1 kiwi = 1 simple carbohydrate
Mangoes	Should yield slightly to touch but should not be soft.	1/3 of whole or 1/3 cup diced = 1 simple carbohydrate
Nectarines, peaches and pears	Are ripe when slightly soft at stem end and not greenish but yellowish. Peaches and nectarines should have a pink blush as well. To help with the ripening, place nectarines, peaches, pears and plums in a brown paper bag with a banana. As the banana ripens, it releases a natural gas that ripens the fruit as if it were still on the tree.	1 medium fruit = 1 simple carbohydrate
Papaya	Choose those mostly yellow, that yield slightly to pressure and have a pleasant aroma.	3/4 cup fruit = 1 simple carbohydrate
Pineapple	Is ripe when it has deep-green leaves at the crown, heaviness for its size and a sweet aroma (not fermented or acidic). It should yield slightly when pressed with finger.	2 slices or 1/3 cup chunked or crushed = 1 simple carbohydrate
Plums	Should not be rock hard but plump and firm to the touch.	2 small plums = 1 simple carbohydrate
Watermelon	Should be purchased with a smooth surface, dullish sheen and a creamy yellow underside.	1 cup diced melon = 1 simple carbohydrate

TABLE 14

DRIED FRUIT

Fruit	Serving Equivalent
Dried apple rings	1/2 ounce = 1 simple carbohydrate
Dried apricots	4 large halves = 1 simple carbohydrate
Dates (unsweetened, pitted)	2 = 1 simple carbohydrate
Dried peaches, pears	1 = 1 simple carbohydrate
Prunes	2 large = 1 simple carbohydrate
Raisins	2 tablespoons or 1 small box = 1 simple carbohydrate

CHAPTER FOUR

VITAMINS AND MINERALS: FOOD IS THE BEST SOURCE

COMMANDMENT VII
THOU SHALT GET YOUR VITAMINS AND MINERALS FROM FOOD, NOT PILLS

Can good nutrition be put into a capsule? *No!* Do you need to take vitamin-mineral supplements? *It depends on your life-style choices.* Do you skip breakfast? Lunch, too, sometimes? Do you travel a lot? Eat out frequently? Drink alcohol frequently? Smoke? Take contraceptive pills? Have a high-stress career or home life? Drink coffee constantly?

If you answered yes to many of these questions, your nutritional state is at high risk! If you were to continue on your same life-style course, you would quite possibly benefit from supplemental vitamins and minerals. However, supplements are not the only answer. You can remedy the situation by subtly rearranging life to include balanced, wholesome meals and snacks at regular intervals each day. It is often a simple matter of learning what to grab and when to grab it!

You would not be alone if you opted for a quick-fix life-style change. Sixty million other Americans spend nearly three billion dollars a year on vitamin and mineral pills. Sadly, this whole idea of a quick fix in a pill is often based on a false security that goes something like this: If you have a poor diet and an unhealthy life-style, you can fill in the gaps with a pill. If you are under intensive stress and have no energy, just take a vitamin to overcome the problem.

Unfortunately supplementation doesn't ever address the real problems or meet the real needs. It can never replace a life-style of self-care. Pills have little to do with the foundations of building a healthy life-style. They concern themselves only with the "interior decorating."

What Are Vitamins and Minerals Anyway?

Vitamins are organic molecules that the body does not produce on its own but cannot do without. As chemical catalysts for the body, they make things happen! Though vitamins do not give energy, they help the body convert carbohydrates to energy and then help the body use it.

Minerals, unlike vitamins, are inorganic compounds. Some minerals are building blocks for structures such as bones and teeth. Others work with the fluids of the body, giving them certain characteristics. Some thirty minerals are important in nutrition, though in small amounts when compared to vitamins.

Any varied diet with enough calories should provide the essential vitamins and minerals. For most people there is no need to take artificial vitamins, either in pill form or as part of "fortified" products. Rather than supplementation, your goal should be to improve your eating patterns to assure adequate intake of all nutrients. The best source of vitamins and minerals is, and always has been, *food!* (See Tables 15 and 16 below and on page 32 for vitamin and mineral sources.)

TABLE 15
VITAMIN SOURCES

Vitamin	Sources
A	liver, spinach, deep-yellow vegetables, sweet potatoes and carrots and fruits such as apricots
B complex	whole grain products, peanuts, dried beans, dark green leafy vegetables
C	citrus fruit, strawberries, cantaloupe, cauliflower, green peppers, tomatoes, potatoes
D	fortified milk and milk products
E	vegetable oils, margarine, wheat germ
K	broccoli, spinach, other leafy vegetables

Vitamins

Vitamins are either fat-soluble or water-soluble. Fat solubles (A, D, E and K) are absorbed through the intestinal walls and can be stored in the body fat for long periods of time. Water-soluble vitamins (B complex and C) cannot be stored in the body for long because they dissolve in water and are released in the urine.

Because fat-soluble vitamins accumulate in the body, you can get into a toxic state from taking mega-doses or amounts that are more than ten times the RDA (Recommended Daily Allowance). In these mega-amounts the vitamins are no longer being used as vitamins but as drugs, carrying drug side effects. Most people are not aware of this when they start taking megadoses of vitamins and minerals. They figure that if a little is good, a lot is better. At best, using vitamins or minerals as a sort of insurance policy is a waste of money. At worst, they can be highly toxic. Toxicities can bring on a host of maladies, from flu-like symptoms to organ damage, and can be fatal.

TABLE 16
MINERAL SOURCES

Mineral	Sources
Calcium	dairy products, green leafy vegetables, salmon, tofu, legumes
Chloride	table salt
Chromium	brewer's yeast, cheese, whole grains
Copper	oysters, nuts, liver, whole grain bread and cereals, mushrooms
Fluoride	fluoridated drinking water
Iodine	iodized salt, seaweed
Iron	red meats, dried beans and peas, whole grain breads and cereals, prunes, raisins
Magnesium	dairy products, whole grains, legumes, nuts, green leafy vegetables
Manganese	nuts, whole grain breads and cereals, vegetables, fruits
Molybdenum	meats, grains, legumes
Phosphorus	dairy products, meat products, legumes, nuts, whole grains
Potassium	cream of tartar, tomatoes, bananas, cantaloupe, citrus fruits, dried fruits, dark green vegetables, lentils, bright-orange vegetables
Selenium	Varied diet provides adequate sources; consistently good are seafood, liver and meats; beware of supplementation — easily toxic.
Sodium	table salt, sea salt, dairy products, cured meats, most packaged and canned foods, pickled food, baking soda; more than enough is found in the foods we eat.
Zinc	red meat, milk, liver, seafood, eggs, whole grain cereals; beware of supplementing with more than 15 milligrams in addition to diet — easily toxic.

At one time the water-soluble vitamins were considered harmless in megadoses. This is no longer the case, as some studies are showing that even the water-soluble variety can lead to problems when taken in large quantities over a period of time. B6 and niacin are two such vitamins. A toxicity of B6 has caused neuromuscular paralysis, and excess niacin can cause liver damage.

How About Minerals?

Some minerals are stored like the fat-soluble vitamins and, like them, are toxic if taken to excess. These are iron, copper, choline, magnesium, selenium, manganese, iodine, zinc and fluoride. Other minerals do not appear to accumulate in the body and are readily excreted, so toxicity is not as great a risk.

Who Needs Vitamins and Minerals?

Who needs vitamins and minerals? *Every human being!* Who would need a vitamin and mineral *supplement*? If you are eating well, there is no need for supplements unless you are part of a group at high risk of a vitamin-mineral deficiency. These groups include chronic dieters whose nutrition gets cut with their calories (it's not possible to get the nutrients you need in fewer than 1,200 calories a day); those chronically ill; heavy drinkers and smokers; pregnant and nursing mothers; and those who have a limited intake of food choices (such as a strict vegetarian eating only plant products).

In addition, there are three problem minerals in the American diet: We get far too much sodium and far too little calcium and iron. Iron and calcium merit special attention. Twenty percent or more of American women have severely low iron stores and may be suffering from iron deficiency anemia. Calcium deficiency is linked to women's high risk of osteoporosis. (See page 40 for tips on how to "pass the salt.")

Anemic? Not Me!

Anemia, caused from a lack of iron in the diet, is the most common nutritional deficiency disease in the country. Symptoms include immune disorders, fatigue, muscle weakness and childhood learning problems. Studies have shown that the overwhelming majority of women take in less iron than they need. Again, more than 20 percent of American women are at high risk of anemia, particularly during their menstrual periods. Men are generally not in such danger,

TABLE 17

FOODS HIGH IN IRON

most dried beans
clams
lean beef and veal
dark green, leafy vegetables
peanuts
dried fruits (especially apricots,
raisins and prunes)
tuna, shrimp and sardines
poultry
whole grains and cereals

except when they may have blood loss from a disease (such as ulcers) or from dieting in a way that robs their body of valuable iron and protein.

To prevent anemia, women must make sure they take in as much iron as possible through dietary sources. A woman's daily requirement is 18 milligrams. (See Table 17 for a list of foods high in iron.)

Eating Tips to Fight Anemia

Eat small, frequent meals throughout the day. This allows the body to absorb iron more effectively. The more iron you put in at one time, the less the body absorbs.

Have protein with every snack and meal, as protein enhances your iron absorption.

Eat fruits high in vitamin C (citrus, strawberries and pineapple) and vegetables from the cabbage family (broccoli, cabbage and cauliflower) at your meals and snacks. Vitamin C enhances your absorption of iron.

Avoid drinking tea, colas and coffee with your meals or snacks, as these contain tannic acid, which hinders your absorption of iron.

Iron Supplements?

It is not uncommon for women who eat a well-balanced diet to require additional iron, especially when their caloric intake is restricted for weight loss. Your need can be confirmed by getting a check of your hemoglobin or hematocrit, which shows the iron stores in your cells. If you are anemic, or borderline low, it is wise to take a well-absorbed iron supplement for at least six to eight weeks as you make positive changes in your eating patterns. If additional iron is called for, the best form is ferrous gluconate. One brand name of this is Fergon. You might split a daily dose and take it in two installments.

Ammunition to Fight Osteoporosis

Osteoporosis is a painful and crippling loss of bone mass that is eight times more common in women than in men and is characterized by stooped posture and an increased risk of fractures. It usually begins earlier in life but worsens after menopause. Although this disease is commonly seen in the elderly, it is not a normal part of aging. It can be prevented. The ammunition: calcium and exercise, along with proper hormone balance.

Calcium. Women have a particularly high need for calcium for three reasons. First, they mature faster and earlier than men, which means they have a lower bone density from the very beginning. Second, pregnancy, nursing and menopause increase the need for calcium. Third, many women miss out on proper exercise, which helps build stronger bones. Recent studies show that most women don't get half the calcium they need.

Unfortunately, osteoporosis can be the pay-later penalty for skimping on calcium now. The symptoms again are fragile, break-prone bones, a bent-over posture and a loss in height. The symptoms first appear in the mid-fifties and early sixties, but the condition takes years to develop, having actually started in the mid-thirties. The hormonal change at menopause speeds up the bone loss; estrogen replacement is often recommended to counteract this. Adequate calcium in the earlier years can help you build stronger bones to diminish your chances of osteoporosis later on. Adequate calcium in your later years can help you to halt the process. Unfortunately, only 42 percent of the population consumes the recommended daily allowance of calcium. The people who need it most consume the least: 80 percent of teenage and middle-aged women consume half of their RDA.

Exercise. Recent studies have shown that exercise seems to be a vital factor in promoting excellent bone growth and maintenance throughout life. A well-planned exercise routine may not only stimulate the development of strong bone mass but may also halt any bone loss. Exercise keeps bones stronger and thicker; without regular exercise, bones may shrink, weaken and become porous. Exercise increases the circulation and flow of nutrients to the bone, encouraging new bone growth and strengthening.

The best types of exercises to build strong bones are weight-bearing exercises, such as brisk walking, jumping rope and bicycling. Bones stressed from such exercises become stronger and denser. Swimming, although an excellent aerobic exercise, is not as effective in strengthening bones. It is recommended that exercise be done at least every other day, for twenty-five to thirty minutes. Good exercise and good nutrition work together for strong bones, a strong heart and a healthy body!

How Much Calcium Do You Need?

All people need calcium throughout their lifetime, about 800 milligrams or three servings of a high-calcium food each day. Children and pregnant women have higher needs, requiring 1,200 milligrams or four servings of high-calcium foods each day. Women over the age of thirty-five, however, need 1,400 milligrams of calcium or five servings of high-calcium foods each day. This is a particularly difficult requirement to meet from dietary sources alone, and calcium supplements may be necessary. Calcium is important for many reasons beyond its prevention of osteoporosis. A lack of sufficient calcium in the diet can also lead to gum disease, high blood pressure and even colon cancer. (See Table 18 for a list of foods high in calcium.)

Calcium Supplements?

If you require calcium supplements, consider these facts:
• Calcium carbonate and calcium citrate are the forms best absorbed.
• Calcium will be better absorbed when taken with a meal or a small snack.
• Taking calcium at bedtime will allow the best use of it.
• Two calcium preparations, dolomite and bone meal, have been found to be occasionally contaminated with lead and should be avoided.

What's the Bottom Line?

Some people say that today's food cannot possibly provide all your vitamins and minerals. They've heard that today's crops are critically deficient in nutritional value. That simply isn't true. The nutritive value is as high, or higher, than ever before. Nutrient-deprived soil cannot produce high-yield crops; the chemical structure of the crop will not allow it. And the crop production from our country's farms is as high as it has ever been.

Qualified research shows repeatedly: There is no

TABLE 18

FOODS HIGH IN CALCIUM

Portion Equaling 1 Serving of High-Calcium Food

milk or nonfat plain yogurt .... 1 cup
cheese .... 1-1/2 ounces
cottage cheese .... 1-1/2 cups
part-skim ricotta cheese .... 1/2 cup
salmon, canned .... 5 ounces
collard or turnip greens .... 1 cup
broccoli .... 2 cups
tofu or fortified soy milk .... 1 cup
dried beans, cooked .... 2-1/2 cups

better source of nutrition than food, which has been perfectly created to meet the needs of the human body. Vitamin supplements were created by man, for profit.

The beautiful thing about good, balanced nutrition is this: Everything fits together in such a perfect way that just focusing on these ten basic principles will allow adequate intake of essential nutrients. You don't have to be continually analyzing your intake to see if you've had your zinc today.

No single food supplies your daily requirement of all the vitamins and minerals. There is no one perfect food. Many trace vitamins and minerals are found in just a few foods. In addition, foods contain many hidden protective factors that we are just beginning to learn about. Eating a variety of foods in their whole form is the time-tested answer to the vitamin-mineral question.

No matter what anybody says, some people just can't shake the belief that a vitamin pill will give extra insurance. To these people I recommend a single, balanced multivitamin-mineral supplement taken every other day or a half taken daily. I encourage my clients to take only a supplement that offers 100 to 150 percent of the RDAs for all the nutrients. If the levels are higher than this (some supplements contain 1,000 percent of the RDAs), they're very imbalanced and should be avoided.

Don't waste money on vitamins or minerals that contain substances for which there is no proven nutritional need, such as lecithin and vitamin P or vitamin F. Others are arsenic, cadmium, carnitine, choline, cobalt, coenzyme Q, nickel, PABA, silicon, tin, vanadium, vitamin B15 and vitamin Q.

CHAPTER FIVE

WATER: AN ESSENTIAL NUTRIENT

COMMANDMENT VIII
Thou Shalt Drink at Least Eight Glasses of Water a Day

Increasing one's water intake to meet the body's needs can seem to produce some quite miraculous results. However, most of us Americans grew up drinking just about anything but water! We list our favorite beverages as soda, coffee, tea, juice, Kool-Aid — with water being used for washing down pills, bathing and brushing teeth. But when you see how vital water is for the proper functioning of the body, it can quickly become your beverage of choice.

Water makes up 92 percent of our blood plasma, 80 percent of our muscle mass, 60 percent of our red blood cells and 50 percent of everything else in our bodies. What an important ingredient to good health! Although often ignored, water is as essential a nutrient as the other five: carbohydrates, proteins, fats, vitamins and minerals. A human can survive many days, even months, without food. But the human body can survive only three to five days without water.

Water has many vital functions. It is *the* vehicle the body must use to flush out the waste produced in normal body functions. In weight loss, the body requires even more water to carry out the breakdown waste from the fat. Adequate water also prevents the build-up of uric acid within the body, which in excess leads to gouty arthritis.

Being a mild laxative, water is essential for proper bowel function, activating the fiber you eat to form a bulky mass that moves through the GI tract easily and quickly. Water first thing in the morning, with the juice of a lemon, makes a great waker-upper for your system.

Water is the only liquid you consume that doesn't require the body to work to metabolize or excrete it. The body has to work overtime to process and excrete the colorings and chemicals in sodas. Many other beverages, although fluid-based, actually remove more water than contained in the beverage itself. Many beverages, such as tea, coffee and sodas, contain tannic acid, a waste product that interferes with iron absorption and competes for excretion with the other bodily waste products such as uric acid. Even juices do not provide the solid benefits of pure, wonderful water, since they require the body to work to process the substances they contain.

Water is essential for maintaining proper fluid balance. As you avoid excess salt, take in adequate protein and increase your water intake, your kidney function will increase. This three-point approach releases excess stores of water, much like priming a pump. Water is *the* natural diuretic!

Water is essential for maintaining muscle tone, allowing muscles to contract naturally, which prevents dehydration. Water also works to keep the skin healthy and resilient.

I am often asked, How much water do I need?

My answer is always the same: Eight to ten glasses each day. As you begin to meet this need by drinking more water, your natural thirst for it will increase. As you learn what water does for your body, your motivation for drinking it will grow. Water drinking is habit forming; the more you drink, the more you want!

Try filling a two-quart container with water each morning, then make sure it's all gone before you go to bed. I have developed a habit of drinking an 8-ounce glass of water right *after* each meal and snack throughout the day. This ensures at least six glasses, with the others easily fitting in. I don't encourage people to gulp down their meals with any beverage, even water. This dilutes the digestive enzymes in the mouth. Sip while eating if you would like, but drink your beverage before or after the meal. Some of us find that a glass of cool, clear water before we begin to eat can slow down our fast-paced life. Remember, many of us are not just fast-food eaters; we are *fast* eaters! If you are prone to excess stomach acid, water on an empty stomach will not be wise for you. You will do much better drinking water right after your meal, while the food is present, thereby neutralizing the acids.

If you drink tap water, the taste may improve after refrigerating it for twenty-four hours (the chlorine dissipates). Water is refreshing with an added slice of fresh lime or lemon, and bottled water or seltzer is a nice treat.

CHAPTER SIX

FOOD TRAPS: ROBBERS OF WELLNESS

COMMANDMENT IX
THOU SHALT CONSUME A MINIMUM OF SUGAR, SALT, CAFFEINE AND ALCOHOL

Up to this point all the commandments have focused on the nutrients vital to wellness. This commandment addresses the need to avoid foods and substances that do not benefit the body and can cause serious detriment if taken to excess. These substances serve as weapons against your physical well-being and can easily cause a problem with overindulgence and even addiction.

When we eat for wellness, it's easy to see how our bodies were created. The body so reinforces positive changes that old negative eating patterns lose much of their appeal. Why eat foods that rob your health, energy and well-being? When you feel good, really good, you want to hold on to good health.

In New Testament times the apostle Paul penned to the Corinthians, " 'Everything is permissible for me' — but not everything is beneficial. 'Everything is permissible for me' — but I will not be mastered by anything" (1 Corinthians 6:12). Eating the typical American diet, we are being mastered by many foods and many substances. As we look at the culprits one at a time, we can learn, as Paul did, that we needn't be in bondage to anything.

Sugar: How Sweet It Isn't!

Called by many names — honey, brown sugar, corn syrup, fructose — sugar is sugar! Much of our problem with sugar lies in the fact that it is hidden in nearly every packaged product on the grocer's shelf. American consumption of sugar has grown to 125 pounds per person per year. If you have been raised on a typical American diet, you have been raised on a diet high in simple sugars and refined carbohydrates. Consider that the average can of soda contains 10 to 12 teaspoons of sugar, and you will see the overwhelming quantities of sugar the typical American consumes — 132 pounds per year! How about you?

"But I just have a sweet tooth!" Actually we all have a sweet tooth; we're all created with a natural preference for foods with a sweet taste. Our problem is that this natural preference has taken on an unnatural drive, fueled by a lifetime of poorly chosen foods and erratic eating patterns.

The health problems associated with sugar are controversial. Some voices call it "white death," and others see no problem other than empty calories. There are problems with sugar.

Refined sugar *has* been shown to cause dental cavities, obesity and high triglycerides; it wreaks havoc in the control of diabetes and hypoglycemia. Actually, most high-sugar snacks (candy bars, cookies, donuts and so forth) are also loaded with saturated fats and calories; it's a triple threat to your well-being!

In addition, continual choosing of refined, highly concentrated sugar foods prevents us from choosing other nutrient-rich foods. The resulting junk (nutrient-poor) diet is often to blame for the ill effects of a high-sugar diet. Many nutrients are easily lost in a junk diet: iron, chromium and thiamine are just a few. The absence of these nutrients will result in a wide range of effects on personality, attention span, mental performance, sleep patterns, GI function and energy levels. Our tendency is to blame the junk food, but it is more likely the fault of the junk diet (the lack of good food).

Even occasional eating of high-sugar foods is impossible for some. Those sensitive to blood sugar fluctuations *will* be hurt by "just a little bit" — not by the calories but by the effect it has on their bodies. The seesaw effect that sugar has on some seems to result in a "the more you have, the more you want" syndrome, laying the foundations for sugar dependency or abuse.

Here is how it works: A heavy sugar intake causes a pleasurable rise in blood sugar that will be followed by a quick fall a few hours later. That dip in blood sugar triggers "eating for a lift" to relieve fatigue. Usually the food is again high in sugar, and the seesaw effect continues. If sweets aren't available, the affected blood sugar will leave you vaguely dissatisfied with anything else. "If I just had something sweet...." Couple this sensation with erratic eating patterns, and eating can get out of control. For some sensitive systems even a small amount of sugar foods can cause blood sugar fluctuations that set the craving process in motion.

It may be necessary to withdraw from eating sweets long enough to allow your blood sugar levels to stabilize, to allow your energy and appetite for good foods to return. Does nibbling a little bit of sweets lead to a lot? Does a "the more you have, the more you want" syndrome kick in when you eat something sweet? If the answer is yes, do not set up sugar as a forbidden fruit in your life. Rather acknowledge that you are making the choice not to allow *any* food to take power over you. No food tastes good enough to rob you of your freedom and well-being!

Healthy tip: Cut back on your daily use of sugar or sweets and eat fruit to satisfy your natural craving for a sweet taste. Sugar abuse is not worth robbing yourself of precious energy and stamina.

How About Sugar Substitutes?

As you become aware (and possibly alarmed) at your intake of sugar, be careful not just to replace it with artificial sweeteners. As long as you continue to use either sugar-laden foods or sugar substitutes, you will keep your taste buds alive for sugar! Your goal is to reduce your need for everything to taste sweet. By allowing your taste buds to change, your desire for sweetness can be met in a safer way. Try fruits and other naturally sweet foods — God's natural provision for our inborn preference for sweets.

Also remember that there are no absolutes in the safety of chemicals, be it saccharin or aspartame or any new one to come along. The long-term effects of their use will not be known for years. As bad as sugar may be, and whatever the health hazards associated with its overuse, at least it's not a chemical. It has been used for centuries.

When in doubt, leave it out!

Salt — Don't Pass It!

"Please pass the salt" is a common and *overused* phrase. We need to shake the habit. The taste for salt is conditioned; as you use less of it, your tastes will change so that you will enjoy foods more without it. Be patient with yourself and your family but begin to cut back gradually on your use of salt in cooking and eliminate completely those snacks that are *triple threats*: high in salt, fat and calories.

Salt's chemical name is sodium chloride — with sodium being the more important in terms of health. Everyone requires some sodium, but there's more than enough naturally present in foods to supply this requirement. Most Americans consume five to twenty-five times more than they need.

Excessive sodium is a factor in many diseases, the most prevalent being hypertension and kidney disease. Excess salt causes temporary build-up of body fluids in your system. This makes it harder for your heart to pump blood through the cardiovascular system, and the result may be high blood pressure. About one in every five persons is predisposed to this salt/blood-pressure connection, so it's wise to practice prevention and cut back on excess salt in your eating. Accept the challenge: Learn to cook and enjoy foods without added fat and salt! *An ounce of prevention is worth a pound of cure!*

See Table 19 for a list of high-sodium foods.

How to Shake the Salt Habit

Cut back on your use of highly processed foods and salty snacks. This will substantially reduce your sodium intake.

Leave the salt shaker off the table. This will help break the "salt before you taste" habit. You'll quickly begin to enjoy the natural flavor of foods without covering them with salt. Try substituting herbs and spices for some of the salt.

Cook with herb blends rather than salt. This will add new flavors. Use one of the wonderful salt-free blends from your grocery or try making your own (try the recipes on page 82). Keep the herb blends in a large-holed shaker right by the stove where your salt used to be. *You can automatically cut a recipe's salt amount by half of what is called for.* If you use herbs in its place, you can cut the salt down to a quarter of the original amount.

Breaking the Caffeine Habit

A relatively mild stimulant, caffeine is among the world's most widely used and addictive drugs. Ironically, caffeine remains an acceptable way of artificially stimulating the brain at a time when society is being exhorted to "just say no." Caffeine, which allows mental clarity and mood elevation, works by blocking one of the brain's natural sedatives, a chemical called adenosine. Like other drugs, there is a

TABLE 19

WATCH OUT FOR THESE HIGH-SODIUM FOODS!

- any food pickled or brine-cured, including sauerkraut, pickles and olives

- any food salt-cured or smoked, including ham, bacon and sausage

- any cold cut, including bologna, hot dogs, pastrami and salami

- condiments, including soy sauce, ketchup and chili sauce

- convenience foods, such as canned vegetables, soups and frozen meals downside to caffeine. Because it is a central nervous system stimulant, even small amounts of it can cause side effects such as restlessness and disturbed sleep, heart palpitations, stomach irritation, fibrocystic breast disease and diarrhea. It can promote irritability, anxiety and mood disturbances. Caffeine can also aggravate premenstrual syndrome symptoms in women.

The amount required to cause a stimulant effect is estimated to be the amount in one to two cups of brewed coffee or three glasses of iced tea (about 250 milligrams). It adds up quickly! I encourage my clients to cut back their daily caffeine consumption to not more than this 250 milligrams. If, after cutting back to this amount, they continue to have caffeine's side effects, I encourage them to withdraw altogether. Try it. Be careful though. Caffeine withdrawal may cause a zombie-like fatigue and even headaches and may last for up to five days. Set a goal and cut back *slowly*. The good news is by eating more evenly throughout the day, your energy and moods will be elevated without a caffeine kick. You can say good-bye to being a caffeine junkie!

There are five major sources of caffeine:

Coffee: The amount of caffeine in coffee depends on a number of factors: how it's brewed and how long; whether it's ground or instant. Brewed, ground coffee contains the highest level of caffeine, packing 85 milligrams per 5-ounce cup. Instant coffee is slightly lower, containing 65 milligrams per cup. This is not a significant enough difference to choose instant coffee; just reduce your intake of both. Also look at the size of cup from which you typically drink. Many mugs hold upwards of 12 ounces of coffee, with about 250 milligrams of caffeine.

Decaf coffee has just a few milligrams of caffeine per cup. Many "withdrawers" do well to come off slowly by drinking a mixture of half decaf and half caffeinated. Be sure to look for naturally decaffeinated coffees (Swiss water process); they are decaffeinated without the chemicals.

Tea: A cup of tea will typically have about a third of the caffeine of a cup of brewed coffee; the longer the tea brews the higher the caffeine level. There are a number of decaffeinated teas available.

Sodas: Generally the cola beverages have the highest levels of caffeine (36 to 50 milligrams per serving), but look at all soda labels, as some of the fruit-flavored sodas contain caffeine. Some, such as Mountain Dew and Dr. Pepper, contain almost as much caffeine as coffee and tea. This is a matter of great concern for children. In the body of a 60-pound child, two or more such beverages are equivalent to the caffeine in eight cups of coffee for a 175-pound man.

Of course, the major problem with soda is not the caffeine; it's the incredibly high concentration of sugar! Most sodas contain 10 to 12 teaspoons of sugar per can; the diet sodas simply replace the sugar with chemicals.

Chocolate: Cocoa beans have a high caffeine content. The caffeine content of a cup of hot chocolate is usually one-quarter the amount in a cup of brewed coffee. One ounce of baking chocolate contains about one-third the caffeine of a cup of coffee.

Over-the-counter drugs: Read labels carefully! Stimulants for keeping you awake and many diet pills, decongestants and headache pills supply as much caffeine as two cups of regular, brewed coffee.

Don't Mix Alcohol With Wellness

Alcohol is one of the most common and addictive drugs of our time. The U.S. Department of Agriculture Dietary Guidelines suggest, "If you drink alcoholic beverages, do so in moderation — and don't drive." What is considered moderate? One light beer, 4 ounces of wine or 1 1/2 ounces of liquor a day is acceptable, but it appears that your health hazards escalate dramatically the minute you drink more.

This recommendation comes from much medical research that implicates excess alcohol as a major risk factor in many killer diseases: cancer, cirrhosis and fatty liver and congestive heart failure. Cirrhosis of the liver is one of the fastest-growing illnesses in the United States.

Alcohol is also the major cause of malnutrition in the United States. And there is increasing evidence of the effect of alcohol consumption by pregnant mothers on their developing babies; studies have shown that babies born to mothers who drink have lower IQs and higher rates of heart and joint defects. Even babies born to mothers who drink in moderate quantities have been shown to be affected negatively. For this reason pregnant women are advised not to drink, even in small amounts. When in doubt, leave it out!

The good news is that healthy Americans are beginning to drink less; they are limiting themselves to one drink and making that one "light." If you drink, try ordering a white wine spritzer or light beer. Or skip the alcohol altogether and enjoy a refreshing mineral water and lime.

Healthy tip: Reduce or eliminate alcohol consumption. Drinking sets you up for excessive eating and undisciplined behavior.

CHAPTER SEVEN

THE SUPER-QUICK WEIGHT-LOSS DIET

Gotcha, didn't I?

Go back to the introduction and begin to reread. By the time you get here again you will know there are *no* quick ways of losing weight permanently and healthfully. Diets always begin with firm resolve and white-knuckle discipline until the pain of living without food becomes unbearable. And then....

Diets: Treating the Symptoms, Missing the Problem

Going on a diet is similar to taking throat lozenges for a strep throat infection. The lozenges soothe the pain and even make the redness go away! But treating only the symptoms allows the infection to run rampant and worsen. And as soon as you go off the throat lozenges, the strep infection rears its ugly head. It's the same with dieting: The weight comes back after going off the diet.

COMMANDMENT X
THOU SHALT NEVER GO ON A FAD DIET

Why *is* it so easy to gain weight and so hard to lose it? Why is it so hard to keep weight off? What is the answer? The solution begins with an acknowledgment: Weight is not the problem; it is only a symptom. One's eating patterns and perspectives about food are the problem. We eat, not to meet our bodies' physical needs for nourishment, but for other reasons, often emotional. My experience has taught me that freedom comes only in dealing with the problem, not the symptoms.

I consider the word *diet* to be a nasty four-letter word. It speaks defeat and depression and means *temporary!* We go *on* diets only to go *off* them. We are "good" only to be "bad." We are "legal" and then we "cheat." We must stop setting ourselves up for a starvation/gorge existence, with our weight shooting up and down like a yo-yo. We don't need to look at weight loss as a punishment of eating awful-tasting and worse-looking foods or of swallowing pills, potions or supplements. A way of eating for life cannot exclude any major food group or nutrient or claim any food to be magic.

It's a lot easier to diet than to change eating habits, so there is a tremendous market for the quick-fix diet. Because more than 95 percent of the people who go on a fad diet regain the lost weight within a year or sooner, the market is continuous.

There are millions of dollars to be made by those willing to take advantage of the American obsession with dieting. We will buy and drink anything if we think it will make us lose weight. It boils down to a belief in magic, an instant cure! We want desperately to believe a new diet will work, and sometimes it will for a short time. We want to believe that our lives will change as quickly as our weight. But even thinness doesn't solve all of life's problems, so we return to overeating. *Diets don't work;* they modify behavior only temporarily.

It's time to break the diet mentality with a nutrition consciousness that works for life. You *can* feel better, have abundant energy from morning till night and look more radiant and healthy. You *can* take charge; you *can* change. Now that you have a new plan of eating and the knowledge to undergird it, you never need to diet again!

You may say, But this will take too long! I want to be thin now! Well, the truth is, this *will* take longer, but the results will last. You won't be fighting the same battles day after day, month after month, year after year. You won't even be *able* to eat the same way anymore; you'll be too aware of what you're doing! You will be free because you have a new relationship with food and are no longer using it in a life-damaging way.

The Dieting Dilemma

Being free to control your appetite has to include freedom from the scale and freedom from dieting. Obsessive, unhealthy, deprived *dieting* is no more of a freedom than obsessive, unhealthy *overeating*. Being physically free begins by choosing a way of eating and living that is comfortable enough so you can live with it for the rest of your life.

Understand that the human body is "fearfully and wonderfully made" (see Psalm 139:14). Our early ancestors were subject to the ups and downs of feast and famine; only those who could maintain a steady weight could survive. You see, the body was created with fat cells for storing food energy for emergencies — famine.

A human baby produces a certain number of fat cells, depending upon genetics and how he or she is fed. The baby never loses these cells, and the body can add more if overfed for an extended period of time.

It appears that the more fat cells we have, the hungrier we feel; they are continually signaling the brain to feed them.

If we drastically cut our food intake by going on a fad or self-imposed diet, our bodies will slip into a starvation mode. Our metabolism will slow down, using fewer calories than usual. And to make matters worse, when we're wanting to lose weight, each fat cell appears to have a built-in gauge which tries to maintain in itself a certain amount of fat.

This is the reason for plateaus in dieting (which will occur even in balanced, sensible weight loss). The body recognizes a certain weight it has been before by the amount of fat in the fat cells, and it will do everything it can to maintain that level. In a plateau the body will attempt to slow down metabolically, hold fluid and even increase the appetite — all attempts to maintain the body's weight. In healthy weight loss the plateau will be broken in three or four weeks; the body releases the gauge. But when the diet is an unbalanced, unhealthy one, the body holds on to its weight even more stubbornly and will regain what is finally lost even more quickly. You don't have to go back to gorging to gain back your weight lost with a fad diet; your body does it for you.

You will not so easily fall into this trap if you follow the healthy pattern of eating I've outlined here in the Ten Commandments of Great Nutrition. You will be feeding your body in such a way that it will best deal with the symptoms of plateau action. The metabolism may start to slow, but your even eating throughout the day will help to keep it burning relatively high. Your body's blood sugars may fluctuate to increase your appetite, but your balanced, frequent eating will hold them stable. Your body may retain fluid, but your new healthy way of eating and drinking water will force the fluids to be released. Most important, you are not starving the body, setting yourself up for an eventual gorge. You are learning a fabulous lifetime pattern of eating and living. *Eating to lose weight is a lot more fun than starving.*

Fallacies About Fad Diets

All fad diets are variations on four themes (or schemes!) of deception: fasting or semi-starvation (fewer than six hundred calories per day); the food-combining diet; the high-carbohydrate, low-protein diet; and the high-protein, low-carbohydrate diet. Let's look at each and see how it works for you in the short run and against you in the long run.

Fasting or semi-starvation. Going without all food for weight loss can be just as damaging for the overweight person as binging. It is extreme and extremely unhealthy! Although there is a proper place for fasting in our spiritual lives, it is important not to fast for the wrong motives. Do not fast with the impure, improper motive of weight loss or "cleansing the body." Starving will certainly prompt weight loss, but as seen in concentration camps during the war, what you lose is primarily water and muscle weight. This may look great on the scale, but it will look *terrible* on your body! To make matters worse, starvation so slows down the body's metabolism that it takes up to a year for it to normalize. This is why you gain back the weight so quickly. After starvation, even a return to normal eating (not the usual binge) will cause your body to store the calories as fat. What comes off will come back on…and on…and on.

The food-combining diet. This type of diet typically has you eating protein just one time a day. But if you don't balance your intake of carbohydrate and protein, you are not able to use the protein you eat in an optimal body-building way.

Again, your body cannot store excess protein; it's a use-it-or-lose-it nutrient. You *will* lose weight on such a diet, but you'll also lose your protein nourishment, immunities and well-being. Many people on this type of plan become anemic and protein malnourished, all in the name of health.

The high-carbohydrate, low-protein diet. This type of diet so robs your body of essential protein that it throws off your fluid balance and dehydrates your body. It appeals to your body's desire for carbohydrates (usually deprived in the typical fad diet), but it deprives your body just the same. You can lose weight quickly on a protein-deficient diet, but initially it's just water weight. Continued use of this low-protein diet will begin to tear down your muscle mass; the body must have protein to repair and rebuild from normal wear and tear on the body.

The high-protein, low-carbohydrate diet. This type of fad diet has turned America against energy-giving carbohydrates with the lie that they make us fat. This diet comes packaged in a book with a lot of hype and promotion or in a formula to mix up or in freeze-dried or prepackaged meals. It works by totally unbalancing the body. Remember that carbohydrate is *the* energy fuel for the body. Without carbohydrate, protein and fat begin to be used for energy, throwing off a waste product called ketones. This state of ketosis will cause the body to dehydrate and lose a great deal of water weight.

This is how a high-protein, low-carbohydrate diet can promise you a quick weight loss (such as ten pounds in ten days). But initially you're losing water weight only. The scale does not have a measurement for fat, water or muscle weight; it just gives you a total poundage. We tend to play tricks with it. When we lose five pounds, we're just sure it's five pounds of fat. If we gain five pounds, we're just sure it's water gain! *The number on the scale can never be an accurate measure of your progress!* Water weight returns just as quickly as it leaves.

TABLE 20

How to Determine Your Ideal Weight

Men

Start your calculations from a base height of 5 feet and base weight of 106 pounds. Add 6 pounds for each inch over 5 feet. If you are medium-framed, this is your ideal weight. If you consider yourself small-framed, multiply that figure by .90. If you are large-framed, multiply that figure by 1.10.

Example
5-foot, 10-inch large-frame male should weigh:
106 pounds plus (10 x 6) = 166 pounds x 1.10 = ideal weight of 183 pounds

Women

Start your calculations from a base height of 5 feet and base weight of 100 pounds. Add 5 pounds for each inch over 5 feet. If you are medium-framed, this is your ideal weight. If you consider yourself small-framed, multiply that figure by .90. If you are large-framed, multiply that figure by 1.10.

Example
5-foot, 5-inch medium-frame female should weigh:
100 pounds plus (5 x 5) = 125 pounds

Remember that ideal weight is just a ball-park figure;
the weight on the scale cannot reflect body muscle, body fat or fluids.

If you stay on these unhealthy diets for more than two weeks, you will lose more than just water weight. You will begin to lose your muscle mass. And because muscle weighs more than fat, you will lose much more quickly on the scale (translated: success). But the weight you gain back (and you always do!) is fat (translated: failure). Years of this kind of dieting will leave you in terrible shape. Losing muscle weight only to gain back fat causes you to go from a larger pear shape to a smaller pear shape, back to a larger pear shape, down to a smaller pear shape, until you begin to deposit the regained fat in new places and finally grow into a pumpkin shape!

The only desirable kind of weight to lose is fat, through a leaning down process that comes from a balanced intake of nutrients. On an unbalanced diet, you lose your money, your energy and your health — a risk not worth taking!

Burn Fat, Not Muscle

The key to any successful, healthy weight loss is to lower your percentage of body fat — not to lose pounds of muscle and water. Unfortunately, the average American body contains more fat than it should. For men, a good percentage of body fat is 16 to 19 percent of body weight. A good percentage for women is 22 to 25 percent. Lower percentages of body fat are common among well-conditioned athletes. This is both healthy and desirable. Higher levels of body fat appear to increase the body's risk of disease.

Calories certainly do count in weight control, but how and when you eat those calories is extremely important to obtain optimal fat loss.

To preserve muscle mass and burn fat while dieting, it is necessary to eat balanced meals and snacks of carbohydrate and protein, evenly distributed throughout the day. This, in combination with an adequate amount of food, keeps the body out of starvation and prevents the metabolism (the campfire) from slowing down, sabotaging your weight-control efforts. Fat loss doesn't show on the scale as quickly as loss of muscle and water weight; ideally you should lose no more than one to two pounds per week. This may seem slow, but losing the right kind of weight will make you look and feel great! Fat comes off wherever fat is, not just in your face and chest. (See Tables 20 and 21 above and on page 46 to determine your ideal

TABLE 21

HOW TO DETERMINE YOUR DAILY CALORIC NEEDS

If you are female, multiply your ideal weight by 11. If you are moderately active, multiply your ideal weight by 13. If very active (burning at least 500 calories each day through exercise or physical work), multiply your ideal weight by 15.

If you are male, multiply your ideal weight by 12. If moderately active, by 15. If very active, by 20.

The total will be the approximate number of calories you need each day to maintain your weight. To lose 1 pound each week you must lower your daily caloric intake by 500 calories below this maintenance level.

Example: I weigh 125 pounds and am moderately active. Multiplying my weight by 13 gives a daily caloric need of 1,625. To lose 1 pound each week I need to take in 1,125 calories each day. I want only 20 percent of these calories to come from fat — or 36 grams per day.

weight and your daily caloric needs.)

As I have said before, a calorie is indeed a calorie, but how and when you eat those calories makes quite a difference in how they are burned. You don't want to eat all your calories at one time in the evening when the metabolism has slowed down in response to being starved all day. In such a case the body can convert even a decreased number of consumed calories each day to fat because it's not burning as well as it would if the same number of calories were eaten in smaller quantities more evenly spaced throughout the day.

Keep Your Metabolism Revved Up

The two keys to keeping your metabolism burning are simple: Keep eating proteins with carbohydrates and keep exercising. Research shows that most people with weight problems not only eat too much, but they also exercise too little. Controlling your intake of food is not an alternative to exercise, nor is exercise an alternative to healthy eating. Both are important to total wellness. Exercise *decreases* your appetite while it *increases* your metabolic rate. Some studies show that metabolism continues working at a higher rate for up to three hours after proper aerobic exercise. Exercise also serves as a powerful stress release, often being the ticket to proper stress management.

Cutting Your Appetite

Many people find that their biggest health challenge is in controlling *how much* they eat. Even if they are eating food that's good for them, they eat too much of that good food. If this is you, it will be excit-

ing for you to find that food through the day keeps a ravenous appetite away! Portion control is a benefit of appetite control. When you're eating right things at the right time, you do not so easily fall into the wrong things at the wrong time. You don't have to rely on iron-will discipline to control your food intake. By following an eating plan that meets the physical needs of your body, you *will* be in control. (See Tables 22-24 on pages 48-53 for generalized meal plans.)

While you can't go through life weighing and measuring everything you eat, you may want to do so when you first start on your new nutrition plan till you get used to the proper portion sizes for you. If you are eating in the proper timing and balance, you will be satisfied with much less food, so you should be able to stick to these amounts.

Healthy Hints for Appetite Control

Try not to have more than two cups of beverages containing caffeine per day. In addition to its health risks, caffeine will stimulate your appetite! Try to buy coffee decaffeinated by the Swiss water method to avoid the chemicals used in most decaffeination. Look for this on the label. If the label says nothing, beware!

Eat the fruit and vegetables on your plate first. They cause a quicker rise in your blood sugar and will make you feel full more quickly.

Eat slowly. It takes twenty to twenty-five minutes for your brain to get the message that your stomach is satisfied. Dine — don't eat!

Warm foods are more satisfying than cold. Cold foods stimulate more gastric acid to be produced and will not satisfy, but often intensify, hunger.

Water is the best beverage you can drink to replace fluid after exercise. If you are not getting enough fluid to meet your body's need, you may crave salty foods.

Stay out of tempting territory. Don't buy problem foods and snacks in the first place, or keep them out of sight. A glimpse of a tempting food is enough to alert your brain mechanism and start your gastric juices flowing.

Always have your healthy snack handy: at home, in your car or in your desk drawer. Several small meals a day deposit less fat than one or two large meals, even if you eat the same food and the same amount of food. The secret of healthful snacking is to plan ahead. If you don't have the right food available, you'll reach for the wrong food! Or, just as poor a choice, you will not eat at all. Both alternatives set the stage for disaster later in the day.

Never go to the grocery store hungry. Everything will look good! Eat first; shop later. Take a grocery list with you and stick to it.

Recognize that television advertisements are not in the least concerned with your health or long life! They are expertly designed to tempt you and convince you that you desire something you neither want nor need. Don't be conned!

All alcoholic beverages are loaded with empty calories and have absolutely no nutritional value.

Choose crunchy foods over soft foods. Psychologically we need to chew; it releases stress and tension.

TABLE 22

HAVE IT YOUR WAY
WEIGHT-LOSS MEAL PLAN FOR WOMEN

Breakfast (within 1/2 hour of arising)

Complex Carbohydrate .... 1 slice whole wheat bread
OR 1/2 whole wheat English muffin
OR 3/4 cup cereal with raw bran added (begin with 1 teaspoon bran, gradually increasing to 2 tablespoons)

Protein .... 1 ounce part-skim cheese
OR 1/2 cup nonfat plain yogurt
OR 3/4 cup skim milk for cereal
OR 1 egg (limit whole eggs to 3 times per week) or 1/4 cup egg substitute

Simple Carbohydrate .... 1 small piece fresh fruit

Morning Snack

Carbohydrate .... 3 whole grain crackers
OR 1 small piece fresh fruit
OR 1 rice cake or Wasa bread

Protein .... 1 ounce part-skim cheese or lean meat
OR 1/2 cup nonfat plain yogurt with 1 teaspoon all-fruit jam

Lunch

Complex Carbohydrate .... 2 slices whole wheat bread
OR 1 baked potato
OR 1 whole wheat pita bread

Protein .... 2 ounces part-skim cheese
OR 2 ounces cooked poultry, fish or lean roast beef
OR 1/2 cup cooked legumes

Simple Carbohydrate .... 1 small piece fresh fruit
OR 1 cup noncreamed soup

Healthy Munchie (optional) .... raw vegetable salad with no-oil salad dressing

Added Fat (optional) .... 1 teaspoon mayonnaise (or 1 tablespoon light mayonnaise)
OR 1 teaspoon margarine (1 tablespoon reduced-calorie margarine)
OR 1 teaspoon olive oil or canola oil
OR 1 tablespoon salad dressing

Afternoon Snack

Repeat earlier snack choices.

Dinner

Complex Carbohydrate.............. 1/2 cup rice or pasta
OR 1/2 cup starchy vegetable

Protein .... 2 to 3 ounces cooked chicken, turkey, fish, seafood or lean roast beef
OR 1/2 cup cooked legumes

Simple Carbohydrate................. 1 cup nonstarchy vegetable
OR 1 small piece fresh fruit

Healthy Munchie (optional) ...... raw vegetable salad with no-oil salad dressing

Added Fat (optional) .... 1 teaspoon margarine (1 tablespoon reduced-calorie margarine)
OR 1 teaspoon olive oil
OR 1 tablespoon salad dressing

Evening Snack

1 small piece fresh fruit
OR 3 cups microwave light popcorn

Free Items

raw vegetables, mustard, vinegar, lemon juice

TABLE 23

HAVE IT YOUR WAY
WEIGHT-MAINTENANCE MEAL PLAN FOR WOMEN
AND WEIGHT-LOSS MEAL PLAN FOR MEN

Breakfast (within 1/2 hour of arising)

Complex Carbohydrate..............2 slices whole wheat bread
OR 1 whole wheat English muffin
OR 1-1/2 cups cereal with raw bran added (begin with 1 teaspoon bran, gradually increasing to 2 tablespoons)

Protein.......................................2 ounces part-skim cheese
OR 1 cup skim milk for cereal
OR 2 eggs (limit whole eggs to 2 times per week) or 1/2 cup egg substitute

Simple Carbohydrate ....1 piece fresh fruit

Morning Snack

Carbohydrate.............................5 whole grain crackers
OR 1 small piece fresh fruit
OR 2 rice cakes or Wasa breads

Protein.......................................2 ounces part-skim cheese or lean meat
OR 2 tablespoons natural peanut butter (limit peanut butter to one time per day)
OR 1 cup nonfat plain yogurt with 1 teaspoon all-fruit jam

Lunch

Complex Carbohydrate..............2 slices whole wheat bread
OR 1 baked potato
OR 1 whole wheat pita bread

Protein.......................................2 to 3 ounces part-skim cheese
OR 2 to 3 ounces cooked poultry, fish or lean roast beef
OR 3/4 cup cooked legumes

Simple Carbohydrate ....1 piece fresh fruit
OR 1 cup noncreamed soup

Healthy Munchie (optional).......raw vegetable salad with no-oil salad dressing

Added Fat (optional) .... 1 teaspoon mayonnaise (1 tablespoon light mayonnaise)
             OR 1 teaspoon margarine (1 tablespoon reduced-calorie margarine)
             OR 1 teaspoon olive oil or canola oil
             OR 1 tablespoon salad dressing

Afternoon Snack

Repeat earlier snack choices
OR 1/2 cup trail mix (recipe on page 111)

Dinner

Complex Carbohydrate.............. 1 cup rice or pasta
             OR 1 cup starchy vegetable

Protein .... 3 to 4 ounces cooked chicken, turkey, fish, seafood or lean roast beef
             OR 1 cup cooked legumes

Simple Carbohydrate................ 1 cup nonstarchy vegetable
             OR 1 piece fresh fruit

Healthy Munchie (optional) ...... raw vegetable salad with no-oil salad dressing

Added Fat (optional) .... 1 teaspoon margarine (1 tablespoon reduced-calorie margarine)
             OR 1 teaspoon olive oil
             OR 2 tablespoons sour cream
             OR 1 tablespoon salad dressing

Evening Snack

Repeat earlier snack choices
OR 3/4 cup cereal with 1/2 cup skim milk

Free Items

raw vegetables, mustard, vinegar, lemon juice, no-oil salad dressing

TABLE 24

HAVE IT YOUR WAY
WEIGHT-MAINTENANCE MEAL PLAN FOR MEN

Breakfast (within 1/2 hour of arising)

Complex Carbohydrate .... 2 slices whole wheat bread
OR 1 whole wheat English muffin
OR 1-1/2 cups cereal with raw bran added (begin with 1 teaspoon bran, gradually increasing to 2 tablespoons)

Protein .... 2 ounces part-skim cheese
OR 2 tablespoons natural peanut butter (limit peanut butter to one time per day)
OR 1 cup skim milk for cereal
OR 2 eggs (limit whole eggs to 2 times per week) or 1/2 cup egg substitute

Simple Carbohydrate .... 1 piece fresh fruit

Morning Snack

Carbohydrate .... 5 whole grain crackers
OR 1 piece fresh fruit
OR 2 rice cakes or Wasa breads

Protein .... 2 ounces part-skim cheese or lean meat
OR 2 tablespoons natural peanut butter (limit peanut butter to one time per day)
OR 1 cup nonfat plain yogurt with 1 teaspoon all-fruit jam

Lunch

Complex Carbohydrate .... 2 slices whole wheat bread
OR 1 baked potato
OR 1 whole wheat pita bread

Protein .... 3 to 4 ounces part-skim cheese
OR 3 to 4 ounces cooked poultry, fish or lean roast beef
OR 1 cup cooked legumes

Simple Carbohydrate .... 1 piece fresh fruit
AND 1 cup non-creamed soup

Healthy Munchie (optional) .... raw vegetable salad with no-oil salad dressing

Added Fat (optional) .... 1 teaspoon mayonnaise (1 tablespoon light mayonnaise)
OR 1 teaspoon margarine (1 tablespoon reduced-calorie margarine)
OR 1 teaspoon olive oil or canola oil
OR 1 tablespoon salad dressing

Afternoon Snack

Repeat earlier snack choices
OR 1/2 cup trail mix (recipe on page 111)

Dinner

Complex Carbohydrate.............. 1 cup rice or pasta
OR 1 cup starchy vegetable

Protein .... 4 ounces cooked chicken, turkey, fish, seafood or lean roast beef
OR 1 cup cooked legumes

Simple Carbohydrate................. 1 cup nonstarchy vegetable
AND 1 piece fresh fruit

Healthy Munchie (optional) ...... raw vegetable salad with no-oil salad dressing

Added Fat (optional) .... 2 teaspoons margarine (2 tablespoons reduced-calorie margarine)
OR 2 teaspoons olive oil
OR 2 tablespoons sour cream
OR 2 tablespoons salad dressing

Evening Snack

Repeat earlier snack choices
OR any Power Snack (see pages 12 and 111-113)
OR 1 cup cereal with 3/4 cup skim milk

Free Items

raw vegetables, mustard, vinegar, lemon juice, no-oil salad dressing

CHAPTER EIGHT
STRESS-BUSTERS: EXERCISE AND NUTRITION

No one needs a definition for stress. Most of us feel we are experts at it! But stress is prompted by different things in different people. What is challenging to you may be incredibly stressful to me. And intense, crisis-oriented stress is different from a day-to-day feeling-out-of-control stress. This chronic type of stress takes a particular toll on the body. It has been said that in this modern age things don't get better or get worse — they just get different!

Because we are three-part beings, we have a three-part response to stress; we respond spiritually, emotionally and physically. Our emotional and spiritual reaction to stress is set according to the emotional and spiritual atmosphere in which we live. If our emotions are thriving in an atmosphere of love, stress can stretch us into new and healthy places. If our spirits are thriving in an atmosphere of faith, the stress can allow growth and a birth of vision.

Our physical response to stress is more universal. It is set by the elaborate programming with which we were created. We were created to survive, and our bodies were finely tuned to ensure it.

Fight or Flight

We respond to stress with a "fight or flight" mechanism. Our bodies recognize the stress we experience as danger, something like a grizzly bear in our path. To survive, we were created either to run (the flight) or to fight this dangerous bear. When stressed, the body goes into a conservation mechanism to allow optimum defense. In this state of conservation, (1) the body's metabolism slows, storing excess energy for the fight or flight; (2) the body's blood sugar fluctuates, stimulating an appetite for higher-calorie foods to provide the needed energy; and (3) the body will retain excess fluids to keep the body in proper hydration for the defense.

This metabolic slow-down explains the physical side of quick weight gain in stressful times. Certainly overeating due to the stress also plays a part, but while in the stress response the body does a lot more damage with what comes in.

As the blood sugars fluctuate, energy drops, mood drops, but appetite soars! Yes, there's a physical reason you are apt to be so tired and cranky in stressful times. And, yes, there's a physical reason you crave M & Ms when you get stressed! Double whammy this with the emotions asking for food to tranquilize the stressful feelings, and iron-will discipline crumbles.

As for fluid retention, the extra fluid leads to a bloated, sluggish feeling. The stress response also affects GI motility, so it is not unusual for GI irritation, constipation or diarrhea to accompany stress.

Because the stress we experience is not a grizzly bear that we can fight or run from, we never get a stress release. Because we have to "grin and bear it" rather than fight it, our bodies stay in the stress response — with all its accompanying symptoms. And, interestingly, research even shows that the body's physical response appears to be the same for both positive and negative stress; the body can't discern the difference.

The Nutritional Strategy

A strategy of good nutrition can provide a deflective shield against the physical symptoms of stress. Properly timed and balanced eating can gear up the body's slowed metabolism. As the blood sugars fluctuate in response to stress, right foods at the right time can provide an undergirding of support, keeping them even and high. Proper intake of proteins and fluids helps restore proper fluid balance.

Good nutrition is never more important than when we're stressed. But good eating usually goes out the window in times of stress — just when we need it most as our defensive shield. And exercise usually gets put on the back burner or even kicked off the stove!

Exercise: Your Ticket to Stress Release

As much as good nutrition can serve as a defensive shield for the body in stress, exercise is *the* offensive tool — the sword in your hand to cut off the stress response of the body.

In the body's fight-or-flight reaction to stress, the brain secretes chemicals that tell the body it is in danger. These chemicals are responsible for the symptoms of stress, from a slowed metabolism to gastrointestinal distress. Because it simulates the fight or flight, aerobic exercise allows the release of stress-busting chemicals called *endorphins*. Like morphine, the endorphins medicate the stress sensor, telling the body the danger is gone. So exercise can be your way of taking control of stress, rather than letting it control you. When your life is most stressful, when you have the *least time* to exercise, you have the most to gain from it.

How often do you need to exercise? The answer depends on your individual goals. A person actively seeking fitness needs to be exercising four to five times each week. A person working to maintain good fitness should be exercising three to four times each week. A person under intensive stress may need some form of exercise every day. *It is the physical way to process that stress effectively!*

Exactly What Does Exercise Do for You?

Exercise increases your metabolism and decreases your appetite! Exercise and nutrition are a great combination for the body and the mind. Both increase your self-esteem, improve your general appearance and give you a wonderful sense of well-being.

Exercise improves your quality of sleep, allowing you to wake up feeling more rested and refreshed.

Exercise helps to lower blood pressure.

Aerobic exercise increases your protection against heart disease by improving your heart's condition and increasing your HDL cholesterol (the good guy!). It helps make your heart more efficient by setting up new cardiac pathways, reducing your risk of heart problems. Any exercise that raises your pulse to a training rate (gets you breathing hard) is an aerobic exercise. The benefits occur from achieving that increased pulse rate and maintaining it for at least twenty minutes three times a week. Many exercise experts encourage gradually increasing your exercise time up to an hour every other day.

Exercise breaks the plateaus or "set points" of weight loss. It is an external way of boosting the metabolism, offsetting the body's natural lowering of the metabolic rate to keep the body at a certain weight.

Exercise helps in diabetes management, making the cells of the body more accepting of insulin. The subsequent improved blood sugar control, along with the accompanied improvements in circulation and weight control, help form a counterattack against diabetes.

Any weight-bearing exercise, even walking, will increase the density of the bones, preventing calcium loss and making them less prone to injury and brittleness.

Exercise helps with arthritis management. Non-abusive exercise helps keep joints mobile and provides valuable stress release.

Exercise is nature's best tranquilizer. Just thirty minutes of aerobic exercise a day is one of the tried and true methods of releasing tension.

Exercising for Life!

Despite the benefits of exercise, it is difficult to find a program we can enjoy and stick to. As a result, too many of us have a history of start-and-stop exercising. Others drive themselves to work out but derive little pleasure from it. Others simply avoid exercise altogether. If you fall into one of these categories, you probably haven't found the form of exercise that suits you best. To jump on the fitness bandwagon — and stay on it — you need to select an exercise that matches your life-style, fills your fitness needs and seems enjoyable. You may be convinced that no form of exercise will ever seem enjoyable. But keep in mind your new perspective about exercise: It can be a "sword in your hand" to cut off the stress mechanism and lower your level of stress. Who could give up that opportunity?

The major aerobic activities include brisk walking, running, swimming and bicycling. Then there's aerobic dance, which combines the toning benefits of calisthenics with a good heart workout and stress release. A number of routines will fit your needs, but you'll stick with the ones you find the most fun, and the exercises you'll find most enjoyable are those you feel you can handle. If you have difficulty with eye-hand coordination, you may feel frustrated by a sport like tennis but do well with swimming or walking, which requires less coordination. If you are not naturally flexible, you may be happier with bicycling than ballet.

Consider the shape you are in. If you are overweight, any activity in which you pound land forcibly on your feet may stress your joints by placing too much weight on them. In such cases, try riding a stationary bike or swimming instead of running or aerobic dance.

I advise all newcomers to regular exercise to consider walking. Begin by measuring off a mile and walking it briskly. How long did it take you to walk that mile? Now gradually increase your pace until you walk it in fifteen minutes. Then add a second mile and work up to walking the two miles in thirty minutes. Then add a third mile and work till you can walk the three miles in forty to forty-five minutes. By starting with something you can already do, anytime, anywhere, you'll be more apt to build a natural routine.

Remember that exercise is something you do as an act of kindness to your body, not as a punishment. "No pain, no gain" is a lie. The truth is "Gain through no pain!" So start slow and avoid overtaxing yourself. The biggest mistake people make is doing too much, too soon. Be sure to warm up before exercise and cool down afterward. By warming up your muscles — stretching them, then beginning your exercise at a slow pace — you help prevent injury. Cooling down — reducing the pace of your exercise, then stretching the muscles — helps stop them from tightening up and cramping. Be sure to set realistic goals for yourself and gradually build up to a good pace. Do not try to win the Olympics the first time out. You will end up in the emergency room — or vowing never to exercise again.

If you're over thirty-five, most exercise experts encourage you to see a health professional for an "all-points" check before beginning an exercise program.

Write *exercise* into your daily and weekly schedule book. Look at your schedule and determine the best time for you to exercise: first thing in the morning, on the way to work, before lunch, on the way home or after work. Whenever it is, your exercise time has to be a priority commitment — as if it were a business appointment you simply could not cancel. Your well-being is that important!

Remember that good eating is a must for effective exercise. A person who is eating sporadically with poor nutrient balance will not achieve optimal building of lean body mass or increased energy levels. Never go into an exercise session without having eaten properly beforehand.

As vital as good nutrition is to total wellness, it is only one of the spokes in the wellness wheel. The proper combination of balanced eating and balanced exercise is an unbeatable way to total well-being. But you can't store fitness. It's consistent exercise that gives you more energy, better concentration, less depression, better sleep and ammunition against disease. Commitment to an exercise routine that goes hand in hand with good nutrition is one of the greatest gifts you can ever give yourself.

Let it be something you choose to do for life!

CHAPTER NINE

DON'T MAKE RULES— DEVELOP HABITS

Often we get so caught up in the rules of a diet that we miss the most important part of a life-style strategy: changing attitudes and perspectives about food and eating to allow a change of habit. Some eating is habitual as an automatic response to various life situations. Old habits can be triggered into action by memories, nostalgia, even friends. Change toward a life-style of wellness must include a change of attitude and relationship with food. To live free over food *and* dieting means being able to enjoy food without abusing it. It means walking around not feeling deprived!

A major challenge in your personal change will be dealing with family and friends who are losing a familiar you. When they see glimpses of a new you, family and friends often feel they have more to lose than to gain. Why? Being human, they dislike change. As unhealthy as you may have been, the status quo is comfortable for them.

Prepare for others' reactions. Who will try to sabotage you? If you can expect others' negative actions and comments, you can minimize their negative effect on you.

Many people express their love by feeding others rich and "special" foods. If you are on the receiving end of such an unhealthy arrangement, you need to show lovingly that food and love are not synonymous to you. Your "food provider" will gradually learn to express his or her love in other ways.

If you cook for a family, you may see this tendency in yourself. In wanting to please them, you may hesitate to feed them the same healthy, energy-building foods that you are eating. "My family doesn't have the problem; I do. They won't want to give up their favorite foods." But you do not need to contribute to the unhealthiness of others any longer! I see a great number of people who feed others all the foods they feel they "can't eat." Don't be a party to the same behaviors that have entrapped you.

"Just Say No!"

"Just say no!" is a powerful campaign against drug use in children. The irony of such a campaign is that we, as adults, can't even say no to a chocolate chip cookie! How can we think our children can say no to drugs? Peer pressure didn't die in high school; it is alive and well no matter what one's age.

How do you say no? Never say, "I *can't* eat this." Say, "I don't care for any, thank you." You will be communicating strength and decisiveness *and* making a positive confession. The truth is, you *can* eat anything; there are just some foods you choose not to eat!

I have my clients practice saying no to the rearview mirror while driving, to the bathroom mirror while shaving, even to their make-up mirrors. Just practicing the word, seeing the word form on their lips, prepares them to "just say no" to unhealthy eating. There is no need to explain why you are saying "No, thank you" when you're offered a food that doesn't fit into your wellness plan. There is no need to feel guilty either, especially when the person doing the offering is a friend who knows the efforts you are making to be free over food. A caring friend will respect your desire for freedom and will understand a simple "No, thank you."

You will hear things like "Come on, you can splurge tonight. You deserve a little fun once in a while!" "Oh, just a little bit won't hurt!" Even, "I think you are carrying this too far. This nutrition thing is taking over your life." Prepare for discouraging words and temptations. Again, answer with a simple "No, thank you." It is your life and your choice for a healthy one. Remember, you are the only person capable of gaining the health you desire for yourself. Another person cannot force or prevent your changing. Their words and actions may have an effect on you, but ultimately *you* make the decisions for your actions.

Be Prepared

As you make any dietary change, your body needs time to adjust physiologically and emotionally. As you start to keep the Ten Commandments of Great Nutrition, you may experience a somewhat uncomfortable physical adjustment lasting at least five or six days. Expect the following:

Days 1 and 2: You will be slightly sluggish and irritable and a little dissatisfied with your eating.

Day 3: One of your most difficult days, as your body will begin to feel the chemical change. It may seem that every cell is crying out for food, particularly something sweet! Expect this day to be a struggle, but not an impossible one to overcome.

Day 4: If you make it through day 3 without overeating, this one won't be so difficult.

Day 5: The day of the ravenous appetite; you can expect to be hungry for food, not necessarily sweets, just food! You can eat a meal and think: That was a good appetizer. What else is there to eat?

Days 6 and 7: It is getting easier. You begin to have more energy, and your appetite is more in your control. You are on the road to a lifetime of good eating.

When most people start a "diet" on Monday morning, they never make it past Monday afternoon's "arsenic hour." Even if they do, when Wednesday's third-day withdrawal pains hit, the diet usually goes out the window. If they make it past Wednesday, they are destined to fail when Friday's fifth-day "hungries" hit. Then it's the weekend, and why get started again till Monday? This pattern is repeated week after week. *The third and fifth days are always the most difficult; circle them on your calendar in red.*

I know this sounds more like withdrawal from a strongly addictive drug than simply allowing your body to adjust to a healthy way of eating. But the reality is, putting *in* the healthy foods means leaving *out* the unhealthy, and that means a chemical change — a withdrawal of sorts. I would rather you know what to expect than to give up in defeat as soon as you get started. In the past, when withdrawal pains of a new diet plan began, you may have soothed them with food. This time you can speak back to them, knowing they are necessary but temporary!

Cravings: Real or Imagined?

Even after you have adjusted physically to the new way of eating, you will at times crave certain favorite foods. You miss that old friend! But it's not necessarily your taste buds that are noticing the loss. When you crave that particular food, evaluate your day. Did you get off your routine of eating the right foods at the right time? Did you go too long without a meal or snack? Did you miss out on a proper balance of carbohydrates and proteins? If so, the physical you is sending out a message: "Feed me! I *need* food!" At the same time, the emotional you may be sending a message: "Feed me! I *want* food!" The emotional you is missing the comfort of that old favorite. In your memory a certain food may symbolize happier times; without it you feel deprived.

These cravings can be the undoing of your new walk of wellness, and the best way to handle cravings is to prevent them by keeping your physical system in balance. A regular, balanced diet is especially important when you are most stressed and most vulnerable to the emotional messages that signal you to eat. When the feelings get too hot to handle, it *seems* simpler to return to the old way of eating than to stay on the course of healthy eating.

Breaking Patterns

Much of our eating is based on habitual patterns. Even when we have embraced a new life-style of eat-

ing, a party or a birthday will come along and tempt us to fall back to traditional fare. Old ways are comfortable and sometimes so subtle that we aren't even aware of this power. Let's look at some common unhealthy patterns and how they can be broken.

Tips for the "Taster"

A lot of our eating is not done consciously. While cooking, it's easy to pop in a taste of this here, a bite of that there, a little more of those and a spoonful of that! While cleaning the table, we remember our childhood teachings about wasting food. ("You need to clean your plate to help the starving children in Asia.") Stop. All those "tastes" can easily add up to an entire meal's worth of calories!

Here's how you can break the tasting chain:

If you feel you must taste what you are preparing to adjust the spices, keep a measuring teaspoon available for the tasting. This helps reduce the amount you taste. If you add spices, do so in precisely measured amounts. Once you get a recipe just right, record exact amounts of ingredients so you can trust the recipe without having to taste next time.

Mom wasn't exactly telling you the truth about cleaning your plate to save starving children! Your unhealthiness from overeating has never helped the hunger effort. If you want to aid these children, send money or support a charity. Don't overeat!

Remember this: Wasting food is wasting food, be it in a body or in a trash can. The difference: It doesn't hurt the trash can, but it may hurt your health!

Come and Dine

We are not just fast-food eaters; we are *fast* eaters! We need to slow down and dine even to begin to hear our body's natural satisfaction signals. The appetite is satisfied by a triggering system in which the body tells the brain, "You are full. Stop eating!" But this trigger takes twenty to twenty-five minutes to kick in. By eating in a fast and frenzied style, you can consume enormous quantities of food before you feel satisfied. *Slow down your eating and give your body a chance for natural portion control!* Here's how:

Make dining a separate experience, not an activity synonymous with watching TV or reading. (This will prevent the TV from becoming an emotional trigger — it's time to eat.)

Be sure to dine only while sitting at the dining table, not over the sink. This applies to snacks as well as meals. Eating over the sink or in front of an open refrigerator does not equate with dining satisfaction — only mindless eating!

Begin your meal with fruit as an appetizer. This simple carbohydrate will start raising your blood sugar, allowing your appetite regulator to be satisfied by the time you finish your meal. Fruit as an appetizer will also prevent the drowsiness that often follows a meal; it's natural sugar is quickly released as energy into your bloodstream (within fifteen to twenty minutes).

Serve salad or raw vegetables as your second course. Most people find this slows down the meal itself and provides them with bulk for dulling their appetite.

Never serve food "family style." This leads to the clean-out-the-bowl habit and makes portion control difficult, if not impossible. Serve food onto plates at the stove, putting leftovers away before you sit down to eat. Then "going for more" will require more effort. You might even practice leaving a few bites on your plate, which will put a dent in the clean-plate syndrome!

Completely chew and swallow before putting more food on the fork. We are usually so busy shoveling the food in that we don't realize we have forks, poised and ready, at our mouths while we're still chewing the prior bite! Practice putting your fork down at least every third bite.

Eat your small protein portion intermittently between the other items on your plate. Once the meat is gone, we tend to feel that we are only "finishing up."

Meal Planning

The art of cooking doesn't stop at the stove. It is part of the concept and planning of the meal, the presentation and everything in between. When planning meals, consider what tastes good together and what looks good together, such as color and texture contrasts. Pair something hard with something soft, something crisp with something creamy. A plate with everything soft and creamy will be as unappealing as a plate of all white foods (steamed fish, mashed potatoes, lima beans and applesauce — yuk!). Instead, go for bright colors that help make the dish look fresh and alive.

These meal suggestions may provide a good start for you.

Perfect Breakfasts That Are Quick, Easy and Delicious!

1) Cheese Danish (page 87)
2) Oatmeal With a Difference (page 86)
3) Framed Egg (page 86)

4) Everyday French Toast (page 89)
5) Oatmeal Pancakes (page 91)
6) Quick Breakfast Shake (page 98)
7) Breakfast Parfait (page 88)
8) Cheese Apple Slices (page 87)
9) Muffin and More (Oat Bran Muffin — page 179; 8 ounces skim milk or nonfat plain yogurt; fresh fruit)

Wonderful Lunches

Don't skip lunch, and don't get into a rut either! For a lunch that will refresh you and keep your energy high, try one of these delicious and fast, complete meals:

1) Seafood Salad (page 105)
2) Rolled Delite (page 104)
3) Chicken Waldorf Salad (page 106)
4) Grilled Cheese of the Nineties (page 104)
5) Pita Pizzas (page 104)
6) The "Smithwich" (page 103)
7) Quesadillas (page 106)
8) Carrot-Cheese Melt (page 105)

Easy, Delicious and Healthy Dinners

Having a basic format to work from can be invaluable. Start with the following ideas. They are perfectly balanced and easy, and everyone will like them. Freeze properly portioned leftovers in freezer bags or containers for quick meals when you need them most!

1) Oven-baked Chicken — protein (page 129)
   Peas Rosemary — complex carbohydrate and fat (page 190)
   Steamed Cabbage — simple carbohydrate
   Fresh Carrot Salad — simple carbohydrate (page 194)

2) Marvelous Meat Loaf — protein and complex carbohydrate (page 147)
   Corn on the Cob — complex carbohydrate
   Colorful Green Beans — simple carbohydrate (page 186)
   Romaine Salad — healthy munchie

3) Hawaiian Chicken — protein (page 132)
   Wild Rice Pilaf — complex carbohydrate (page 170)
   Green Beans With Mushrooms — simple carbohydrate (page 186)
   Sliced Tomatoes — healthy munchie

4) Salmon of the Day — protein (pages 140-142)
   Baked Sweet Potato — complex carbohydrate
   Steamed Broccoli — simple carbohydrate
   Waldorf in Disguise — simple carbohydrate
   (page 193)

5) Chili con Carne — protein, complex carbohy-
   drate and simple carbohydrate (page 134)
   Romaine Salad — healthy munchie
   Sliced Melon — simple carbohydrate

6) Basque Chicken or Stir-fry Chicken With
   Cashews and Snow Peas — protein and
   complex carbohydrate (pages 128/132)
   Steamed Asparagus — simple carbohydrate
   Spinach and Apple Salad — healthy munchie
   and fat (page 193)

7) Italian Swiss Steak — protein (page 147)
   Whole Wheat Pasta — complex carbohydrate
   Steamed Yellow Squash — simple
   carbohydrate
   Romaine Salad — healthy munchie

8) Easy Chicken and Rice — protein (page 127)
   Caesar Salad — healthy munchie and fat
   (page 192)
   Fresh Berries — simple carbohydrate

9) Spaghetti Pie — protein, complex carbohydrate and simple carbohydrate (page 134)
   Marinated Vegetables — healthy munchie
   (page 194)

Party Well

There's nothing like a party to bring out the worst in our old habits and attitudes about food. Parties are like mini-vacations — a time to let go. Use these party tips to help your choices be naturally wise — and naturally better!

Always eat a healthy snack before going to parties, open houses and so forth, so your "appetite for the appetizers" will be in control. You're then better prepared to taste what you choose with wisdom; you won't be eating out of hunger. Stay away from the food table; fix your plate and talk elsewhere!

Never, never starve the day of a big party or meal. You will only throw off your metabolism and set yourself up for disaster. Instead, eat small, evenly spaced meals throughout the day, keeping your metabolism and appetite in better control.

Never tell people you are dieting; it is self-sabotage. You will instantly be talked into eating everything. If you feel you must say anything, say, "No, thank you." Don't look pitiful in a corner. No one ever notices that the life of the party isn't eating!

Remember, it's not the big parties that are a problem, but your day-by-day eating. Avoid the "I've blown it now" syndrome.

Always offer to bring an appetizer or salad so that you are sure of at least one healthy choice.

Don't give a food-focused party; when you are in charge, plan other activities besides eating.

Holiday Dinners That Celebrate Life!

For centuries holidays have centered around the sharing of food. This year allow your holidays to be a celebration of the healthy life you have found. Holiday food does not have to be sinful to be enjoyable, nor does the meal have to be the center of the celebration. The dinner should be just one part of a glorious day that celebrates life!

Here are some healthy holiday menu plans that will please even your skeptical guests.

New Year's Dinner
Mixed Green Salad
Celebration Roast (page 145)
New Year's Black-eyed Peas (page 190)
Steamed Broccoli With
Tangy Chive Sauce (page 187)
Fresh Fruit Salad

New Year's Dinner With Football Fever
Fresh Vegetable Platter With Dips (pages 115-117)
Sliced Turkey and Roast Beef Platters
Taco Platter With Skinny Dippers (page 118)
Assorted Whole Wheat Bread and Rolls
Lettuce Leaves and Tomato Slices
Fresh Fruit
Date Bars (page 200)

Easter Dinner
Mixed Green Salad
Rosemary Roast Lamb (page 149)
Cauliflower With Happy-Daise Sauce (page 188)
Banana Blueberry Bread (page 177)
Wild Rice and Mushrooms (page 169)
Fresh Fruit Pie (page 203)

Fourth of July With Flair
Fresh Vegetable Platter With Dips (page 115-117)
Chicken Hawaiian (page 120)
Corn on the Cob
Eggplant-Squash Casserole (page 155)
Watermelon Quarters

Fourth of July Traditional
Marinated Vegetables (page 194)
Cole Slaw With a Difference (page 194)
Grilled Hamburgers on Whole Wheat Buns
Lettuce Leaves and Tomato Slices
Hollowed Watermelon With Fresh Fruit

Thanksgiving Dinner
Fresh Vegetable Platter With Dips (page 115-117)
Roast Turkey (page 132)
Turkey Gravy — The Healthful Way (page 79)
Wild Rice and Mushrooms (page 169)
Sweet Potatoes Glorious (page 191)
Green Beans With Mushrooms (page 186)
Apricot Pecan Bread (page 177)
OR Oat Bran Muffins (page 179)
Raisin Pie (page 203)

Christmas Dinner
Cranberry Salad Mold (page 195)
Roasted Chicken With
Water Chestnut Sauce (page 125)
Peach Halves
Wild Rice Pilaf (page 170)
Spinach With a Twist (page 189)
Southern-Style Corn Muffins (page 181)
Baked Ambrosia (recipe on page 212)

An Italian Supper
Antipasto (page 192)
Lasagna (page 172)
Broccoli With
Orange and Sweet Red Pepper (page 187)
Raspberry Freeze (page 211)

Menu for a Mexican Fiesta
Chilled Broccoli Salad (page 195)
Quesadillas (page 106)
Chicken Enchiladas (page 129)
Vanilla Poached Pears (page 207)

Avoiding the "I've Blown It Now" Syndrome

Making changes in eating behavior is a lot like running a marathon; it takes pacing, consistency and endurance. Those who jump out ahead, thinking they can take a short cut, will either burn out or get disqualified! Yet no amount of falling down can stop a runner determined to finish. That person just keeps running with eyes more closely focused on the track.

Overcoming Setbacks

Know that one lapse in your healthy pattern of eating does not ruin all the health previously obtained. Once you've started on the right track, your health will never be ruined with one extravagant meal, one hot dog at a ball game or one slice of birthday cake.

A lapse in your healthy life-style is just that, a lapse, a time when you made a less-than-ideal choice. Do not let it become a relapse, another relapse, another relapse and finally a collapse.

There is no atonement or "making up" for a poorly chosen meal. Do not try to fast the next day or punish yourself with restrictive dieting. Just choose to get back on track with your nutritious life-style of healthy eating.

Listen to your body and how bad it feels after eating poor-choice foods. Your body has been so wonderfully designed that it will reinforce your decision to eat in a healthier style. You are avoiding high-fat and highly sweetened foods because they are wellness-robbers; no food is worth feeling so bad! Expect GI distress, bloating and sluggishness.

If you are a scale-watcher, you will be disheartened by the jumps you see three to four days following a lapse in your good eating. (The scale may reflect up to four pounds of fluid retention.) The gain is only temporary, but the heavy and bloated feeling should remind you why you are choosing to eat in a healthier way.

Realize that there will be vulnerable times — hectic schedules, fatigue, personal obligations — that seem to draw you back to old, predictable patterns. Overcoming each difficult time will make the next time easier.

Live one day at a time, one meal at a time. Some days will work out as you had hoped they would, and some won't. The joys and rewards come from continuing to see changes in your attitudes, your body and your life. Remember, this is about healthy eating, not about dieting. Do not think in terms of "legals" or "cheatings," "goods" or "bads," "on it" or "off it." Think in terms of feeling great and being healthy.

DINING OUT: MAKING HEALTHY CHOICES

New research shows that America spends 40 percent of its food dollars dining away from home; dining out is no longer just for special occasions. For the health-conscious, dining out presents a culinary challenge: to enjoy fine food without compromising health.

The health dangers of dining out lie mostly in the hidden fats; the typical restaurant meal will give the equivalent of twelve to fourteen pats of butter! Never be timid about ordering foods in a special style. You are paying (and paying well!) for the meal and the service and deserve to have foods prepared to your preference. Learn to be discriminating, not intimidated!

A Discriminating Guide

Plan ahead. When you're in charge, choose a restaurant that you know and trust for quality food and a willingness to prepare foods in a healthful way upon request. More and more restaurants recognize that this trend toward healthy eating is not a passing fad; many progressive and responsible restaurants have begun to offer healthy menu selections. Supporting these restaurants will help to establish this tremendous service to the discerning diner.

Read between the lines. Think before you order! Menus are filled with clues about what the selections contain. Avoid these words:

- à la mode (with ice cream)
- au fromage (with cheese)
- au gratin (in cheese sauce)
- au lait (with milk)
- basted (with extra fat)
- bisque (cream soup)
- buttered (with extra fat)
- casserole (in some type of cream sauce)
- creamed (in extra fat)
- crispy (means fried)
- escalloped (with cream sauce)
- hash (with extra fat)
- hollandaise (with cream sauce)
- pan-fried (in fat)
- sautéed (fried with extra fat)

If you see these words in the description of an appealing entrée, be bold enough to ask for the entrée prepared in a special way. If the description says "buttered," ask for it without the added butter. If the description says "pan-fried," ask for it grilled or poached instead. Entrées poached in wine or lemon juice are good choices, as are those simmered in tomato sauce. A baked potato or a side of pasta with red sauce is often a better choice than rice pilaf, which is prepared with oil.

Ask questions. Remember, it's your health, your money and your waistline. If you have concerns about the way something will be prepared, discuss it kindly with the server. Don't be intimidated by the server or the people you are with.

Make special requests. Learn to say "on the side" and "no butter." Even though not stated on the menu, most foods will be prepared with fat, and more will be added before it is served to you. Ask for your salad dressing "on the side" (then apply sparingly; add extra lemon juice or vinegar for moistness). Order meats, fish or poultry broiled or grilled without butter and with sauces on the side. When fresh vegetables are available, ask for them steamed without butter. If you order a baked potato, ask for it without butter or with sour cream, butter, salsa, cottage cheese or mustard to the side.

Monitor extra fats — the pats of butter, the cream in coffee, not to mention the whipped cream on dessert! If the restaurant brings bread and rolls to the table, ask them to remove the butter (if no one in your party objects!). It's too easy to find yourself spreading that roll liberally with butter. Good crusty rolls really don't need the extra fat, especially when they are heated. (Request it!) The heat brings out natural flavor and makes them more satisfying. When the dessert tray comes by, ask for fresh berries (a much healthier choice than mousse).

Controlling Portions

Believe me: As an adult there are no rewards for cleaning your plate. Restaurant portions can be obscenely large, yet we often eat them, thinking ourselves virtuous. Many restaurants are answering the cry of *too much* by offering luncheon options at dinner time. You have other choices: Smaller appetizer selections are often just right and make a fine meal with an à la carte salad.

If you are dining with a willing companion, try ordering one meal (and an extra plate) to share. And don't forget "take home." You can often better enjoy what's left as an elegant lunch the next day.

Never eat "all you can eat" at brunches, buffets or covered-dish dinners — affairs that can easily become feeding frenzies! Instead, revise your perspective from "I need to get my money's worth" to "Look at all I have to choose from."

Healthful Dining Strategies

Let's look at the good and bad qualities of various

cuisines and restaurants. Think about this information as you consider eating well when eating out.

Breakfast Out

• If you buy breakfast later than normal, eat a snack when you first get up to gear up your metabolism and begin to stabilize your body.

• Always order whole wheat toast *unbuttered*. You be in control; you may add one teaspoon, if desired.

• Grits may be substituted for a serving of bread, but be sure to order them unbuttered.

• It's usually safer to order à la carte so you are not paying for, or tempted by, the abundance of unhealthy food in the "breakfast specials" or buffets.

• Be bold and creative. Rather than accepting French toast with syrup and bacon, ask for it prepared with whole wheat bread, no syrup and a side dish of fresh berries or fruit. Many restaurants will substitute cottage cheese or an egg for the breakfast meat.

• Many restaurants serve oatmeal and cereal even though it's not on the menu. It's a nice whole grain carbohydrate. Don't forget to ask for low-fat milk or yogurt, and top it with fresh berries or a banana.

• Always look for a protein and a carbohydrate — more than a Danish!

Healthy Choices:
• cereal with skim milk and fruit
• French toast (with whole wheat bread) and berries
• fresh fruit with cottage cheese or yogurt, whole wheat toast
• fresh vegetable egg-white omelet and toast
• scrambled egg substitute and unbuttered whole wheat toast

Fast-Food Restaurants

• Just say no to sauces: It's the mayonnaise, special sauces and sour cream that triple the fat, sodium and calories in fast foods; always order your food *without* them! And undress your salad; a single packet of regular dressing can contain as much fat as a double cheeseburger.

• Shun the cheese. The varieties commonly used by the fast-food chains are high in fat, cholesterol and calories.

• Stuffed potatoes may seem a healthy addition to the fast-food menu, but not with the cheese sauces they hold — often the equivalent to nine pats of butter per potato! Try chili or broccoli and salsa instead.

• Chicken is a lower-fat alternative to beef, but not when it's batter-fried! One serving of chicken nuggets has more than twice the fat of a regular hamburger. A chicken sandwich is no health package either. This greasy sandwich has enough fat to equal eleven pats of butter. The new grilled chicken sandwiches are much better, as long as you order them without the dressing and sauces.

• Salad bars can be a good way to add fiber and nutrients to a meal, but it's only the salad vegetables that do so. Leave the mayonnaise-based salads, the croutons and the bacon bits on the bar. Use little dressing, adding extra lemon juice or vinegar for moistness.

• Croissant sandwiches aren't a whole lot more than breakfast on a grease bun. Most croissants have the fat equivalent of more than four and a half pats of butter and the toppings add insult to injury!

• Frozen yogurt, although lower in fat and cholesterol, contains more sugar than ice cream. It is *not* a perfectly healthy substitute.

Don't get discouraged and think you can't ever eat fast food and still be healthy. You can still have a healthy fast-food meal; the goal is to learn to make wise choices. Learn what and how to order fast food. Here is a guide to help you:

Burger King

Healthiest Choices:
• B.K. Broiler Chicken Sandwich (without ranch dressing or mayo)
• Hamburger Deluxe (no mayo!) — for women
• Whopper (no mayo!) — for men

You may order a side salad with any of the above meals (with the light Italian dressing). Some Burger King restaurants have also begun to offer fresh fruit.

Worst Choices:
• Breakfast or Burger Buddies
• Chicken Sandwich
• Croissan'wich With Sausage, Egg and Cheese
• Double Whopper With Cheese
• Scrambled Egg Platter With Sausage

Chick-Fil-A

Healthiest Choices:
• Grilled Chicken Salad (no-oil salad dressing)
• Grilled Chicken Sandwich (no mayo)

McDonald's

Healthiest Choices:
• Chunky Chicken Salad (with your own crackers for carbohydrate)
• Hamburger (small)
• McLean Deluxe Sandwich (no mayo)

Worst Choices:
• Big Mac
• Chicken McNuggets
• Quarter Pounder With Cheese
• Sausage Biscuit With Egg
• Sausage McMuffin With Egg

Wendy's

Healthiest Choices:
• Baked Potato (plain, without cheese sauce; get with chili instead)
• Grilled Chicken Sandwich (without honey mustard; it's in a fat base)
• Jr. Hamburger (without mayo)
• Salad Bar (use raw vegetables as desired; avoid potato salad, macaroni salad and so forth; use garbanzo beans or chili for protein)

Worst Choices:
• Big Classic
• Crispy Chicken Nuggets
• Fish Fillet Sandwich
• Hot Stuffed Baked Potato
• Jr. Swiss Deluxe

Hardee's

Healthiest Choices:
• Chicken 'n' Pasta Salad
• Grilled Chicken Sandwich (no mayo!)
• Hamburger (no mayo!)

Worst Choices:
• Bacon Cheeseburger
• Big Country Breakfast With Sausage or Ham
• Big Deluxe Burger
• Fisherman's Fillet
• The Lean 1 (18 grams of fat!)
• Mushroom 'n' Swiss Burger

Taco Bell

Healthiest Choices:
• Soft Taco
• Taco
• Tostada With Red Sauce

Worst Choices:
• Mexican Pizza
• Nachos BellGrande, Nachos Supreme
• Soft Taco Supreme
• Taco BellGrande
• Taco Salad (with 61 grams of fat — 905 calories!)

Arby's or Rax

Healthiest Choices:
• Arby's Roasted Chicken Sandwich (no mayo!)
• Rax Turkey (no mayo!)
• Roast Beef Sandwich (no sauce!)

Pizza Places

Healthiest Choices:
• personal-size cheese pizza, with vegetables if desired (eat three quarters and save the remaining quarter for a snack)
• thin-crust 13-inch (medium) cheese pizza, with vegetables if desired (no sausage or pepperoni): 2 slices for women; 3 slices for men

Worst Choice:
• thick-crust or deep-dish pizza with sausage or pepperoni

Sub Shops or Delis

Healthiest Choices:
• mini-sub (turkey, roast beef, no oil or mayo)
• snack sub — 6 inches (turkey, roast beef, cheese, no oil or mayo)

Worst Choice:
• tuna subs — loaded with fat!

Deli and grocery stores will usually make you turkey, roast beef or Jarlsberg Lite sandwiches (ask for 3 ounces of meat on sandwich).

Health or Natural Food Restaurants

• Do not feel safe here by any means! Although you will have an opportunity to get whole grains and fresh vegetable salads, the fats and sodium can still sneak in quite deceptively. Beware of sauces and high-fat cheeses smothering the foods and high-fat dressings on salads and sandwiches. Many foods are prepared as they would be at a fast-food restaurant — but with healthier-sounding names. With judicious selections, you can do well here.

• Again, the salads and salad bars may be lovely, but follow the guideline of dressing to the side, used sparingly. Many salad bars have a protein source in cottage cheese, grated cheese or chopped eggs. (Aim for the egg whites, not the yolk.)

• If you have a cheese dish, use no other added fats; the cheese will contain enough for the day. Always ask if they can use mozzarella cheese. (It is almost always partly skimmed of fat.)

Healthy Choices:
• bean soup with salad (dressing on side)
• chef-type salad with whole grain roll (no ham or cheese)
• fruit plate with nonfat plain yogurt or cottage cheese and whole grain roll
• pitas stuffed with vegetables and meat or mozzarella cheese
• stir-fry dishes (ask for "light on the soy sauce")
• vegetable-egg white omelet with whole grain roll
• vegetable soup and half a turkey sandwich (avoid tuna or chicken salads)

Italian

• Portion control is very important here. Although pasta with red sauce is a relatively low-fat choice, a plateful is five times too much! Order a side portion or an appetizer serving of pasta with steamed seafood or grilled chicken or fish.

• Alfredo sauce is deadly, as is any white sauce. Ask for red sauce substitution.

• Garlic bread sticks are rolled in butter, then garlic. Special order without butter, and you'll receive them straight from the oven!

Warning words: Alfredo, cheese sauce, cream sauce, fried, pancetta, parmigiana, prosciutto, saltimbocca, white sauce

Healthy Choices:
• cioppino (seafood soup) or minestrone
• clams, mussels or scallops linguine with red sauce
• grilled chicken with pasta marinara
• grilled fresh fish with pasta marinara
• pasta e fagioli and salad

Mexican

• Ask that your salad be brought in place of the chips. It will help stop the "munch a bunch" syndrome!

• Beware of margaritas. They are loaded with salt and sugar — to say nothing of the alcohol.

• Order à la carte; whole-meal selections are laden with high-fat side dishes, such as refried beans (made with pure lard).

• Ask that the sour cream and cheese be omitted from your dish. The cheese is a high-fat cheddar or Monterey Jack with 10 grams of fat per ounce.

• Ask for guacamole on the side; 2 tablespoons contain the fat of a pat of butter.

• Never, never eat the fried tortilla shells that contain Mexican salads. Think of them as inedible, hard, plastic bowls. They are sponges for the grease they are cooked in!

Warning words: chimichangas, chorizo, con queso, fried, guacamole, served in a tortilla shell, shredded cheese, sour cream, tortilla chips

Healthy Choices:
• black bean soup or gazpacho
• chicken burrito or tostada
• chicken enchiladas
• chicken fajitas (without added fat)
• chili with salad
• soft chicken tacos

Oriental

Chinese, Korean, Thai or Vietnamese food can be an excellent choice for dining out, as stir-frying is the main method of cooking. This terrific technique cooks the vegetables quickly, retaining the nutrients; done properly, it uses very little oil.

• Order dishes lightly stir-fried (not deep-fried like egg rolls) and without heavy gravies or sweet and sour sauces.

• Half a dinner portion is appropriate, with

steamed brown or white rice. (Fried rice is just that, fried!)

• Ask for food prepared *without MSG* and be careful with the soy sauce you add. (Both are loaded with sodium!)

• Order sushi only at highly reputable restaurants that serve the freshest fish from the best sources.

Warning words: deep-fried, battered, fried, crispy, cashews, fried noodles, duck, bird's nest, tempura, tonkatsu (fried pork), torikatsu (fried chicken)

Healthy Choices:
• bamboo-steamed vegetables with scallops, chicken or whole steamed fish
• moo goo gai pan (with no MSG and little oil)
• tofu with vegetables (no MSG, little oil)
• udon (noodles) served with meat and vegetables
• won ton, hot and sour, or miso soup
• yakitori (meats broiled on skewers)

Seafood

• Order fresh seafood when possible — steamed, boiled, grilled or broiled without butter. For dipping, a small amount of cocktail sauce is a better choice than butter (2 dips in butter = 50 calories). Remember, when fried, small seafood items such as shrimp and oysters are deadly in terms of fat and calories; because the surface area is high, more breading adheres, absorbing more fat. All seafood can be low-fat and low-sodium if grilled *without butter* and served without sauces.

Healthy Choices:
• fresh fish of the day — grilled or poached, without butter, sauce to the side
• lobster, crab meat, crab claws (1/4 cup = 1 serving protein)*
• mesquite-grilled shrimp
• scallops (grilled or broiled without butter)
• seafood kabobs, grilled without butter
• steamed clams, mussels, oysters or shrimp*

*Crab, lobster and shrimp contain cholesterol and must be eaten without saturated fat to be acceptable.

Steak Houses

• As with Italian restaurants, portion control is the key here. A 16-ounce steak or prime rib will give you five times more protein than needed. Order the smallest cut available (often a petite-cut fillet), and don't hesitate to take some home! You may do well to cut off an appropriate portion and separate it from the other on your plate. (Try this before you begin to eat, when control is at its highest!)

• Remember always to have a complex carbohydrate and a protein source, never just meat and salad alone. Your carbohydrate may be a roll, a side of pasta or a baked potato.

Healthy Choices:
• charbroiled shrimp (grilled without butter)
• Hawaiian chicken
• petite-cut fillet
• shish-kabob or brochette (grilled without butter)
• slices of London broil (no sauces or gravies)

CHAPTER ELEVEN

AT THE GROCERY STORE: VOTE FOR VARIETY

For many people, healthful eating means eating in a rut that seems safe, even comfortable. We don't want to think about what we're going to eat. It's easier just to have a bowl of the same cereal for breakfast, a turkey sandwich for lunch, and always a piece of chicken for dinner. Why such a rut? Some people don't trust themselves to make healthy choices. Others are trying to work magic, thinking that only a certain combination of foods will work. Some people punish themselves with the same old boring foods, thinking they are paying some sort of penance. Some just don't care enough about themselves to do anything differently, feeding themselves with as much forethought and effort as they'd feed a dog with a can of dog food. And for some it just seems easier.

If you eat in this kind of rut, you face major problems ahead. You are setting yourself up to overindulge the minute you taste anything more exciting. Then, once you get off track, it will be difficult to get back on track — if "on track" for you means returning to the same old boring rut! As long as you stay in a rut, healthy eating will at least subconsciously be a punishment rather than an enjoyable way of life.

Vote for Variety!

There are also many nutritional reasons to break the rut. Consider these vital factors:

Various foods may contain nutrients that we still know nothing about. Eating a variety of foods in their whole form provides exposure to more possibly "hidden" nutrients.

There is no one perfect food. Many nutrients are found in minute quantities in a few foods, so only a wide variety of foods can assure your meeting all of your nutritional needs.

If your weekly diet covers the broadest possible range of foods, you will limit your exposure to any one potential risk factor, such as pesticides, hormones, bacteria or toxins.

The recipe ideas in this book will encourage you to put variety into your meal planning. An old food prepared a new way is the beginning of change! The recipes include many foods from the grocery list on page 75 — items I recommend you keep on your pantry and refrigerator shelves. These are only suggestions, and you may find other products that meet the same requirements.

The Healthy Gourmet's Shopper's Guide

Dairy

These should be skim or part-skim.

Yogurt is very high in nutrients, particularly calcium and protein, but must be plain and nonfat. The flavored varieties are very high in sugar and are to be avoided. Eat yogurt as a snack with your own unsweetened fruit or all-fruit jam added for sweetness. It is also great as a substitute for high-fat mayonnaise and sour cream and as a marinade for chicken.

Although cheese is a tremendous source of protein, most varieties are also tremendously high in fat and cholesterol. Use the low-fat cheeses routinely (less than 5 grams of fat per ounce), others just for an occasional nibble. Use other cheeses such as Parmesan or feta in very small amounts — no more than 1 ounce per serving.

Best Choices:
- egg whites or egg substitutes
- nonfat plain yogurt
- skim and 1 percent low-fat milk
- skim and part-skim milk cheeses
    cheddar cheese, part-skim
    cottage cheese, part-skim or nonfat (1 percent or less)
    farmer's cheese
    Jarlsberg Lite
    Laughing Cow Reduced Calorie cheese
    light cream cheese (tub)
    mozzarella cheese, part-skim or nonfat
    Parmesan cheese
    ricotta cheese, part-skim or nonfat
    sap sago

Do Not Use:
- heavy cream
- whole milk
- whole milk cheeses

Grains, Cereals and Crackers

Look for grains and breads with the word "whole" as the first ingredient. Avoid products with wheat flour, enriched wheat flour or unbleached wheat flour listed first in the ingredients — these are actually white and refined.

Best Choices:
- barley
- brown rice
- cornmeal
- couscous
- millet
- old-fashioned oats
- whole grain crackers without coconut oil, palm oil or lard
- whole wheat bread, English muffins, pita breads
- whole wheat flour for yeast breads
- whole wheat pastry flour for muffins
- whole wheat (or buckwheat) pasta
- whole wheat flour tortillas
- wild rice

Do Not Use:
- white pasta
- white refined flour breads and other bakery products
- white rice

Oils

Never use more than 1 teaspoon per serving. The best choice in small amounts is monounsaturated oil.

Best Choices:
- canola oil
- olive oil

Do Not Use:
- bacon drippings
- coconut oil
- fatback
- ham hocks
- hydrogenated soybean oil
- lard
- palm oil
- hydrogenated frying oils
- vegetable shortening

Proteins

Each portion should be a maximum of 4 ounces.

Do Not Use:
- organ meats such as chitterlings, kidneys and sweetbreads

Beans

black beans, garbanzo beans, Great Northern beans, kidney beans, lentils, pinto beans, split peas, soybeans, other soy products such as tofu

Beef

Beef is very dense in weight, so a good portion size is three ounces even though it looks quite small. Buy only lean cuts, as evenly red as possible without heavy marbling, and trim all fat before and after cooking.

Leanest Cuts:
- arm
- fillet
- flank
- hamburger ground from the cuts listed (do not use beef labeled "lean ground beef")
- London broil
- round and eye of round
- round bone chuck
- sirloin tip and steak (wedge and round bone)

Do Not Use:
- corned beef

Fish and Seafood

Fish and seafood are wonderful — and as versatile in their use as chicken. An extra bonus: fish is lightweight, meaning you can eat a larger piece than you can of beef, for the same number of ounces. Try fish charbroiled on the grill with lemon, in addition to the standard broiling procedures.

Best Choices:
- cold-water fish:
    bluefish
    mackerel
    salmon
    swordfish
    tuna
- mild fish:
    cod
    flounder
    grouper
    orange roughy
    sea bass
    snapper

- shellfish (only hard mollusk type)
  clams
  mussels
  oysters
  scallops

Lamb

Lamb, except for the leg and loin chops, is very high in fat. Be very careful to trim all fat.

Leanest Cuts:
- leg
- loin chops

Pork

Leanest Cuts:
- center-cut chops
- picnic pork

Do Not Use:
- bacon
- sausage

Poultry

Only eat the white meat, skinned before cooking. Cornish hens are extremely lean. Fryers are less fatty than roasters, but don't fry them! Young turkeys are less fatty than older birds. Boneless, skinless chicken breasts may be worth the price because of the time saved in preparation. Also, try ground turkey in place of ground beef. You may buy a turkey breast and have it ground for you so that the skin and other fats are not included in the grinding process.

Do Not Use:
- capon (70 percent fat)
- duck (79 percent fat)
- goose (85 percent fat)

General Guide:
1/2 breast, cooked = 2 to 3 proteins
1 leg and 1 thigh, cooked = 3 proteins

Veal

Leanest Cuts:
- chuck
- leg
- loin chops
- round
- rump
- shoulder chops

Do Not Use:
- breast or flank (They are up to 70 percent fat.)

Vegetables

Canned vegetables, unless specifically marked, will be very high in salt and very low in nutrients and flavor. When buying frozen vegetables, always buy those frozen plain *without* sauces. Only frozen peas and lima beans will be frozen with salt when frozen plain.

Best Choices:
- fresh when possible
- frozen, when truly fresh not possible

Sugars

Avoid using added sugar in recipes. When using other sweeteners, use in small amounts.

Best Choices:
- all-fruit jams
- fruit juices and purées, frozen unsweetened concentrates
- honey

Do Not Use:
- canned fruits and drinks
- pre-sweetened cereals
- products with sugar among the first five ingredients (may be called by many names: corn syrup, high fructose corn syrup, brown sugar, dextrose, fructose, maltose, sucrose, molasses, maple syrup)

Hint: 4 grams sugar = 1 teaspoon sugar

Salt

Do not use more than 1/8 teaspoon per serving.

Do Not Use:
- pickled or brine-cured foods (dill or sweet pickles, relishes, olives, sauerkraut, anchovies)
- salt-cured or smoked foods (bacon, corned beef, sausage, hot dogs, deli meats such as ham, cold cuts, salami, pastrami, wursts)
- salted snack foods (salted-top crackers, salted popcorn, snack chips, pretzels, salted nuts)
- canned foods, unless labeled "no added salt" (soups, vegetables and tomato products are particularly high in sodium)
- condiments, used in limited amounts (barbecue sauce, low-sodium bouillon cubes, celery salt, garlic salt, chili sauce, ketchup, meat sauces, mustard, MSG, no-oil salad dressings, low-sodium soy sauce, Worcestershire sauce)

Hint: 1 teaspoon salt = 2,100 milligrams of sodium

Organically Grown Foods

What is the top-rated concern of today's health-conscious consumer? According to an annual survey conducted by the Food Marketing Institute, the number-one worry since 1985 has been the safety of our food supply. The public is looking for assurances that the food they consume is pure and safe to eat. Unfortunately, with little regulation over organically grown foods and minimal consistency in state standards, these assurances cannot be made with any degree of certainty.

No universal definition exists for organically grown foods. However, the generally accepted belief is that organically grown foods are those grown in soil enriched with organic fertilizers (such as compost) rather than with chemical or synthetic fertilizers and pesticides. Organically processed foods such as meats and grain products have not been treated with hormones, antibiotics, synthetic additives, preservatives, dyes or waxes.

Research has not yet established that there is a significant nutritional benefit to using organically grown foods over those grown with more traditional farming methods. Most research studies have found pesticide residues in foods grown using both methods; this is attributed to long-term soil conditions and rain run-off. Also, there are no federal regulations for foods organically grown. At this time only seventeen states have passed statutes or regulations defining organic food and set standards for its production. With the lack of legislation it becomes a challenge to procure foods that have certifiably been organically grown.

Here are some tips for purchasing quality organically grown or processed foods:
- Buy locally grown foods when possible. Local producers are less likely to use chemical treatments than producers who must ship their food long distances.
- Buy in-season fruits and vegetables. Out-of-season produce is often imported and may be only spot-checked for residues of pesticides and other chemicals.
- Talk to your grocer about their organic products. What foods are available? Who certifies the organic foods they carry? How frequently can it be supplied?
- Expect organically grown foods to cost more even though they frequently have small insect holes and/or surface blemishes. These blemishes are due to the fact that strong pesticides have not been used. You need not be concerned about their appearance.

Pam Smith's Healthy Grocery List

GRAINS
- ❑ Brown Rice: ❑ Instant
  - ❑ Long-grain ❑ Short-grain
- ❑ Wild Rice
- ❑ Cornmeal
- ❑ Whole Wheat Bagels
- ❑ Whole Wheat Bread — 100%
  (whole is the first word of
  ingredients)
- ❑ Whole Wheat English Muffins
- ❑ Whole Wheat Hamburger Buns
- ❑ Whole Wheat Pasta: ❑ Elbows
  - ❑ Flat ❑ Lasagna ❑ Spaghetti
  - ❑ Spirals
- ❑ Whole Wheat Pastry Flour
- ❑ Whole Wheat Pita Bread
- ❑ _____ ❑ _____

CEREALS *(whole grain and less than 5 grams of added sugar)*
- ❑ Cheerios (General Mills)
- ❑ Grape-Nuts
- ❑ Grits
- ❑ Muesli (Ralston)
- ❑ Nutri-Grain (Kellogg's):
  - ❑ Almond-Raisin ❑ Wheat
- ❑ Oats: ❑ Old-fashioned
  - ❑ Quick-cooking
- ❑ Puffed Cereals: ❑ Rice ❑ Wheat
- ❑ Raisin Squares (Kellogg's)
- ❑ Shredded Wheat (Nabisco)
- ❑ Shredded Wheat 'N Bran (Nabisco)
- ❑ Unprocessed Bran: ❑ Oat ❑ Wheat
- ❑ Wheatena
- ❑ _____ ❑ _____
- ❑ _____ ❑ _____

CRACKERS
- ❑ Crispbread: ❑ Kavli ❑ Wasa
- ❑ Crispy Cakes
- ❑ Harvest Crisps 5-Grain (not all
  whole grain, but good for variety)
- ❑ Rice Cakes
- ❑ Ry-Krisp
- ❑ _____ ❑ _____

DAIRY
- ❑ Butter
- ❑ Cheese (low-fat — less than 5
  grams of fat per ounce):
  - ❑ Cheddar:
    - ❑ Kraft Light Naturals
    - ❑ Weight Watchers
      Natural
  - ❑ Cottage Cheese 1%
  - ❑ Farmer's
  - ❑ Jarlsberg Lite
  - ❑ Light Cream Cheese:
    - ❑ Philadelphia Light (tub)
  - ❑ Mozzarella: ❑ Nonfat
    - ❑ Part-skim
    - ❑ String Cheese

- ❑ Nonrefrigerated:
  - ❑ The Laughing Cow
    Reduced Calorie
- ❑ Parmesan
- ❑ Ricotta: ❑ Nonfat
  - ❑ Part-skim
- ❑ Egg Substitute
- ❑ Eggs
- ❑ Fleischmann's Squeeze Spread
- ❑ Milk (Skim or 1%)
- ❑ Nonfat Plain Yogurt
- ❑ _____ ❑ _____

CANNED GOODS
- ❑ Soups:
  - ❑ Pritikin
  - ❑ Progresso: ❑ Black Bean
    - ❑ Lentil
- ❑ Tomatoes: ❑ Paste ❑ Sauce
  - ❑ Stewed ❑ Whole
- ❑ _____ ❑ _____

FRUITS
- ❑ Apples ❑ Apricots ❑ Bananas
- ❑ Berries ❑ Citrus ❑ Cherries
- ❑ Dates (unsweetened, pitted)
- ❑ Grapes ❑ Kiwi ❑ Lemon/Lime
- ❑ Melon ❑ Nectarines ❑ Peaches
- ❑ Pears ❑ Pineapple
- ❑ Plums ❑ Raisins
- ❑ _____ ❑ _____

VEGETABLES
- ❑ Asparagus ❑ Broccoli
- ❑ Cabbage ❑ Carrots ❑ Cauliflower
- ❑ Celery ❑ Corn ❑ Cucumbers
- ❑ Green Beans ❑ Greens ❑ Kale
- ❑ Mushrooms ❑ Onions ❑ Peas
- ❑ Peppers ❑ Red Potatoes
- ❑ Romaine Lettuce ❑ Spinach
- ❑ Squash ❑ Sweet Potatoes
- ❑ Tomatoes ❑ White Potatoes
- ❑ Zucchini
- ❑ _____ ❑ _____

BEANS AND MEATS
- ❑ Beans and Peas: ❑ Black
  - ❑ Chick-peas/Garbanzo Beans
  - ❑ Kidney ❑ Lentils ❑ Navy
  - ❑ Multi-beans ❑ Split Peas
  - ❑ Pinto ❑ _____
- ❑ Beef (lean): ❑ Deli-sliced
  - ❑ Ground Round
  - ❑ Round Steak
- ❑ Fish and Seafood:
  - ❑ fresh ❑ frozen
- ❑ Lamb: ❑ Leg ❑ Loin Chops
- ❑ Poultry:
  - ❑ Chicken: ❑ Boneless Breasts
    - ❑ Parts ❑ Whole Fryer
  - ❑ Turkey: ❑ Breast ❑ Ground
    - ❑ Sliced ❑ Whole

- ❑ Veal: ❑ Chuck ❑ Leg Chops
  - ❑ Loin Chops ❑ Round
  - ❑ Rump ❑ Shoulder Chops
- ❑ Water-packed Cans: ❑ Chicken
  - ❑ Salmon ❑ Tuna
- ❑ _____ ❑ _____

MISCELLANEOUS
- ❑ All-Fruit Jam:
  - ❑ Clearbrook Farms
  - ❑ Polaner
  - ❑ Smucker's Simply Fruit
  - ❑ Welch's Totally Fruit
- ❑ Baking Powder
- ❑ Baking Soda
- ❑ Boullion Cubes: ❑ Beef ❑ Chicken
- ❑ Cooking Oils:
  - ❑ Canola ❑ Olive
- ❑ Cornstarch
- ❑ Fruit Juices (unsweetened):
  - ❑ Apple ❑ Apple-Cranberry
  - ❑ Grape ❑ Orange
- ❑ Garlic: ❑ Cloves ❑ Minced
- ❑ Honey
- ❑ Mayonnaise: ❑ Light
  - ❑ Miracle Whip Light
- ❑ Mustard
- ❑ Nonstick Cooking Spray
- ❑ Nuts/Seeds, Dry-roasted, Unsalted:
  - ❑ Peanuts
  - ❑ Sunflower Kernels
- ❑ Pasta Sauce: ❑ Pritikin
  - ❑ Ragu Chunky Gardenstyle
- ❑ Peanut Butter (natural)
- ❑ Popcorn:
  - ❑ Orville Redenbacher's Light
    Natural Microwave
  - ❑ Plain Kernels
- ❑ Salad Dressing:
  - ❑ Bernstein's Low Calorie
  - ❑ Good Seasons ❑ Kraft Free
  - ❑ Pritikin
  - ❑ Richard Simmon's Spray
- ❑ Soy Sauce (low-sodium)
- ❑ Spices & Herbs: ❑ Allspice
  - ❑ Basil ❑ Black Pepper
  - ❑ Cayenne Pepper
  - ❑ Celery Seed ❑ Chili Powder
  - ❑ Cinnamon ❑ Curry
  - ❑ Dill Weed ❑ Garlic Powder
  - ❑ Ginger ❑ Mustard
  - ❑ Nutmeg ❑ Oregano
  - ❑ Onion Powder ❑ Paprika
  - ❑ Parsley ❑ Rosemary
- ❑ Vanilla Extract
- ❑ Vinegars: ❑ Balsamic ❑ Cider
  - ❑ Red Wine ❑ Tarragon
- ❑ White Wine Worcestershire Sauce
- ❑ _____ ❑ _____
- ❑ _____ ❑ _____
- ❑ _____ ❑ _____
- ❑ _____ ❑ _____
- ❑ _____ ❑ _____

GREAT SAUCES,
MARINADES
AND MORE

Few people these days have the time or inclination to spend all afternoon preparing the dinner meal each day. When it comes to cooking, many people feel strongly that "if it takes longer to cook it than to eat it, FORGET IT!"

This guide presents a simple way to plan ahead for quick, nutritious meals. By spending just an hour on a weekend to put together some of the basics of each night's meal, your dinners will be healthy delights with a minimum of effort.

Sauces, Marinades and Stocks

You will always want to have stocks on hand for steaming vegetables, cooking pasta and rice, and making sauces, for they provide flavor in a light way. Cook stocks in large quantities and, before freezing or storing, chill the stock and allow all the fat to rise to the surface. Skim off this fat and freeze the stock in either pint-sized containers or ice cube trays (store frozen cubes in plastic bags, all ready for use; 1 cube = 1/4 cup stock).

Every time you prepare vegetables, add the cooking water to a stock jar kept in the freezer. This will provide a continuous supply of stock for stews and soups.

Marinades give moisture and tenderness to meat and are perfect for use in grilling. By allowing meat to soak in a marinade before cooking, you will greatly enhance the flavor of the meat — which makes for scrumptious eating!

Meal-planning Basics

Do each of these once a week:
• Prepare the marinade for Hawaiian Chicken (recipe on page 132). Marinate enough boneless chicken breasts for two meals. Half the chicken can be sliced and stir-fried with vegetables one night; half can be grilled another night.

• Cook a big pot of brown rice. It can be heated during the week as needed, or you can measure it out into servings and freeze them in freezer bags or containers to be reheated in boiling water or in the microwave.

• Cook a big pot of whole wheat pasta for quick heat-ups during the week.

• Make a pot of Perfect Tomato Sauce (recipe on page 78) or choose a favorite commercial brand (without sugar or salt) to have on hand. It's the perfect beginning to any Italian dish. It can be tossed with pasta, used to make Pita Pizzas (recipe on page 104) or Lasagna (recipe on page 172) or as a topping for meats.

• Cook a pot of pinto beans. They can be used one night in a beans and rice dish and another night puréed and spread on warm tortillas with shredded lettuce, chopped tomatoes and picante sauce as bean burritos.

• Cut up a variety of fresh vegetables: zucchini, broccoli, cauliflower, mushrooms, carrots and the like. Part may be marinated in no-oil Italian salad dressing for a quick salad or Marinated Vegetables (recipe on page 194); the remaining portion may be steamed or stir-fried.

• For extra quick stir-frying use frozen bags of assorted vegetable mixes. The vegetables are already cut and can be fully cooked in four minutes. Bags of frozen peas can also be used for a quick complex carbohydrate.

• Make a basic salad of torn romaine lettuce topped with a tomato, no-oil Italian salad dressing and a sprinkle of Parmesan cheese.

• Sliced melon or fresh strawberries are a refreshing and quick complement to any meal.

SAUCES

PERFECT TOMATO SAUCE

2 teaspoons olive oil
1 cup onion, chopped
1 cup green pepper, chopped
2 teaspoons dried parsley
2 bay leaves
1 tablespoon fresh garlic, minced
2 teaspoons dried basil
1 teaspoon dried oregano
1/2 pound fresh mushrooms, sliced
1 teaspoon salt (optional)
1 small can (6 ounces) tomato paste
1 large can (28 ounces) tomato purée
1 cup tomatoes, chopped
1/4 teaspoon black pepper

Sauté in oil the onion, green pepper, parsley, bay leaves, garlic, basil, oregano, mushrooms and salt. When onions are soft, add tomato paste, tomato purée, chopped tomatoes and pepper; reduce heat to low.

Cover and simmer for at least 45 minutes.

Makes 10 servings

1 serving (1 cup) = 1 simple carbohydrate

The perfect beginning for any Italian dish!

QUICK PASTA SAUCE

2 teaspoons olive oil
1 small onion, chopped
1 green pepper, cut into small pieces
2 cloves garlic, minced
1 teaspoon dried oregano
1 teaspoon dried basil
1 tablespoon dried parsley
1/2 teaspoon creole seasoning
4 cans (28 ounces each) whole
    tomatoes, drained
nonstick cooking spray

Coat a heavy skillet with nonstick cooking spray. Add oil; heat over medium heat and add onions and green pepper. Sauté for a few minutes until tender; add garlic and sauté 1 additional minute. Add oregano, basil, parsley and creole seasoning. Add tomatoes and sauté 5 additional minutes.

Serve over pasta.

Makes 8 servings

1 serving (1 cup) = 1 simple carbohydrate

WATER CHESTNUT SAUCE

Combine chicken stock, soy sauce, sherry, water chestnuts, onion and pimento in a saucepan; set aside. Combine cornstarch and cold water to make a paste and add to liquid. Cook over medium heat, stirring constantly until thickened.

Makes 3 cups

1/4 cup = "free"

1-1/2 cups chicken stock or low-sodium chicken bouillon
2 tablespoons low-sodium soy sauce
1/4 cup sherry or additional chicken stock
2 cans (5 ounces) water chestnuts, drained and sliced
1 tablespoon dried minced onion
2 tablespoons pimento, chopped
1 tablespoon cornstarch
2 tablespoons cold water

WINE SAUCE

Heat together chicken stock and white wine until boiling. Mix cornstarch and cold water. Add to boiling liquid. Stir until thickened and clear.

Makes 1-1/4 cups

1 serving (1/4 cup) = "free"

3/4 cup chicken stock or low-sodium chicken bouillon
2/3 cup white wine or additional chicken stock
1 tablespoon cornstarch
2 tablespoons cold water

TURKEY GRAVY — THE HEALTHFUL WAY

Heat canola oil in a saucepan. Add garlic and cook for 30 seconds. Stir in cornstarch until smooth. Add stock, bay leaf and wine. Cook until sauce thickens, about 5 minutes, stirring frequently. Remove bay leaf. Serve with turkey.

Makes 2 cups

1 serving (1/3 cup) = 1 added fat

2 tablespoons canola oil
1 clove garlic, minced
1 tablespoon cornstarch
1-1/2 cups defatted chicken or turkey stock, heated (may use low-sodium chicken bouillon)
1 bay leaf
1/4 cup white wine or additional chicken stock

ALL-PURPOSE MARINADES

MARINADE 1

1/3 cup unsweetened pineapple juice
1/3 cup low-sodium soy sauce
1/3 cup sherry or chicken stock
2 cloves garlic
2 tablespoons fresh parsley or 1
    tablespoon dried
1/2 teaspoon black pepper

Combine all ingredients. Marinate skinned chicken pieces, meat, fish or seafood for 3 to 4 hours or overnight. (The marinade adds no significant calories to the chicken.) Grill.

Makes 1 cup

MARINADE 2

1/2 cup lime or lemon juice
2 teaspoons dried thyme
2 cloves garlic, crushed
1 tablespoon olive oil
1/2 teaspoon salt
1/2 teaspoon black pepper

Combine all ingredients. Marinate skinned chicken pieces, meat, fish or seafood for 3 to 4 hours or overnight. Grill.

Makes 1/2 cup

DRESSINGS

ORANGE YOGURT DRESSING

Combine all ingredients and refrigerate.

Makes 1-1/2 cups

1 serving (1 tablespoon as topping) = "free"

Hint: Make several recipes of this dressing at one time and store in the refrigerator to use as a wonderful topping for fruit.

3/4 cup nonfat plain yogurt
juice of 1/2 lemon
1/2 cup orange juice
dash of salt
dash of cinnamon

TASTY APPLE JUICE DRESSING

In a small bowl combine oil, basil, onion powder, salt and pepper; set aside for 10 minutes, allowing flavors to blend. Stir in apple juice and vinegar. Refrigerate. Use on salads and as a marinade.

Makes 3/4 cup

1 serving (2 tablespoons) = 1 added fat

2 tablespoons canola oil
1-1/2 teaspoons dried basil
1 teaspoon onion powder
1/2 teaspoon salt (optional)
1/8 teaspoon black pepper
1/2 cup unsweetened apple juice
2 tablespoons apple cider vinegar

SEASONING BLENDS

SEASONING BLEND 1

2 teaspoons dry mustard
1 1/2 teaspoons oregano
1 teaspoon marjoram
1 teaspoon thyme
1 teaspoon garlic powder
1 teaspoon curry powder
1/2 teaspoon onion powder
1/2 teaspoon celery seed

Combine all ingredients, mixing well. Store in an airtight container.

SEASONING BLEND 2

1 tablespoon garlic powder
1 tablespoon dry mustard
1 tablespoon paprika
1/2 teaspoon pepper
1 teaspoon basil
1/2 teaspoon thyme

Combine all ingredients, mixing well. Store in an airtight container.

STOCKS

CHICKEN STOCK

Cover chicken with water; add peppercorns. Simmer uncovered for 30 minutes. Add remaining ingredients. Cover and simmer for 2 additional hours. Strain and remove chicken. Use deboned chicken in salads or recipes calling for cubed chicken.

Chill stock until fat can be skimmed off easily. Ready to use or be frozen.

*May substitute 3 pounds beef or veal bones with meat on them for hearty meat stock. Simmer for 4 hours instead of 2 hours.

3 to 4 pounds chicken pieces*
6 black peppercorns
2 carrots, sliced
2 cloves garlic, minced
1 medium onion, chopped
1 stalk celery with leaves, sliced
1 bay leaf
2 tablespoons fresh parsley or 1 tablespoon dried

TRIMMINGS STOCK

Load a heavy pot with scrubbed vegetable tops, peelings and scraps. (These can be collected for up to a week in a plastic bag stored in the refrigerator.) Cover the scraps with water; add a pinch of salt or low-sodium soy sauce. Salt is optional but will draw nutrients into the stock. Add whatever spices and herbs are in reach: bay leaves, onions, rosemary, basil, and so on. Cover the pot and let simmer for 1 to 2 hours, stirring occasionally.

Let cool; strain and refrigerate or freeze (will keep for 8 to 10 days in the refrigerator).

Hint: Everything can be used as scraps — seeds and cores of peppers, broccoli leaves and stalks, outer leaves of greens, onion slices, even cauliflower cores! Go light on the cabbage family, however; it will provide a strong flavor.

scrubbed vegetable tops, peelings and scraps

BREAKFAST

BOUNTIFUL BREAKFASTS

COUNTRY BRUNCH OMELETTE

Coat a small skillet with nonstick cooking spray. Heat oil over medium heat. Add tomatoes, scallions and spinach; sauté until the spinach wilts, about 30 seconds. Remove from heat and set aside.

In a small bowl, beat egg substitute with salt and pepper.

Coat an 8-inch skillet with nonstick cooking spray. Pour one-fourth of the egg mixture into the skillet; stir once and cook over high heat until the eggs begin to set, about 1 minute. Pull omelette gently from sides of skillet, letting the uncooked portion flow under cooked edge; continue cooking until the liquid is set, about 20 seconds.

Sprinkle one-fourth of the cheese and one-fourth of the cooked vegetables over the omelette; fold in half and heat for 2 to 3 additional seconds.

Repeat procedure 3 times for remaining egg mixture, cheese and vegetables. Serve immediately.

Makes 4 servings

1 serving = 2-1/2 proteins and 1 added fat

1 teaspoon olive oil
1/3 cup tomato, peeled, seeded and coarsely chopped
2 tablespoons scallions, chopped
1 pound fresh spinach, torn into bite-size pieces
1-1/2 cups egg substitute
1/4 teaspoon salt (optional)
1/4 teaspoon black pepper
1/2 cup part-skim or low-fat cheddar cheese, shredded
nonstick cooking spray

FRAMED EGG

1 slice whole wheat bread
1 egg white
1 ounce part-skim or low-fat cheddar
    cheese
nonstick cooking spray

Coat a skillet with nonstick cooking spray and heat on medium high.

Cut a hole out of the center of the bread with the rim of a drinking glass or cup. Put bread in heated pan. Pour egg white into hole in center of bread.

Cook over medium heat for 1 minute. Turn bread over with a spatula; top with cheese. Cook 1 additional minute and serve.

Makes 1 serving

1 serving = 2 proteins and 1 complex carbohydrate

OATMEAL WITH A DIFFERENCE

1/3 cup old-fashioned oats, uncooked
3/4 cup skim milk
1/4 cup unsweetened apple juice
1 tablespoon raisins
1/2 teaspoon ground cinnamon
1/2 teaspoon vanilla

Bring oats, milk and apple juice to a boil. Cook for 5 minutes, stirring occasionally. Add raisins, cinnamon and vanilla. Remove from heat; cover and let sit for 2 to 3 minutes to thicken.

This recipe also cooks well in the microwave. Combine all ingredients and cook for 3 to 4 minutes on high.

Makes 1 serving

1 serving = 1 protein, 1 complex carbohydrate and 1 simple carbohydrate

CHEESE-GRITS PIE

1/3 cup quick-cooking grits, uncooked
1 cup water
3 eggs, beaten, or 3/4 cup egg
    substitute
1 cup evaporated skim milk
1/2 teaspoon dry mustard
3/4 cup (3 ounces) part-skim or
    low-fat cheddar cheese, shredded
1 tablespoon dried parsley
1/2 teaspoon hot pepper sauce
1/2 teaspoon salt
nonstick cooking spray

Preheat oven to 350 degrees.

Cook grits in water according to package directions, omitting salt. Combine cooked grits with remaining ingredients, mixing well.

Pour mixture into a 9-inch pie plate coated with nonstick cooking spray. Bake for 30 to 35 minutes or until set. Let stand for 5 to 10 minutes before serving.

Makes 6 servings

1 serving = 2 proteins and 1/2 complex carbohydrate

DANISH DELITE

Preheat oven to broil.

Combine cottage cheese, yogurt and vanilla; mash together until smooth. Spread mixture on bread slice. Arrange fruit on top and sprinkle with cinnamon. Broil for 3 to 4 minutes until heated through.

Makes 1 serving

1 serving = 1 protein, 1 complex carbohydrate and 1 simple carbohydrate

2 tablespoons part-skim or nonfat cottage cheese
1 tablespoon nonfat plain yogurt
1/4 teaspoon vanilla
1 slice whole wheat bread, lightly toasted
1/2 cup fresh fruit (try peaches)
1/8 teaspoon ground cinnamon

CHEESE DANISH

Top muffin with cream cheese; toast in toaster oven until cheese is warm. Sprinkle with raisins.

Makes 1 serving

1 serving = 1 protein, 1 complex carbohydrate and 1 simple carbohydrate

1/2 whole wheat English muffin
1 ounce light cream cheese
2 tablespoons raisins

CHEESE APPLE SLICES

Preheat oven to broil.

Top bread slice with apple slices and raisins. Place cheese on top of apple-raisin layer. Broil until cheese is bubbly.

Makes 1 serving

1 serving = 1 protein, 1 complex carbohydrate and 1 simple carbohydrate

1 slice whole wheat bread
1/2 apple, thinly sliced
1 tablespoon raisins
1 ounce part-skim or nonfat mozzarella cheese

BREAKFAST PARFAIT

1/2 cup nonfat plain yogurt
2 teaspoons blueberry or other flavor
  all-fruit jam
1/4 cup fresh or frozen unsweetened
  blueberries or other fruit
1/4 cup grape-nuts
dash of ground cinnamon

Layer half of yogurt, jam, fruit and cereal parfait-style into a tall glass; repeat layers with remaining yogurt, jam, fruit and cereal. Sprinkle with cinnamon.

Makes 1 serving

1 serving = 1 protein, 1 complex carbohydrate and 1 simple carbohydrate

HOMEMADE GRANOLA

4 cups old-fashioned oats, uncooked
3/4 cup unprocessed wheat bran
1/2 cup whole wheat pastry flour
2 cups wheat germ
1/2 cup oat bran
1/4 cup canola oil
2 tablespoons honey (optional)
1 cup sunflower kernels
1 cup raisins
2 teaspoons vanilla

Preheat oven to 300 degrees.

Mix together oats, wheat bran, flour, wheat germ, oat bran, oil and honey. Spread into a large, shallow pan.

Bake for 45 minutes, stirring every 15 minutes. Add the sunflower kernels during the last 10 minutes of baking. Add the raisins and vanilla at the end of the baking time. Let cool.

Makes 42 servings

1 serving (1/4 cup) = 1 complex carbohydrate, 1 simple carbohydrate and 1 added fat

FRENCH TOAST AND PANCAKES

EVERYDAY FRENCH TOAST

Beat together egg whites, milk, orange juice concentrate, vanilla and cinnamon. Add bread slices one at a time, letting the bread absorb the liquid in the process. May need to let sit for a few minutes.

Coat a skillet with nonstick cooking spray and heat. Gently lift each bread slice with a spatula and place in the skillet; cook until golden brown on each side.

Serve topped with 1/2 tablespoon of all-fruit jam per slice.

Freeze leftovers in individual freezer bags. When ready to use, toast to thaw and heat.

Makes 4 servings

1 serving (1 slice) = 1 proteins, 1 complex carbohydrate and 1 simple carbohydrate

4 egg whites, lightly beaten
1/2 cup skim milk
2 tablespoons frozen unsweetened orange juice concentrate, undiluted
1 teaspoon vanilla
1/2 teaspoon ground cinnamon
4 slices whole wheat bread
2 tablespoons all-fruit jam
nonstick cooking spray

SPECIAL BANANA FRENCH TOAST

4 egg whites or 1/2 cup egg substitute
1 banana, peeled and mashed well
1/2 cup skim milk
1/2 teaspoon ground cinnamon
4 slices whole wheat bread
2 tablespoons all-fruit jam
nonstick cooking spray

Combine egg whites, banana, milk and cinnamon in a pie plate; beat well. Soak bread slices in banana mixture.

Coat a skillet with nonstick cooking spray and heat on medium. Place bread slices in hot skillet. Spoon an additional teaspoon of banana mixture over each slice of bread. Cook until golden brown on both sides.

Top with 1/2 tablespoon of all-fruit jam per slice.

Freeze leftovers in individual freezer bags. When ready to use, toast to thaw and heat.

Makes 4 servings

1 serving (1 slice) = 1 protein, 1 complex carbohydrate and 1 simple carbohydrate

CRUNCH TOAST

4 egg whites or 1/2 cup egg substitute
1/2 cup skim milk
1/2 cup Nutri-grain wheat cereal,
  crushed
4 slices whole wheat bread
1/2 cup nonfat plain yogurt
1 can (8 ounces) unsweetened crushed
  pineapple
nonstick cooking spray

Beat egg whites with milk in a pie pan; set aside. Place cereal in another pie pan.

Coat a skillet with nonstick cooking spray and heat on medium.

Dip each bread slice into egg mixture and then into cereal, coating both sides. Cook until browned on both sides.

Mix yogurt and pineapple; warm if desired. Serve on top of toast.

Freeze leftovers in individual freezer bags. When ready to use, toast to thaw and heat.

Makes 4 servings

1 serving = 1 protein, 1 complex carbohydrate and 1 simple carbohydrate

Place all ingredients in a blender or food processor and blend for 5 to 6 seconds. Drop by tablespoonfuls into a skillet coated with non-stick cooking spray. Turn pancakes when bubbles appear on surface; cook 1 additional minute.

Serve with Fresh Fruit Syrup (recipe on page 95) or all-fruit jam.

Freeze leftovers in individual freezer bags. When ready to use, toast to thaw and heat.

Makes 4 pancakes

1 serving (1 pancake) = 1 protein and 1/2 complex carbohydrate

These pancakes are a delightful meal-in-one — protein and carbo-hydrate!

2 egg whites
1/2 cup part-skim or nonfat ricotta cheese
1 tablespoon canola oil
1/4 cup plus 2 tablespoons old-fashioned oats, uncooked
1/8 teaspoon salt
Fresh Fruit Syrup or all-fruit jam
nonstick cooking spray

Cover the raisins with boiling water and let soften for 20 minutes; drain well.

In a mixing bowl, beat egg whites lightly with milk; stir in apple juice. Mix oats with baking powder and add to egg mixture. Fold in raisins.

Coat a skillet with nonstick cooking spray. Heat on medium high. Spoon pancake batter into the hot skillet; turn when bubbles break on the surface of the pancakes. If you prefer a thinner pancake, add more apple juice to batter.

Freeze leftovers in individual freezer bags. When ready to use, toast to thaw and heat.

Makes 10 pancakes

1 serving (1 pancake) = 1 complex carbohydrate

This is another delicious version of Oatmeal Pancakes.

1/2 cup raisins
boiling water
2 egg whites
1/2 cup skim milk
1/4 cup apple juice
2 cups quick-cooking oats, uncooked
1 tablespoon baking powder
nonstick cooking spray

WHEAT MIX

4 cups whole wheat pastry flour
1 teaspoon salt
1 cup nonfat dry milk powder
2-1/2 tablespoons baking powder
1/4 cup canola oil

Mix together flour, salt, milk powder and baking powder. Slowly pour in oil, continuing to mix until completely moistened.

May be stored in the refrigerator for 1 month. Use to make Wheat Mix Pancakes (recipe follows).

Makes 5 cups

WHEAT MIX PANCAKES

1-3/4 cups Wheat Mix (see above recipe)
1 cup water or club soda (club soda makes the pancakes even lighter!)
2 egg whites or 1/4 cup egg substitute, beaten
1 tablespoon honey
topping (see recipes on pages 94-97)
nonstick cooking spray

Combine wheat mix, water or club soda, egg whites and honey; stir gently until completely moistened.

Drop by quarter-cupfuls into a hot pan that has been coated with nonstick cooking spray. Cook until bottom is lightly browned. Flip and cook until bottom is set.

Serve pancakes with one of the toppings on pages 94-97 and a protein of your choice.

Freeze leftovers in individual freezer bags. When ready to use, toast to thaw and heat.

Makes 10 pancakes (5-inch diameter)

1 serving (2 pancakes) = 1-1/2 complex carbohydrates and 1 added fat

Preheat oven to 425 degrees.

Mix flour, baking powder and salt. Stir in milk; beat in eggs one at a time.

Coat a large 12-inch cast-iron skillet with nonstick cooking spray. Spread oil over bottom of skillet and heat over medium heat. Pour all batter into skillet. Cook for 1 minute. Transfer skillet to oven and bake uncovered for 20 minutes until pancake is golden and puffy.

While baking, sauté apples with lemon juice and cinnamon in a pan coated with nonstick cooking spray. Spread fruit on pancake when done.

Slice into 6 wedges to serve.

Freeze leftovers in individual freezer bags. When ready to use, toast to thaw and heat.

Makes 6 servings

1 serving = 1 protein, 1 complex carbohydrate and 1 simple carbohydrate

1 cup whole wheat pastry flour
1/2 teaspoon baking powder
1/2 teaspoon salt
1 cup skim milk
5 eggs or 1-1/2 cups egg substitute
2 teaspoons canola oil
3 cups fresh apples, sliced
juice of 1/2 lemon
1 teaspoon ground cinnamon
nonstick cooking spray

TOPPINGS, SYRUPS AND JAMS

CINNAMON-RAISIN APPLESAUCE

1/2 cup unsweetened applesauce
1 teaspoon ground cinnamon or
    apple-pie spice
1 tablespoon raisins

Combine all ingredients, mixing well.

Makes 1 serving

1 serving = 1 simple carbohydrate

SPICED PINEAPPLE

1/4 cup unsweetened crushed
    pineapple
1 teaspoon vanilla
1/4 teaspoon ground cinnamon

Combine all ingredients, mixing well.

Makes 1 serving

1 serving = 1/2 simple carbohydrate

FRUITED YOGURT TOPPING

1 cup nonfat plain yogurt
1/2 cup fruit or 2 tablespoons all-fruit
    jam
ground cinnamon to taste

Combine all ingredients, mixing well.

Makes 2 servings

1 serving (1/2 cup) = 1 protein and 1 simple carbohydrate

FRESH FRUIT SYRUP

Blend fresh fruit and apple juice in a blender until smooth. Pour into a small saucepan and simmer for 5 minutes. Mix cornstarch with water and lemon juice; add to fruit mixture. Simmer until thick.

Makes 2 cups

1 serving (1/3 cup) = 1 simple carbohydrate

2 cups fresh fruit (strawberries, banana, berries, peaches)
1/2 cup apple juice
2 tablespoons water
1 tablespoon cornstarch
1 tablespoon lemon juice

PINEAPPLE SYRUP

Heat together pineapple juice and apple juice. Mix together cornstarch and water. Add to hot juice and heat until thickened.

Makes 2-1/2 cups

1 serving (1/3 cup) = 1 simple carbohydrate

2 cups unsweetened pineapple juice
1/2 cup apple juice
2 tablespoons cornstarch
1/2 cup water

BANANA JAM

Combine apple juice concentrate and cornstarch in a heavy saucepan; stir until smooth. Add remaining ingredients, stirring well.

Cook over medium heat, stirring constantly until thickened and bubbly. Cook an additional 3 to 5 minutes.

Remove cloves and cinnamon stick. Spoon into jars. Keep refrigerated.

Makes 3 cups

1 teaspoon = "free"
2 tablespoons = 1 simple carbohydrate

1 can (6 ounces) frozen unsweetened apple juice concentrate, thawed and undiluted
2 tablespoons cornstarch
3 cups ripe bananas, sliced
3 tablespoons lemon juice
2 whole cloves
1 cinnamon stick (2 inches)

APRICOT WONDER JAM

1 can (20 ounces) unsweetened
   crushed pineapple
1 cup dried apricots
1 cup unsweetened pineapple juice
1/2 cup golden raisins
1/2 teaspoon ground ginger

Drain pineapple, reserving juice. Add water to the juice to equal 1-1/2 cups liquid. Combine juice mixture, apricots, pineapple juice and raisins. Bring to a boil; cover and simmer for 20 minutes.

Pour mixture into a blender container. Add pineapple and ginger. Cover and blend until smooth.

Return mixture to saucepan. Bring to a boil, stirring constantly.

Ladle into clean jars, leaving a 1/4-inch headspace at the top of each jar. Wipe jar rims and adjust lids. Process in boiling water for 10 minutes (after water boils).

Makes 4-1/2 pints

1 teaspoon = "free"
1 tablespoon= 1 simple carbohydrate

SPICED WALNUT PEAR DELITE

2 pears, chopped
1/2 cup unsweetened pineapple,
   chopped
1/4 cup walnuts
1/4 cup unsweetened pitted dates
1/4 teaspoon ground cinnamon
1/8 teaspoon ground ginger
dash of ground cloves

Combine all ingredients in a blender; process until smooth. Refrigerate.

Makes 2 cups

1 teaspoon = "free"
2 tablespoons = 1 simple carbohydrate and 1 added fat

RAISIN BUTTER

1-1/2 cups raisins
3/4 cup orange juice
1/8 teaspoon ground cinnamon
dash of ground cloves

Combine all ingredients in a saucepan; bring to a boil. Reduce heat and simmer uncovered for 10 minutes.

Pour mixture into a blender and process until smooth. Refrigerate.

Makes 2 cups

1 teaspoon = "free"
1 tablespoon = 1 simple carbohydrate

HALF-HOUR APPLE BUTTER

Combine all ingredients in a heavy saucepan, stirring well. Bring to a boil; reduce heat and simmer uncovered for 10 minutes, stirring often. Remove from heat and let cool.

Pour into a blender and process until smooth. Refrigerate.

Makes 3 cups

1 teaspoon = "free"
2 tablespoons = 1 simple carbohydrate

1 jar (25 ounces) unsweetened applesauce
1/2 teaspoon ground cinnamon
1/4 teaspoon ground allspice
1/8 teaspoon ground ginger
1/8 teaspoon ground cloves

MORE TOPPING IDEAS

• All-fruit jam (sweetened with juices rather than sugar)

   1 teaspoon = "free"
   1 tablespoon = 1 simple carbohydrate

• Fresh fruit syrup (purchase a commercial brand or make your own; see recipe on page 95)

   1 teaspoon = "free"
   1 tablespoon = 1 simple carbohydrate

• Frozen bananas, thawed, blended and warmed

   1 serving (1/4 cup) = 1 simple carbohydrate

• Light cream cheese, thinned with fruit juice and vanilla

   1 serving (2 tablespoons) light cream cheese = 1 protein

• Light cream cheese and fresh fruit

   1 serving (2 tablespoons) light cream cheese = 1 protein

• Part-skim or nonfat cottage cheese and fresh fruit

   1 serving (1/4 cup) cottage cheese = 1 protein

• Natural peanut butter, thinned with apple juice and warmed

   1 serving (2 tablespoons) = 1 protein

BREAKFAST IN A BLENDER

QUICK BREAKFAST SHAKE

1/2 cup frozen unsweetened fruit
1 cup skim milk
2 tablespoons nonfat dry milk powder
2 tablespoons wheat germ
1 tablespoon oat bran
1 teaspoon vanilla

Blend frozen fruit in blender until slushy. Add remaining ingredients, continuing to blend until smooth.

Makes 1 serving

1 serving = 2 proteins, 1 complex carbohydrate and 1 simple carbohydrate

ORANGE-BANANA SHAKE

1 cup nonfat plain yogurt
1 banana
1/2 cup unsweetened orange juice
2 tablespoons nonfat dry milk powder
1 egg white, coddled*
1 teaspoon vanilla
1 teaspoon honey
1 tablespoon oat bran
1 tablespoon wheat germ

Combine all ingredients in a blender and blend until smooth.

Makes 1 serving

1 serving = 2 proteins, 1/2 complex carbohydrate and 2 simple carbohydrates

*Coddle an egg by immersing the whole egg (in its shell) into boiling water for 30 seconds. This destroys the bacteria found in raw eggs.

Combine all ingredients in a blender and blend until smooth.

Makes 2 servings (may freeze one for later)

1 serving = 2 proteins, 1/2 complex carbohydrate and 2 simple carbohydrates

*Coddle an egg by immersing the whole egg (in its shell) into boiling water for 30 seconds. This destroys the bacteria found in raw eggs.

1-1/2 cups frozen unsweetened peaches
2 egg whites, coddled*
1 teaspoon honey
1/4 cup unsweetened orange juice
1/4 cup skim milk
1/8 teaspoon ground cinnamon
1 tablespoon oat bran
2 tablespoons wheat germ

BANANA-PEANUT BUTTER SHAKE

Combine all ingredients in a blender and blend until smooth.

Makes 2 servings

1 serving = 2 proteins, 1/2 complex carbohydrate and 2 simple carbohydrates

*Coddle an egg by immersing the whole egg (in its shell) into boiling water for 30 seconds. This destroys the bacteria found in raw eggs.

2 cups skim milk
2 egg whites, coddled*
1 banana
1 tablespoon natural peanut butter
1 teaspoon honey
1/2 tablespoon oat bran
2 tablespoons wheat germ
2 tablespoons nonfat dry milk powder
1 tablespoon sunflower kernels

LUNCH

It's 12:15, and your stomach announces that lunchtime has arrived. But where's lunch? If only you had brown-bagged it! But what would you have packed? When would you have found the time to pack it? Should you go the fast-food route — again? Maybe you could just hit one of those vending machines down the hall. (After all, those peanut butter crackers have protein, don't they?) Or maybe the best idea would be to skip lunch altogether. If you wait long enough, the hunger does go away.

Stop! Don't skip lunch, and don't hit the vending machines. Lunch, from this moment on, can have a different meaning. It doesn't have to be a production, and it doesn't have to take time, just a little forethought and planning.

Tips for New Lunchtime Fare

• *Sandwiches can be a perfect lunch package.*

They give you a perfect balance of complex carbohydrate and protein and with the right filling are low-fat as well. Look at the lunch recipes on the following pages for new sandwich ideas beyond bologna.

If you don't have time to make a sandwich fresh daily, make a week's supply at one time and freeze them. The sandwich will be thawed by lunch, ready to be stuffed with lettuce and other vegetables. Mustard freezes well; mayonnaise does not. Get deli meat sliced so that each slice will give you approximately 1 ounce. This will allow for quick and accurate portioning.

• *Fast food doesn't have to be a nutritional evil.*

You do have to be responsible, however, for ordering the healthier choices. See chapter 10 — Eating Right When Eating Out — for learning survival in the fast-food lane!

• *If the right food isn't available, in a tight time squeeze you will be apt to reach for the wrong food!*

Have easily stored food items available (such as low-fat cheeses, whole grain crackers, dried fruits or trail mix) that can be substituted for vending machine fare. A cooler and a thermos can also do wonders for expanding your lunchtime choices.

• *Life in a rut is NO FUN!*

It is easy to have the same hamburger or turkey sandwich every day, but some variety adds a lot in terms of both excitement and nutrition. In winter you might fill an insulated container with a hearty soup or stew. On hot days pack a cold main dish salad in an insulated container. Be sure to review the pages ahead for great ideas of lunches that are perfectly balanced and perfectly delicious!

Stamp Out Brown-Bag Bugs

If the lunch you are packing is going to sit unrefrigerated for several hours, how you pack it is as important as what you pack. Even the healthiest menu won't prevent the brown-bag bugs — food poisoning. Food poisoning symptoms can strike anytime from 20 minutes to 24 hours after consumption of tainted food.

Lunches carried from home often sit in a desk or locker until noon. That long wait at room temperature makes them a perfect breeding ground for salmonella and staphylococcus bacteria. When these organisms become overabundant, food poisoning can result. And because these bacteria and their toxins are odorless, tasteless and invisible to the naked eye, there is no warning that the food has spoiled.

In most cases food poisoning is characterized by vomiting, fever, headache, diarrhea and/or stomach cramps — all symptoms to avoid!

Packing Safety Pointers

• Keep all food clean. Keep cold foods cold and hot foods hot.

• Your hands, countertops, utensils and cutting boards should be washed in hot soapy water and rinsed before and after each food preparation time. A thermos, any plastic containers and the lunch box should be washed and rinsed after each use.

• Bacteria thrives at temperatures between 60 and 125 degrees; food must not be allowed to sit at that temperature for any period of time. Cold foods should be kept at temperatures below 60 degrees maximum and ideally below 40 degrees. Hot foods should be maintained at a temperature above 125 degrees minimum and ideally above 140 degrees. Insulated thermal containers will aid in the fight against room temperatures as they are designed to keep hot foods hot and cold foods cold. Many are designed to double as a bowl and a carrier. What a thermos will *not* do is make cold foods colder or hot foods hotter. Therefore you must give it a good head start. If a cold food or beverage is going into the container, chill it first with ice water or a short stay in the freezer. If hot food is going into the thermos, the container should be preheated with boiling water, and food should be boiling hot when added to maintain desired hot temperatures.

• Sandwiches may be made several days in advance by freezing them. Put a sandwich into the lunch box frozen and allow it to thaw naturally by lunchtime.

Cooked meats and poultry freeze very well. Add vegetables to the lunch box to stack on the sandwich before serving. Mayonnaise tends to make the bread soggy when frozen (as well as add unneeded fat) — avoid it! Mustard is a fine addition and will not make the bread soggy when frozen.

• Freeze your beverage in a plastic container; it will serve as a cold pack to help keep your foods cool. Many lunch boxes also come as mini-coolers — made of Styrofoam and containing their own freezer packs.

• Be creative with lunches. With a little help from wise packing, there is brown-bag safety beyond peanut butter sandwiches!

Brown-Bagged or Otherwise

The Package

2 slices whole wheat bread
or
1 whole wheat pita bread (providing 2 pouches)
or
1 whole wheat English muffin
or
1 taco shell or tortilla

The Contents

lean sliced meats:
turkey, chicken breast, lean roast beef

alone or in combination with:

nonfat or low-fat cheeses:
mozzarella, part-skim milk cheese
or
bean spreads: particularly those made with
garbanzo beans, split peas and kidney beans
or
tofu, egg and flaked fish (such as tuna and salmon):
prepared with a minimum of light
mayonnaise or nonfat salad dressings

The Packaging Materials

lettuce (try romaine) and tomato slices

sliced cucumbers/squash, green pepper rings, alfalfa
sprouts, shredded carrots, fresh mushrooms

tomato and picante sauces

yogurt dressing

mustard and other condiments

WONDERFUL LUNCHES

TUNA TACOS

Preheat oven to 350 degrees.

Heat tacos on a cookie sheet for 5 minutes.

Place tuna in a medium-sized bowl, breaking it into pieces with a fork. Stir in celery, onion, chilies and taco sauce.

Divide lettuce among the taco shells, placing it in the bottom of each shell. Spoon 1/4 cup of the tuna mixture into each shell. Top with diced tomatoes.

Makes 6 servings

1 serving (2 tacos) = 2 proteins, 2 complex carbohydrates and 1 added fat

12 taco shells
2 cans (6-1/2-ounces each)
   water-packed tuna, drained
1/2 cup celery, chopped
1/4 cup onion, chopped
1 can (4 ounces) green chilies, drained
1/4 cup taco sauce
1 tomato, diced
2 cups romaine lettuce, shredded

THE "SMITHWICH"

Stuff each half of pita with half of cheese. Microwave or bake in toaster oven until cheese melts. Stuff each half of pita with half of vegetables and top with salad dressing.

Makes 1 serving

1 serving = 2 proteins and 2 complex carbohydrates

1 whole wheat pita, halved into
   pockets
2 ounces part-skim or nonfat
   mozzarella cheese or any part-skim
   cheese
2 leaves romaine lettuce
cucumber slices
green pepper rings
tomato slices
no-oil Italian salad dressing to taste

GRILLED CHEESE OF THE NINETIES

2 slices whole wheat bread
2 ounces part-skim or low-fat cheddar
   cheese, sliced
apple or tomato slices (optional)
nonstick cooking spray

Coat a skillet with nonstick cooking spray. Place 1 slice of bread in skillet; top with cheese and a few apple or tomato slices, if desired. Top with the other slice of bread. Grill sandwich on both sides until bread is lightly browned and cheese is melted.

Makes 1 serving

1 serving = 2 proteins and 2 complex carbohydrates

PITA PIZZAS

1 whole wheat pita, cut in half into
   rounds (like a Frisbee)
2 tablespoons spaghetti sauce
2 ounces part-skim or nonfat
   mozzarella cheese, shredded

Preheat oven to 375 degrees.

Place the two pita circles on a baking sheet. Spread each with half of the spaghetti sauce and top each with half of the cheese.

Bake for 8 to 10 minutes or until cheese is bubbly.

Makes 1 serving

1 serving = 2 proteins and 2 complex carbohydrates

ROLLED DELITE

1 flour tortilla (10-inch diameter),
   preferably whole wheat
2 tablespoons light cream cheese
1/2 tomato, cut into strips
1/2 cup romaine lettuce, shredded
1/4 cucumber or zucchini, cut into
   strips
1 tablespoon alfalfa sprouts (optional)

Spread tortilla with cream cheese. Top with vegetables and roll up jelly-roll fashion. Secure with toothpicks, if necessary, and cut in half.

Makes 1 serving

1 serving = 1 protein, 1 complex carbohydrate and 1 added fat

SEAFOOD SALAD

Mix together tuna, mayonnaise, mustard, celery, beau monde, dill weed and pepper. Spread on 1 bread slice or stuff half into each pita pocket. Top with lettuce and tomato; top with remaining slice of bread, if appropriate.

Makes 1 serving

1 serving = 2 proteins, 2 complex carbohydrates and 1 added fat

1/2 cup water-packed tuna or salmon
1 tablespoon light mayonnaise
1 teaspoon Dijon mustard
1 stalk celery, chopped
1/4 teaspoon beau monde (optional)
1/4 teaspoon dill weed
black pepper to taste
2 slices whole wheat bread or 1 whole wheat pita, halved
lettuce leaves
tomato slices

CARROT-CHEESE MELT

Mix together cheese and carrots. Spread mayonnaise on 1 bread slice and top with carrot-cheese mixture and remaining slice of bread.

Coat a skillet with nonstick cooking spray and heat on medium high. Place sandwich in skillet and grill on both sides until cheese melts.

Makes 1 serving

1 serving = 2 proteins, 2 complex carbohydrates and 1 simple carbohydrate

2 carrots, coarsely grated
1/2 cup part-skim or nonfat mozzarella cheese, shredded
2 slices whole wheat bread
1 teaspoon light mayonnaise
nonstick cooking spray

RICOTTA FRUIT SUNDAE

Scoop ricotta cheese onto a plate and surround with fresh fruit; sprinkle with granola or cereal.

Makes 1 serving

1 serving = 2 proteins, 1 complex carbohydrate and 1 simple carbohydrate

1/2 cup part-skim or nonfat ricotta cheese
1/2 cup assorted fresh fruit, sliced
1/4 cup granola or grape-nuts cereal

CHICKEN WALDORF SALAD

2 cups chicken, cooked and diced
1 cup bean sprouts
1/2 cup carrots, shredded
1 stalk celery, diced
1 apple, diced (1/2 cup)
1/4 cup raisins
3 tablespoons walnuts, chopped
2 tablespoons light mayonnaise
2 tablespoons orange juice
3 tablespoons nonfat plain yogurt

Combine chicken, bean sprouts, carrots, celery, apple, raisins and walnuts.

In a separate bowl, stir together mayonnaise, orange juice and yogurt until blended. Pour over salad; stir to coat.

Makes 4 servings

1 serving = 2 proteins, 1 simple carbohydrate and 1 added fat.

Serve with whole wheat crackers or stuffed into a pita to make a complete meal.

QUESADILLAS

2 flour tortillas (10-inch diameter),
    preferably whole wheat
2 ounces part-skim or low-fat cheddar
    cheese, shredded
2 ounces part-skim or nonfat
    mozzarella cheese, shredded
1 small tomato, diced
1/4 cup green pepper, finely chopped
1/4 cup fresh mushrooms, sliced
1/2 cup picante sauce (optional)
nonstick cooking spray

Sprinkle half the cheddar cheese, mozzarella cheese, tomato, green pepper and mushrooms on half of each tortilla. Fold over and press edges to seal lightly.

Place on heated griddle that has been coated with nonstick cooking spray. Grill until browned and crisp. Turn over carefully with a spatula and continue to grill until cheese is melted.

Remove from griddle and cut into triangles. Dip into picante sauce, if desired.

Makes 2 servings

1 serving = 2 proteins and 1 complex carbohydrate

WARM SALAD OF PORK AND BLACK-EYED PEAS

Combine black-eyed peas, salad dressing, onions, mushrooms, celery, red pepper and black olives; set aside.

Coat a large skillet with nonstick cooking spray; heat on medium high. Add garlic and stir-fry for 30 seconds. Add pork; stir-fry for 2 to 3 minutes until no pink remains. Remove from heat. Add vegetable mixture to pork in skillet; mix well.

Serve on spinach-lined plates.

Makes 4 servings

1 serving = 3 proteins, 1 complex carbohydrate and 1 simple carbohydrate

10 ounces black-eyed peas, cooked
1/3 cup no-oil Italian salad dressing
1/4 cup green onions, sliced
1/4 cup fresh mushrooms, sliced
1/4 cup celery, sliced
2 tablespoons red bell pepper, chopped
2 tablespoons black olives, sliced
2 cloves garlic, minced
1/2 pound pork tenderloin, cut into thin strips
fresh spinach leaves to line plate
nonstick cooking spray

Soups

Gazpacho

4 cups tomato juice, chilled
1 small onion, well minced
2 cups tomatoes, diced
1 cup green peppers, minced
1 cucumber, diced
1 clove garlic, crushed
juice of 1 lemon or lime
2 teaspoons wine vinegar
1 teaspoon honey (optional)
1 teaspoon dried basil
1 teaspoon tarragon
dash of ground cumin
dash of hot pepper sauce
1 teaspoon salt (optional)

Combine all ingredients and chill for 2 hours.

Makes 8 servings

1 serving (1 cup) = 1 simple carbohydrate

I add thinly sliced cucumber to this refreshing soup for extra crunch. It makes a wonderful lunch with low-fat cheese and crackers.

Combine potatoes, 2 cups cauliflower, carrots, garlic, onion, salt and chicken stock in pot. Bring to a boil; cover and simmer for 15 minutes.

Let cool for 10 minutes. Purée in food processor or blender until smooth and creamy.

Transfer to a double boiler and gently whisk in cheese, milk, dill, mustard and pepper; heat gently.

Meanwhile, steam the reserved 1-1/2 cups cauliflower until crisp-tender. Add to soup and heat through.

Makes 4 servings

1 serving = 2 proteins, 1 complex carbohydrate and 1/2 simple carbohydrate

2 cups potato chunks
3-1/2 cups cauliflower
1 cup carrots, chopped
3 cloves garlic, minced
1 cup onions, chopped
1 teaspoon salt
4 cups chicken stock
1-1/2 cups part-skim or low-fat
  cheddar cheese, shredded
3/4 cup skim milk
1/4 teaspoon dill weed
1/4 teaspoon dry mustard
1/4 teaspoon black pepper

In a nonstick skillet, sauté onion and garlic in olive oil until softened. Add celery, carrots and salt. Add pepper, oregano and basil. Cover and cook over low heat for 5 to 8 minutes.

Add green pepper, zucchini, tomatoes, tomato purée, chicken stock, garbanzo beans and wine, if used. Cover and simmer for 30 minutes.

Heat the soup to a boil and add pasta 15 minutes before serving; boil gently until pasta is tender.

Sprinkle each serving with 1 tablespoon Parmesan cheese; serve immediately.

Makes 8 servings

1 serving (2 cups) = 2 proteins and 2 complex carbohydrates

1 cup onion, chopped
4 to 5 cloves garlic, crushed
1 tablespoon olive oil
1 cup celery, minced
1 cup carrots, cubed
1 teaspoon salt
1/2 teaspoon black pepper
1 teaspoon dried oregano
1 teaspoon dried basil
1 cup green peppers, chopped
1 cup zucchini, cubed
1 cup tomatoes, chopped
2 cups tomato purée
3-1/2 cups chicken stock
1-1/2 cups garbanzo beans, cooked
3 tablespoons dry red wine (optional)
1 cup whole wheat pasta, uncooked
8 tablespoons Parmesan cheese,
  grated

POWER SNACKS

FRUIT BLOCKS

Dissolve gelatin in boiling water. Add juice concentrate and stir until mixed.

Pour into a 9 x 13-inch pan coated with nonstick cooking spray. Chill for several hours. Cut into squares for "building" blocks!

Makes 10 servings

1 serving = 1 simple carbohydrate

3 envelopes unflavored gelatin
3/4 cup boiling water
1 can (12 ounces) frozen unsweetened orange juice or grape juice concentrate, undiluted
nonstick cooking spray

FROSTED GRAPES

Wash grapes and pull from stems. Place grapes on a cookie sheet and freeze into "mini-grape popsicles."

1 serving (12 grapes) = 1 simple carbohydrate

1 bunch seedless grapes (red or green)

TRAIL MIX

Mix all ingredients together and bag in 1/4-cup portions.

Makes 16 servings

1 serving (1/4 cup) = 1 protein and 1 simple carbohydrate

1 cup unsalted, dry-roasted peanuts
1 cup unsalted, dry-roasted sunflower kernels or pumpkin seeds
2 cups raisins

PEACHES AND CREAM SHAKE

2 ripe peaches or 4 canned
   unsweetened peach halves
1 ripe banana, peeled
1 cup skim milk
8 ounces nonfat plain yogurt
1/2 teaspoon vanilla
5 ice cubes

Combine all ingredients in a blender and process until smooth and frothy.

Makes 4 servings

1 serving = 1 protein and 1 simple carbohydrate

QUICK DREAMSICLE DRINK

1/2 cup skim milk
1/2 cup orange juice
1/2 teaspoon vanilla extract

Combine all ingredients and stir. Serve over crushed ice.

Makes 1 serving

1 serving = 1 protein and 1 simple carbohydrate

YOGURT COOLER

1/2 cup nonfat plain yogurt
1/4 cup white grape juice
1/2 cup honeydew or cantaloupe
1 ice cube

Combine all ingredients in a blender and process until smooth.

Makes 1 serving

1 serving = 1 protein and 1 simple carbohydrate

PEANUT BUTTER-COVERED BANANA

2 large bananas, peeled and cut in
   half
1/2 cup natural peanut butter
1/4 cup unsalted, dry-roasted
   sunflower kernels
4 popsicle sticks

Insert popsicle sticks into bananas; freeze. Frost with peanut butter and roll in sunflower kernels. Freeze again on wax paper.

Makes 4 servings

1 serving = 1 protein, 1 simple carbohydrate and 1 added fat

ORANGE SNOW

Cut off tops of oranges, making a zig-zag path around the top of each orange while cutting. Hollow out the inside of each orange, setting pulp aside. Place orange shells in muffin cups.

Combine orange pulp, orange juice concentrate, banana, yogurt and vanilla in a blender and process until smooth.

Fill orange shells with mixture and freeze. Remove from freezer 15 minutes before serving.

Makes 4 servings

1 serving = 1 protein and 1 simple carbohydrate

4 oranges
1 can (6 ounces) frozen unsweetened
    orange juice concentrate, undiluted
1 small banana
2 cups nonfat plain yogurt
1 teaspoon vanilla

APPLE PIE CREAMY

Mix all ingredients together and serve. May also heat or freeze before serving.

Makes 1 serving

1 serving = 1 protein and 1 simple carbohydrate

1/2 cup nonfat plain yogurt
1/4 cup unsweetened applesauce
1 tablespoon raisins
1/2 teaspoon ground cinnamon

YUMMIEBEES

In a food processor, mix together the peanut butter and honey. Add the milk powder and cereal or wheat germ. Process until mixture is smooth and forms a ball.

Cover a plate with wax paper. Using 1 teaspoon at a time, shape the mixture into bee-shaped ovals. Place on the plate.

Dip a toothpick into cinnamon and press gently across the top of "bees" to make stripes. Place an almond slice in each side of "bee" for wings. Chill.

Makes 4 dozen

1 serving (6 "bees") = 1 protein, 1 simple carbohydrate and 1 added fat

1 cup natural peanut butter
3 tablespoons honey
2/3 cup nonfat dry milk powder
1/2 cup grape-nuts cereal or wheat
    germ
toothpicks
ground cinnamon, as needed
sliced almonds, as needed

HEALTHY APPETIZERS AND PUNCHES

Dips and Dippers

Fresh Vegetable Platter

Prepare a natural serving container and use as an edible dish for any of the tasty dips below and on pages 116-117.

Place the container with dip on a platter and surround it with a variety of cut-up fresh vegetables.

natural serving containers:
    green pepper, with top and seeds removed
    small cabbage head, hollowed out
fresh vegetables
dip (see recipes on pages 115-117)

Zesty Dip

Combine all ingredients in a blender or food processor. Process until mixture is the consistency of sour cream. Serve with fresh vegetables for dipping.

Makes 1 cup

2 tablespoons = "free"

1/4 cup = 1 protein

8 ounces part-skim or nonfat cottage cheese
1 tablespoon lemon juice
2 teaspoons celery seeds
1 teaspoon White Wine Worcestershire sauce
1/2 teaspoon garlic powder
1/4 teaspoon onion salt (or 1/8 teaspoon onion powder)
dash of hot pepper sauce

HERB AND GARLIC DIP

1 cup part-skim or nonfat cottage
   cheese
1/2 cup skim milk
2 tablespoons fresh parsley or 1
   tablespoon dried
1/8 teaspoon curry powder
1/8 teaspoon paprika
1 clove garlic
1/2 teaspoon dried basil
1 small red cabbage

Combine cottage cheese, milk, parsley, curry powder, paprika, garlic and basil in a blender or food processor. Process until smooth.

Hollow out the head of cabbage from the top. Cut a slice from the stem end so the cabbage will rest firmly on its base. Fill the cabbage with the dip.

Serve with fresh vegetables.

Makes 1-1/3 cups

2 tablespoons = "free"
1 serving (2/3 cup) = 1 protein

EASY RANCH DIP

2 cups nonfat plain yogurt
1 package ranch-style salad dressing
   mix

Stir together yogurt and salad dressing mix. Serve with raw vegetables.

Makes 2 cups

2 tablespoons = "free"
1/2 cup = 1 protein

YOGURT PIZAZZ!

1 cup skim milk
1/2 cup nonfat plain yogurt
2 tablespoons dried minced onion
2 tablespoons lemon juice
1/2 teaspoon garlic powder
1/2 teaspoon salt (optional)
1/2 teaspoon dried oregano
1 teaspoon dried parsley
1/2 teaspoon onion powder
1/4 teaspoon black pepper

Mix all ingredients together and chill. Serve with raw vegetables.

Makes 1-1/2 cups

2 tablespoons = "free"
1 serving (1/4 cup) = 1/2 protein

Process yogurt, cottage cheese, parsley and thyme in a food processor or blender until smooth. Add half of the tuna and process again until smooth. Add remaining tuna, green pepper, scallion, pimento and horseradish; stir well. Garnish with parsley sprigs.

Makes 1-1/2 cups

1 serving (1/4 cup) = 1 protein

1/2 cup nonfat plain yogurt
1/3 cup part-skim or nonfat cottage cheese
1 tablespoon fresh parsley or 1/2 tablespoon dried
1/4 teaspoon dried thyme
1 can (6-1/2 ounces) water-packed tuna, drained
1/4 cup green pepper, chopped
1 scallion, chopped
2 tablespoons pimentos, chopped
2 teaspoons horseradish
parsley sprigs for garnish

GUACAMOLE-COTTAGE DELITE

Cut avocado in half and remove pit. Scoop out pulp and place in a blender or food processor. Add cottage cheese and process until smooth. Scrape contents into a bowl and combine with remaining ingredients; mix well.

Serve with fresh vegetables.

Makes 1-1/4 cups

1 serving (3 tablespoons) = 1 added fat

1 large avocado
8 ounces part-skim or nonfat cottage cheese
2 green onions, chopped
1/4 green pepper, minced
1 clove garlic, minced
1 small tomato, peeled and chopped
1/2 teaspoon chili powder
1/2 teaspoon ground cumin
2 tablespoons lemon juice

SKINNY DIPPERS

6 corn tortillas
1/2 teaspoon salt (optional)

Preheat oven to 400 degrees.

Cut each tortilla into 6 wedges; place wedges individually on a cookie sheet. If desired, sprinkle with salt. Bake for 10 minutes. Serve hot or cool.

Store in an airtight container.

Makes 36 chips

1 serving (6 chips) = 1 complex carbohydrate

This will make tortilla chips much lower in calories than the classic type.

PITA DIPPERS

whole wheat pita bread

Cut pita bread into triangles. Toast until lightly browned and crispy.

Use as a healthy dipper.

1 serving (1/2 pita) = 1 complex carbohydrate

APPETIZERS

DATE CHEESE BALL

Process all ingredients in a food processor or blender until mixed evenly. Shape into a ball; garnish with grapes and apple wedges.

Best served with crispbread or any whole grain crackers.

Makes 2-1/2 cups

1 serving (3 tablespoons) = 1 protein and 1 simple carbohydrate

2 tubs (8 ounces each) light cream cheese
8 ounces unsweetened pitted dates, chopped
2 tablespoons skim milk
1/2 cup walnuts, chopped
grapes
apple wedges

CAROLYN'S PINEAPPLE CHEESE BALL

Process cream cheese in a food processor. Add pineapple, onion and 1/3 cup chopped pecans. Blend together until smooth.

Form into 2 balls. Sprinkle cheese balls with remaining chopped pecans. The cheese balls freeze beautifully; remove from freezer several hours before serving.

Makes 2-1/2 cups

1 serving (3 tablespoons) = 1 protein and 1 added fat

2 tubs (8 ounces each) light cream cheese
1 can (8 ounces) unsweetened crushed pineapple, drained well
1 tablespoon minced onion
1/2 cup chopped pecans

CHICKEN HAWAIIAN

4 whole chicken breasts, boned
1/3 cup unsweetened pineapple juice
2 cloves garlic, minced
1/3 cup low-sodium soy sauce
1 tablespoon dried parsley
1/3 cup sherry or chicken stock
1 can (15-1/2 ounces) unsweetened
 pineapple chunks

Preheat oven to 350 degrees.

Skin chicken breasts and cut into 1-inch cubes.

Make marinade, stirring together pineapple juice, garlic, soy sauce, parsley and sherry or stock. Place chicken in a baking dish and cover with marinade. Refrigerate for at least 6 hours.

Remove chicken from refrigerator 1 hour before cooking and allow it to come to room temperature. Leave chicken in same pan and place in oven for 20 minutes or until lightly browned.

Serve on wooden toothpicks, alternating chicken with pineapple chunks.

Makes 8 servings

1 serving (1/2 boneless chicken breast and 1/2 cup pineapple) = 2 proteins and 1 simple carbohydrate

DILLY SHRIMP SHELLS

1/2 cup large (3/4-inch) pasta shells
1 teaspoon Dijon mustard
2 teaspoons lemon juice
1 tablespoon fresh dill, snipped
1/4 pound fresh shrimp, cooked and
 peeled, or 1 can (6-1/2 ounces)
 medium shrimp, rinsed and
 drained
lettuce leaves to line plate
lemon slices

Cook pasta in boiling water according to label directions. Drain; rinse with cold water and drain again.

Mix mustard, lemon juice and dill in a medium-sized bowl. Add shrimp and stir to coat well.

Place 1 shrimp in each pasta shell. Arrange on a bed of lettuce. Garnish with lemon slices.

Makes 40 shells

1 serving (5 shells) = 1 protein and 1/2 complex carbohydrate

FRIENDLY PUNCHES

SUMMER SPARKLING PUNCH

Combine orange juice, apple juice and tea. Add club soda just before serving.

Makes 4 servings

1 serving (10 ounces) = 1 simple carbohydrate

1 cup unsweetened orange juice
1 cup unsweetened apple juice
1 cup mint tea
2 cups club soda

SUNRISE PUNCH

Combine pineapple juice, orange juice and sparkling water or club soda. Garnish with orange slices and mint sprigs.

Makes 16 servings

1 serving (6 ounces) = 1 simple carbohydrate

1 quart unsweetened pineapple juice
1 quart unsweetened orange juice
1 quart sparkling water or club soda
orange slices for garnish
fresh mint sprigs (optional)

TART CRANBERRY PUNCH

Place cinnamon sticks, cloves and allspice in the center of a small piece of cheesecloth; tie securely. Combine spice bag and remaining ingredients in a large pan; bring to a boil. Reduce heat; simmer for 5 minutes. Remove from heat; discard spices and orange slices. Serve warm.

Makes 10 servings

1 serving (1 cup) = 1 simple carbohydrate

3 cinnamon sticks (3 inches each)
24 whole cloves
1 teaspoon ground allspice
1 medium orange, sliced
2 quarts apple cider
2 cups water
3 cups fresh cranberries

THE HEALTHY GOURMET'S GUIDE TO LIGHT ENTRÉES

While the words "healthy" and "gourmet" would not appear to be in any way compatible, this guide to preparing foods in a new, light way opens a kitchen door with bright beginnings! The healthy gourmet can prepare foods that are not only enjoyable to both friends and family, but also provide the fuel for a fit and well body. Foods do not have to be fried to be enjoyed — including fish. When frying, food acts as a sponge, soaking up the high-fat/high-calorie shortening or oil. Small foods (oysters, shrimp, fish fingers) that are breaded and fried are particularly dangerous for those who want to cook light. The high surface area allows increased amounts of breading to adhere and fat to soak in. Rather than frying and smothering in sauce or gravy, you can do away with excess fat and calories by learning the art of light cuisine — broiling, grilling, marinading, microwaving, poaching, sautéing, stir-frying and steaming — and by adapting not-so-healthy recipes and making them wonderfully healthy.

Light Cooking Techniques

Second only to buying the best fresh foods to take advantage of their natural flavors is to select the cooking method that best retains the natural moisture in foods. This reduces or eliminates the need for fats, oils and rich sauces.

Grilling and Broiling

These cooking methods can be used far more often than on weekends. Grilling is an ideal cooking method for our purposes, allowing foods to pick up extra flavor and to be cooked with a minimum of added fats.

When grilled over hot coals or broiled on a rack in the oven, meat, fish and poultry lose extra fat as it drips away. Remove as much fat as possible before cooking by skinning chicken and trimming all visible fat from meat; this prevents the fat from cooking into your food. Coat the broiler or grill rack with nonstick cooking spray to prevent sticking, and place the trimmed fat from steaks on the grill separately to allow better smoking and flavor of the meat.

Lemon juice, wine, vinegar and plain yogurt are good main ingredients for low-fat marinades. Combine with fruit juices, herbs or spices for taste. Baste frequently to keep food moist during grilling. Remember: Marinades will give moisture and tenderness, not fat, to the meat. (See page 80 for marinade recipes.)

If grilling fish, choose firm-textured fish fillets or steaks which are about one inch thick rather than thinner ones (thinner foods dry out on the grill). If frozen, the fish should be thawed first. Basting fish with lemon/lime juice or low-sodium soy sauce often while broiling will keep the fish moist. Particularly good for grilling are snapper, sea bass, grouper, salmon, tuna and swordfish. Oysters and clams are also excellent for roasting on the grill. To roast unshucked oysters or clams, wash shells thoroughly; place on grill rack about 4 inches from hot coals; roast for 10 to 15 minutes or until shells begin to open; serve in shells.

Parchment Paper, Aluminum Foil, Cooking Bags and Wax Paper

By encasing the food in an envelope, evaporation is greatly reduced, and the food stays naturally moist and flavorful. Natural casements that may be used are lettuce leaves, cabbage leaves and corn husks.

Special microwave cooking bags are available at most supermarkets, usually in the foil or plastic wrap section. They're great for microwaving fish or chicken.

Poaching

To poach means to immerse a food in a simmering liquid. Poaching is generally reserved for poultry and fish, but lamb and veal can be poached with delicious results. Fish, chicken breasts, eggs and fruits are all especially good for poaching.

When poaching on top of the stove, the pan should be filled with a small amount of barely simmering liquid, with the food placed in the liquid. The pan should be covered so steam doesn't escape; the steam keeps the food moist.

For oven poaching the food is placed in a film of liquid, covered with foil and roasted.

Always allow food to cool in liquid. This permits flavor to be absorbed. When poached, foods stay tender, moist and low in fats.

Some good liquids to use in poaching are chicken stock, fruit juices, lemon juice, tomato juice and wine.

Following is a general time table for poaching foods:

- Boneless breast of chicken — 15 minutes
- Breast of chicken (with bone) — 25 minutes
- Fish fillets — 10 to 12 minutes (until flakes with fork)
- Fruits — 8 to 10 minutes

Sautéing and Stir-frying

Sautéing and stir-frying are both light methods of cooking with a minimum amount of oil. Vegetables will keep their flavor, have a nice texture, and retain those important water-soluble vitamins. By using nonstick cookware and/or a regular skillet coated with nonstick cooking spray, vegetables and meats can be cooked quickly, often with no fat added.

Nonstick cooking sprays allow high heat searing and cooking without sticking. A nonstick cooking spray will "grease" the pan while adding only a minimal amount of fat. By keeping a can of this in your kitchen, you will be able to add only as much additional oil as the flavor of a dish requires and not a drop more. You won't achieve perfect browning of the foods, but you will have fine results as long as you cook at a moderate temperature.

Nonstick pans are sold everywhere, and some are much better than others. As with every other piece of equipment you buy, high quality will pay for itself in the long run. The major quality differences will not be in the nonstick coating, but in the thickness and sturdiness of the pans. Be sure that your nonstick pan is as heavy as possible.

In most recipes calling for foods to be sautéed, the fat can be drastically reduced or omitted. Some foods, such as green pepper and celery, will dry out if cooked with nonstick cooking spray alone, so always use a small amount (no more than 2 teaspoons) of oil for sautéing. You may also sauté them in 1/2 cup chicken or vegetable stock, stirring frequently to prevent burning. This adds a nice flavor to the vegetables.

Foods such as mushrooms, onions, meat, fish and poultry release some liquids as they cook and can easily be sautéed in nonstick cooking spray or a nonstick skillet without oil. Meats can also be browned in this way without using any fat.

Slice vegetables thinly for sautéing and stir-frying. Meat, fish and poultry should be cut into small, even pieces. Heat the pan, add a little oil, toss in the food and shake, toss or stir the food for even browning. Cook only until the vegetables are crisp-tender.

Sautéing and stir-frying in a minimum of olive or canola oil will also allow vegetables to be flavorful with a nice texture and not lose water-soluble vitamins.

POULTRY

ROASTED CHICKEN WITH WATER CHESTNUT SAUCE

Preheat oven to 375 degrees.

Clean chickens well — skin and trim away all fat. Sprinkle outside of chickens with poultry seasoning and seasoning blend. Place half of the apple and half of the celery and carrots in the cavity of each chicken.

Place chickens, breast side up, on rack in roasting pan and cover tightly with aluminum foil.

Bake for 1 hour. When about half done, sprinkle with paprika and uncover.

To serve, place on a bed of parsley with peach halves that have been warmed for 15 minutes in the oven. Serve with Water Chestnut Sauce.

Makes 10 servings

1 serving (split breast) = 2 proteins
1 serving (thigh-leg quarter) = 3 proteins

2 whole frying chickens (about 3 pounds each)
poultry seasoning, as needed
salt-free seasoning blend, as needed
1 small apple, cut in half
2 stalks celery, cut in chunks
2 small carrots, cut in chunks
paprika
fresh parsley to line platter
8 canned unsweetened peach halves
Water Chestnut Sauce (recipe on page 79)

CHICKEN ELEGANTÉ

1/2 teaspoon salt
1/4 teaspoon black pepper
4 chicken breasts, skinned
1 bunch fresh or 1 package (10
    ounces) frozen broccoli
1/2 pound fresh mushrooms
1 teaspoon canola oil
2 medium onions, sliced into thin
    rings
Wine Sauce (recipe on page 79)

Preheat oven to 375 degrees.

Pat chicken breasts lightly with salt and pepper.

Bake for 25 to 30 minutes or until browned. While chicken is baking, steam broccoli. Sauté mushrooms in oil.

Top chicken with broccoli, mushrooms, onions and sauce. Reduce heat to 325 degrees and bake for an additional 30 minutes.

Makes 4 servings

1 serving = 3 proteins and 1 simple carbohydrate

ORANGE CHICKEN

6 chicken breast halves, skinned and
    boned
1 teaspoon paprika
1/8 teaspoon black pepper
1 can (6 ounces) frozen unsweetened
    orange juice concentrate, undiluted
1 teaspoon dried rosemary
1/2 teaspoon dried basil

Preheat oven to broil.

Place chicken breasts on rack of broiler pan. Broil for 3 to 5 minutes on each side or until golden brown.

Remove from oven and place in a 9 x 13-inch baking pan. Reduce oven heat to 350 degrees. Sprinkle with paprika and pepper. Pour orange juice concentrate over chicken. Sprinkle with rosemary and basil.

Bake uncovered for 30 minutes or until done.

Makes 6 servings

1 serving = 3 proteins and 1 simple carbohydrate

INDONESIAN CHICKEN AND FRIED RICE

In a food processor or blender combine onion, garlic, curry powder, salt and red pepper; process for 1 minute (mixture will be lumpy); set aside.

Heat a wok or large, heavy skillet. Add 1 teaspoon of oil.

In a small bowl beat eggs with water. Pour into wok and cook over medium heat until eggs are set. Remove from wok and fold over like an omelette. Cut into 1/4-inch strips and set aside for garnish.

Reheat wok or skillet. Add and heat remaining oil; add onion mixture and stir-fry for 2 to 3 minutes. Add chicken and celery and stir-fry for 3 to 4 minutes. Stir in soy sauce and rice and stir-fry until hot and well mixed.

Garnish with egg strips and cucumbers.

Makes 8 servings

1 serving = 2 proteins, 1 complex carbohydrate and 1 simple carbohydrate

1 medium onion, chopped
3 cloves garlic, peeled
2 teaspoons curry powder
1/2 teaspoon salt
1/2 teaspoon crushed red pepper
2 teaspoons canola oil
2 eggs or 1/2 cup egg substitute
2 teaspoons water
3 whole chicken breasts, skinned and cut into strips
1/4 cup celery, chopped
2 tablespoons low-sodium soy sauce
3 cups brown rice, cooked
1/2 cup cucumber, chopped

EASY CHICKEN AND RICE

Preheat oven to 350 degrees.

Pour chicken broth and water in a large roasting pan. Add brown rice. Top with chicken breasts. Sprinkle with onion, parsley, salt, pepper, garlic powder and tarragon. Cover roasting pan with lid. Bake for 1-1/2 hours, adding the frozen vegetables during the last 30 minutes of cooking.

Makes 4 servings

1 serving = 3 proteins, 1 complex carbohydrate and 1 simple carbohydrate

A wonderful meal-in-one dish!

1 can (15 ounces) clear chicken broth
3/4 cup water
1 cup brown rice, uncooked
4 boneless chicken breasts, skinned
1 small onion, chopped
1 tablespoon dried parsley
1/2 teaspoon salt
1/4 teaspoon black pepper
1/2 teaspoon garlic powder
1 teaspoon tarragon
1 bag (16 ounces) frozen mixed vegetables (such as California mix)

BASQUE CHICKEN

1 large green pepper, cut in strips
1/4 pound fresh mushrooms, thinly
   sliced
2 medium onions, thinly sliced and
   separated into rings
1 frying chicken (about 3 pounds),
   quartered and skinned
2 cloves garlic, minced
1/2 teaspoon salt
1/4 teaspoon black pepper
1/4 teaspoon cayenne pepper
1 cup tomato purée
1/4 cup dry white wine or chicken
   stock
2 teaspoons cornstarch
1 tablespoon water

Preheat oven to 375 degrees.

Place green peppers, mushrooms and onions in a roasting pan. Place chicken pieces over vegetables; sprinkle with garlic, salt, pepper and cayenne pepper.

In a separate bowl mix tomato purée and wine; pour into roasting pan. Bake uncovered for 1 hour or until tender and browned.

Pour liquid and vegetables into a skillet. Mix cornstarch and water; stir into skillet. Bring to a boil, stirring constantly until thickened and clear.

Place chicken in a serving dish. Pour sauce and vegetables over chicken and serve.

Makes 4 servings

1 serving (1/2 small breast and 1/2 cup sauce) = 2 proteins and 1/2 simple carbohydrate

Note: You may add 2 cups of sliced new potatoes to vegetables before cooking to count recipe as whole meal.

CHICKEN DIVAN

1 pound broccoli florets
2 cups chicken broth
2 tablespoons cornstarch
1/4 cup cold water
1/2 cup nonfat plain yogurt
1 tablespoon low-sodium soy sauce
1/2 teaspoon dried oregano
1/2 teaspoon salt
1/4 teaspoon black pepper
1/2 teaspoon dried basil
2 cups brown rice, cooked
1-1/2 cups chicken, cooked and cubed
1/2 cup Parmesan cheese, grated

Preheat oven to broil.

Steam broccoli until crisp-tender.

Heat chicken broth. Mix cornstarch and water and add to broth, stirring until broth is thickened and clear. Remove from heat and fold in yogurt. Add soy sauce, oregano, salt, pepper and basil.

Place brown rice on bottom of a casserole dish and top with steamed broccoli. Pour half the sauce over the top; layer cubed chicken on top. Add 1/4 cup Parmesan cheese to remaining sauce and pour over the chicken. Sprinkle with remaining cheese and place under broiler until lightly browned.

Serve immediately.

Makes 4 servings

1 serving = 2 proteins, 1 complex carbohydrate and 1 simple carbohydrate

Preheat oven to 350 degrees.

Mix together egg whites and water in a shallow dish; set aside.

Combine cereal, garlic powder, pepper and seasoned salt.

Dip chicken in egg mixture and then in cereal mixture, coating well. Arrange in a baking pan coated with nonstick cooking spray.

Bake for 45 minutes or until tender.

Makes 6 servings

1 serving = 2 proteins and 1/2 complex carbohydrate

2 egg whites, lightly beaten
1 tablespoon water
1 cup Nutri-grain wheat cereal, crushed
1/4 teaspoon garlic powder
1/4 teaspoon black pepper
1/4 teaspoon seasoned salt (optional)
6 boneless chicken breast halves, skinned
nonstick cooking spray

Preheat oven to 350 degrees.

In a bowl combine chicken, onion and green pepper. Place 1/3 cup of the chicken mixture and 2 tablespoons of cheese at one end of each tortilla; roll up. Arrange tortillas, seam side down, in a lightly oiled 12 x 7-1/2 x 2-inch baking dish.

Combine eggs, milk, flour, salt, garlic powder and hot pepper sauce; pour over tortillas. Cover and refrigerate for several hours or overnight.

Bake uncovered for 45 to 50 minutes or until set. Sprinkle with remaining cheese. Bake 3 additional minutes or until cheese is melted. Let stand for 10 minutes.

Makes 8 servings

1 serving = 3 proteins and 1 complex carbohydrate

2 cups chicken, cooked and shredded
1/2 cup green onions, sliced
1/2 cup green pepper, chopped
2-1/2 cups part-skim or low-fat cheddar cheese, shredded
8 flour tortillas (7-inch diameter), preferably whole wheat
4 eggs, beaten, or 1/2 cup egg substitute
2 cups skim milk
1 tablespoon whole wheat flour
1/4 teaspoon salt
1/4 teaspoon garlic powder
few drops hot pepper sauce

CHICKEN IN LEMON AND GARLIC

1 broiler-fryer chicken (3 pounds), cut
    up and skinned
2 tablespoons lemon juice
1 clove garlic, crushed
1/2 teaspoon ground ginger
1/2 teaspoon dry mustard
1/4 teaspoon dried thyme
1/4 teaspoon poultry seasoning
1/2 teaspoon salt
1/2 cup dry white wine or chicken
    stock
1/4 pound fresh mushrooms, sliced
nonstick cooking spray

Sprinkle chicken with lemon juice; rub with crushed garlic. Combine ginger, dry mustard, thyme, poultry seasoning and salt; sprinkle over chicken.

Coat a large skillet with nonstick cooking spray; place over low heat until hot. Add chicken and cook for 10 minutes. Turn chicken over; add wine or stock and mushrooms. Cover and simmer for 30 to 40 minutes or until tender.

Makes 4 servings

1 serving (1/2 breast) = 2 proteins

1 serving (1 thigh-leg quarter) = 3 proteins

SKEWERED CHICKEN À LA ORANGE

2 medium carrots, sliced in 1/4-inch
    rounds
1 teaspoon cornstarch
1/4 teaspoon fresh orange peel, grated
    (optional)
1/2 teaspoon salt
3/4 cup orange juice
1 tablespoon sesame seeds, toasted
1 teaspoon lemon juice
2 onions, peeled and quartered
1 green pepper, cut into pieces
1 pound chicken breasts, skinned and
    cut into 1-inch pieces

Preheat oven to broil.

Cook carrots, covered, in a small amount of boiling water for 4 minutes; set aside.

For sauce, combine cornstarch, orange peel and salt; stir in orange juice. Cook and stir until bubbly. Cook 2 additional minutes. Stir in sesame seeds and lemon juice.

Thread carrots, onion quarters, green pepper and chicken pieces alternately onto skewers. Place on rack of broiler pan or grill. Brush with sauce. Broil 3 to 4 inches from heat for 8 to 9 minutes; turn and brush often with sauce.

Arrange on plates. Serve with remaining sauce.

Makes 6 servings

1 serving = 3 proteins and 1 simple carbohydrate

SESAME BAKED CHICKEN

In a small bowl dissolve dry mustard in water. Add curry powder, paprika and garlic powder; mix well until mixture is the consistency of prepared mustard. Add more water if needed.

Rub skinned chicken breasts with mustard mixture and place in baking dish (for quick clean-up, coat with nonstick cooking spray).

Combine bouillon with boiling water. Pour over chicken breasts.

Bake uncovered at 350 degrees for 45 minutes, turning frequently. Increase oven temperature to 425 degrees and sprinkle chicken with sesame seeds. Bake for 10 minutes until golden brown.

Garnish with lemon slices on a serving platter.

Makes 4 servings

1 serving = 2 to 3 proteins and 1 added fat

1 teaspoon dry mustard
3 tablespoons water
2 teaspoons curry powder
1 teaspoon paprika
1 teaspoon garlic powder
4 chicken breast halves
2 teaspoons low-sodium chicken bouillon granules
1 cup boiling water
2 tablespoons sesame seeds
lemon slices
nonstick cooking spray

STIR-FRY CHICKEN WITH VEGETABLES

Mix water, cornstarch, ginger and soy sauce; set aside.

Coat a wok with nonstick cooking spray. Add oil and heat to 375 degrees. Add onion and garlic; stir-fry for 1 minute. Add chicken; stir-fry for 3 to 4 minutes. Add green pepper and tomatoes; stir-fry for 1 minute. Add cornstarch mixture; stir until thickened.

Serve immediately over brown rice.

Makes 2 servings

1 serving = 2 to 3 proteins, 1 complex carbohydrate, 1 simple carbohydrate and 1 added fat

1/2 cup cold water
2 teaspoons cornstarch
1/2 teaspoon ground ginger
2 teaspoons low-sodium soy sauce
2 teaspoons canola oil
1 medium onion, sliced
1 clove garlic, minced
2 split chicken breasts, cut into 1-inch pieces
1 green pepper, cut into strips
2 tomatoes, cut into 6 wedges each
1 cup brown rice, cooked and hot
nonstick cooking spray

STIR-FRY CHICKEN WITH CASHEWS AND SNOW PEAS

2 cloves garlic, minced
2 tablespoons low-sodium soy sauce
1 tablespoon sherry or chicken stock
2 tablespoons cornstarch
2 split chicken breasts, cut into 1-inch
  cubes
2 teaspoons canola oil
20 snow pea pods, sliced
1/2 cup water chestnuts, drained
1/2 cup chicken stock
1/2 cup unsalted raw cashews
1 cup brown rice, cooked and hot
nonstick cooking spray

Mix together garlic, soy sauce, sherry or stock and cornstarch. Marinate chicken pieces in mixture for 15 minutes.

Coat a wok with nonstick cooking spray; add oil and heat. Add chicken; stir-fry for 3 to 4 minutes. Add snow peas and water chestnuts; stir-fry for 30 seconds. Add chicken stock; stir-fry until thickened. Stir in cashews.

Serve immediately over brown rice.

Makes 2 servings

1 serving = 2 to 3 proteins, 1 complex carbohydrate, 1 simple carbohydrate and 1 added fat

HAWAIIAN CHICKEN

1/3 cup unsweetened pineapple juice
1/3 cup low-sodium soy sauce
1/3 cup sherry or chicken stock
2 cloves garlic
1 tablespoon dried parsley
black pepper
4 chicken breasts, skinned, deboned
  and split lengthwise

Mix pineapple juice, soy sauce, sherry or stock, garlic, parsley and pepper. Marinate chicken breasts for 3 to 4 hours or overnight. (The marinade adds no significant calories.) Grill chicken.

Makes 4 servings

1 serving (1 breast) = 2 to 3 proteins

ROAST TURKEY

1 turkey, thawed
celery leaves, as needed
thin onion slices, as needed

Before roasting, place a thin layer of celery leaves and thin slices of onion between skin and breast meat of turkey. They add a rich flavor to the meat and absorb much of the fat from the skin.

Roast the turkey according to package directions.

TURKEY FRIED RICE

In a small bowl, pour soy sauce over turkey; set aside.

Pour oil into a skillet; add rice and "fry" over medium heat, stirring constantly until rice is toasty brown. Add chicken broth; cover and simmer for 45 minutes until all liquid is absorbed. Add turkey, green pepper, celery and onion. Cook uncovered for 5 minutes.

Push rice to side of skillet and add egg, stirring constantly until set. Combine with rice mixture. Stir in lettuce. Serve immediately.

Makes 8 servings

1 serving = 2 proteins, 1 complex carbohydrate and 1 added fat

3 tablespoons low-sodium soy sauce
2 cups turkey, cooked and diced
2 teaspoons canola oil
1 cup brown rice, uncooked
2 cups chicken broth
1/4 cup green peppers, chopped
1/4 cup celery, chopped
2 tablespoons onion, chopped
1 egg, slightly beaten
1/2 cup romaine lettuce, shredded

CINCINNATI FIVE-WAY CHILI

Brown ground turkey with onion and garlic; drain fat. Stir in chili powder, paprika, pepper, cumin, cinnamon and nutmeg. Add tomatoes, beef stock, vinegar, honey and chocolate, if used.

Reduce heat to low. Simmer 30 minutes, stirring occasionally until thickened and flavors are blended.

Makes 4 servings

1 serving = 3 proteins and 1 simple carbohydrate

1 pound lean ground turkey
1 large onion, finely chopped
2 cloves garlic, crushed
1 tablespoon chili powder
1 tablespoon paprika
1 teaspoon black pepper
1/2 teaspoon ground cumin
1/2 teaspoon ground cinnamon
1/4 teaspoon fresh nutmeg, grated
20 ounces tomatoes, crushed
16 ounces beef stock
1 tablespoon red wine vinegar
1 tablespoon honey
1 square (1/2 ounce) unsweetened
  chocolate, grated (optional)

CHILI CON CARNE

1 pound lean ground turkey or
    ground round
2 teaspoons olive oil
1 cup onion, chopped
2 cloves garlic, crushed
1 cup celery, chopped
3 cups green peppers, chopped
1 can (28 ounces) tomatoes, undrained
1 teaspoon dried basil
2 to 3 teaspoons chili powder
1 teaspoon salt (optional)
1/3 teaspoon black pepper
1 medium can (15-1/2 ounces) red
    kidney beans, drained and rinsed

Place ground turkey in a colander; set colander in a glass bowl. Microwave on high for 3 minutes; break into pieces; microwave on high an additional 3 minutes or until browned; stir again; set aside.

In a 3- or 4-quart saucepan, heat oil. Add 3/4 cup onion, the garlic and celery, and 1 cup of the chopped green peppers. Sauté for 5 to 8 minutes over medium heat, stirring occasionally until tender.

Add tomatoes, breaking them up as you stir them in. Stir in the browned turkey, basil, chili powder, salt and pepper. Cover and simmer over low heat for 1 hour. Uncover and simmer an additional 40 to 60 minutes, stirring occasionally to develop flavor. Stir in beans and cook an additional 5 minutes.

Garnish with remaining onions and green peppers.

Makes 6 servings

1 serving (2 cups) = 2 proteins, 1 complex carbohydrate and 1 simple carbohydrate

SPAGHETTI PIE

6 ounces whole wheat spaghetti
    noodles
1 tablespoon olive oil
1/3 cup Parmesan cheese, grated
1 egg, well beaten
1/2 pound ground turkey or ground
    round
1/2 cup onion, chopped
1/4 cup green pepper, chopped
1 can (8 ounces) stewed tomatoes
1 can (6 ounces) tomato paste
3/4 teaspoon dried oregano
1/2 teaspoon salt (optional)
1/2 teaspoon garlic powder
1 cup part-skim or nonfat ricotta
    cheese or part-skim or nonfat
    cottage cheese
1/2 cup part-skim or nonfat
    mozzarella cheese, shredded

Cook pasta according to package directions; drain. Stir oil and Parmesan cheese into hot pasta. Add egg, stirring well. Spoon mixture into a 10-inch pie plate. Use a spoon to shape the spaghetti into a pie shell. Microwave uncovered on high for 3 minutes or until set; set aside.

Crumble ground turkey in a colander placed over a bowl; stir in onion and green pepper. Cover with plastic wrap and microwave on high for 5 to 6 minutes, stirring every 2 minutes (the fat will drain while meat is cooking). Put into a bowl and stir in tomatoes, tomato paste, oregano, salt and garlic powder. Cover and microwave on high for 3-1/2 to 4 minutes, stirring once; set aside.

Spread cottage cheese evenly over pie shell. Top with meat sauce. Cover with plastic wrap and microwave on high for 6 to 6-1/2 minutes. Sprinkle with mozzarella cheese. Microwave uncovered on high for 30 seconds or until cheese melts.

Makes 8 servings

1 serving = 2 proteins, 1 complex carbohydrate and 1 simple carbohydrate

HERB GRILLED CORNISH GAME HENS

Preheat oven to broil.

Wash hens. With kitchen shears, cut away backbone on either side; reserve for later use if desired. Remove all remaining skin and fat. Flatten hens by whacking breast bone to break. Arrange hens and any detached pieces on broiler pan. Squeeze lime or lemon juice on top and season with minced onion, poultry seasoning, basil, garlic powder, rosemary and black pepper.

Broil close to heat for 10 to 12 minutes. Turn over and broil for an additional 12 to 15 minutes or until juices run clear (not red) when thigh is pricked.

Makes 8 servings

1 serving (1/2 hen) = 3 proteins
1 serving (1 whole breast) = 2 proteins

Excellent served with rice pilaf!

4 Cornish game hens, thawed
2 fresh limes or lemons
dried minced onion
poultry seasoning
dried basil
garlic powder
dried rosemary
black pepper

FISH AND SEAFOOD

PAM'S BEST FISH

2 medium onions, chopped
2 stalks celery, sliced
1 teaspoon olive oil
1 teaspoon dried basil
2 cloves or 1 teaspoon garlic, minced
1 tablespoon dried parsley
4 flounder fillets (4 ounces each)
2 tomatoes, chopped
lemon or lime slices
2 cups tomato juice

Preheat oven to 350 degrees.

Sauté onions and celery in oil for 2 to 3 minutes until tender. Add basil, garlic and parsley. Spread over flounder fillets in a baking dish. Cover with chopped tomatoes and lemon or lime slices. Pour tomato juice over the top so that it covers the bottom of the dish.

Bake for 30 minutes.

Makes 4 servings

1 serving = 3 proteins and 1 simple carbohydrate

FLOUNDER FANTASY

Rinse fish; pat dry with paper towels. Sprinkle lightly with salt and pepper (if desired) and dust with flour.

In a medium-sized nonstick skillet heat half of olive oil over medium high. Add fillets and cook for 2 to 3 minutes on each side, turning once, until lightly browned and opaque. Remove to plate.

Add remaining oil to skillet. When heated, add garlic and almonds; cook for 1 minute, stirring frequently. Add wine or stock and stir until most of the liquid has evaporated. Add lemon juice.

Pour sauce over fish. Sprinkle with parsley.

Makes 4 servings

1 serving = 3 proteins and 1 added fat

1 pound fresh flounder or sole fillets
1/2 teaspoon salt (optional)
1/4 teaspoon black pepper
1 tablespoon whole wheat flour
1 tablespoon olive oil
1/2 teaspoon garlic, fresh minced
1/4 cup sliced almonds
2 tablespoons dry white wine or chicken stock
1 tablespoon lemon juice
1 tablespoon fresh parsley, chopped, or 1-1/2 teaspoons dried

STUFFED HADDOCK

Preheat oven to 350 degrees.

Thaw spinach in its own package. Squeeze excess liquid from spinach.

If haddock is frozen, allow to thaw overnight. Separate fish fillets; dry well with paper toweling.

Sauté celery and onion in olive oil in a medium-sized skillet. Add water; cover and cook for 10 minutes or until tender. Stir in spinach and 1/4 teaspoon of salt.

Place half the fillets in a shallow baking pan. Sprinkle with remaining salt, half the lemon juice and half the dill. Spoon spinach mixture over haddock. Layer remaining fillets on top. Sprinkle remaining lemon juice and dill over top.

Cover pan and bake for 20 minutes or until fish flakes easily.

Makes 4 servings

1 serving = 3 proteins, 1 simple carbohydrate and 1/2 added fat

1 package (10 ounces) frozen chopped spinach, thawed
16 ounces haddock, fresh or frozen
1 cup celery, chopped
1/4 cup onion, chopped
2 teaspoons olive oil
1/4 cup water
1/2 teaspoon salt (optional)
2 tablespoons lemon juice
1 tablespoon fresh dill, snipped, or 1 teaspoon dill weed

BROCCOLI-STUFFED FISH ROLLS

4 haddock fillets, fresh or frozen
1 small package (10 ounces) frozen
   broccoli spears
4 green onions, halved lengthwise
3 tablespoons dry white wine or
   chicken stock
1/4 teaspoon salt (optional)
2 tablespoons water
1 cup celery, chopped
1-1/2 teaspoons cornstarch
1 tablespoon cold water
4 cherry tomatoes
nonstick cooking spray

Preheat oven to 400 degrees.

Thaw fish; separate fillets.

Cook broccoli and onions in a small amount of boiling unsalted water for 3 minutes; drain.

Place a fourth of the broccoli and onions across the center of each fillet; roll up fish and fasten securely with toothpicks. Place rolls in 8 x 8 x 2-inch baking dish coated with nonstick cooking spray.

Combine wine or stock, salt and water; sprinkle over fish. Cover and bake for 30 to 35 minutes. Remove to serving platter; keep warm.

Measure pan juices, adding enough water to equal 3/4 cup of liquid. Cook celery in the liquid for 3 minutes.

Combine cornstarch and cold water; stir into celery mixture. Cook and stir until bubbly, then 2 additional minutes.

Pour sauce over fish. Garnish with tomatoes.

Makes 4 servings

1 serving = 2 proteins and 1 simple carbohydrate

FISH ITALIANO

4 grouper fillets (6 ounces each)
1/2 cup Nutri-grain wheat cereal,
   crushed
1/2 cup Parmesan cheese, grated
1/3 cup fresh parsley or 2 tablespoons
   dried
1/2 teaspoon garlic powder
1/2 teaspoon paprika
1/4 teaspoon salt (optional)
1/4 teaspoon black pepper
2 egg whites, slightly beaten
4 lemon slices

Pat fish dry.

Combine cereal, Parmesan cheese, parsley, garlic powder, paprika, salt and pepper in a shallow dish, mixing well.

Dip fish in egg whites and then in crumb mixture, coating well. Arrange in a shallow 2-quart baking dish, with thickest portions to the outside of the dish. Cover with plastic wrap, venting to allow steam to escape, and microwave on high for 8 to 10 minutes or until fish flakes easily with a fork, turning the dish every 2 minutes.

Garnish with lemon slices.

Makes 4 servings

1 serving = 3 proteins and 1 complex carbohydrate

Combine onion, garlic powder and oil in a bowl; cover and microwave on high for 3 minutes, stirring once. Stir in cornstarch, chili powder and undrained tomatoes. Cover and microwave on high for another 3-1/2 minutes, stirring once. Stir in olives and chilies.

Spoon half of sauce into a baking dish coated with nonstick cooking spray. Arrange fillets over sauce with thickest portions to the outside. Drizzle lemon juice over fish; sprinkle with salt. Top with remaining sauce.

Cover with plastic wrap and microwave on high for 7 to 9 minutes or until fish flakes easily when tested with a fork. Let stand a few minutes before serving.

Makes 4 servings

1 serving = 3 proteins and 1 simple carbohydrate

1 medium onion, chopped
1/8 teaspoon garlic powder
2 teaspoons olive oil
1 tablespoon cornstarch
3/4 teaspoon chili powder
1 can (16 ounces) whole tomatoes, chopped
2 tablespoons green olives, sliced (optional)
1 tablespoon green chilies, chopped
4 snapper fillets (6 ounces each)
1 teaspoon lemon juice
1/4 teaspoon salt (optional)
nonstick cooking spray

In a 9-inch glass pie dish arrange tomato slices on the bottom. Sprinkle garlic over the tomatoes and arrange the fish over the top. Sprinkle basil over the fish. Place lemon slices on top; sprinkle with oregano and crumbled feta cheese. If you have time, let it sit for about 30 minutes.

Cover with vented plastic wrap and microwave on high for 4-1/2 to 5 minutes. Let stand for 5 minutes.

Makes 4 servings

1 serving = 3 proteins

1 ripe tomato, sliced
2 cloves garlic, finely minced
1 pound red snapper fillets (1/2-inch thick)
1 teaspoon dried basil
1 lemon, thinly sliced
1/2 teaspoon dried oregano
1/3 cup feta cheese, crumbled

SWORD IN THE BAG

1 tablespoon whole wheat flour
1 pound fish fillets
1 cup tomatoes, chopped
1 small onion, sliced
1 teaspoon dried basil
1 teaspoon dried thyme
2 teaspoons garlic, minced

Shake the flour around in a microwave cooking bag*; add fish. Add tomatoes, onion, basil, thyme and garlic. Tie a knot in the top of the bag and poke 6 or 7 slits in the bag.

Place on a microwave-safe plate and cook on high for about 5 minutes, rotating the bag halfway through the cooking time. Let stand about 4 minutes before cutting the bag open.

Serve the fish with its wonderful sauce-in-the-bag!

Makes 4 servings

1 serving = 3 proteins

*Special microwave cooking bags are available at most supermarkets, usually in the foil or plastic wrap section. They're great for microwaving fish or chicken; swordfish, tuna steaks and shark are especially good!

POACHED SALMON

2 teaspoons olive oil
1 onion, chopped
2 cloves garlic, minced
1 teaspoon dried dill weed
1/4 teaspoon black pepper
1 tablespoon dried parsley
1-1/2 cups Chablis or other dry white
   wine or chicken stock
1/2 cup water
4 salmon steaks or other fish fillets
   (1-inch thick)
lemon slices
nonstick cooking spray

Coat a skillet with nonstick cooking spray. Add oil and heat. Add onions and sauté lightly. Add garlic, dill weed, pepper and parsley; sauté for 30 seconds. Add wine or stock and water. Bring to a boil. Add salmon steaks or fish fillets; cover and simmer for 8 minutes or until fish flakes easily.

Remove from skillet. Garnish with lemon slices.

Makes 4 servings

1 serving = 3 proteins

Preheat oven to 375 degrees.

Combine vinegar, mustard, dill weed and garlic in a glass baking dish. Add salmon and marinate for 10 minutes. Turn salmon over and marinate an additional 10 minutes.

Cut 4 sheets of aluminum foil into 8 x 8-inch squares. Place 1 salmon steak in the center of each sheet of foil. Divide green peppers, tomatoes and scallions evenly over the top of each salmon steak. Drizzle a fourth of the marinade over each salmon steak. Fold and pinch foil to seal fish inside.

Bake for 15 to 20 minutes. Remove from foil and serve immediately.

Makes 4 servings

1 serving = 3 proteins

1/4 cup apple cider vinegar
1/2 teaspoon Dijon mustard
1/2 teaspoon dill weed
1/4 teaspoon garlic, minced
4 salmon steaks, each 1-inch thick
   (about 1 pound)
1 green pepper, sliced
1 tomato, thinly sliced
1 scallion, minced

GRILLED SALMON

Combine allspice, cardamon, garlic and lime juice.

Arrange salmon steaks in a single layer in a shallow dish; cover with marinade. Let stand for 15 minutes; turn salmon over and let stand for an additional 15 minutes.

Grill salmon for 5 minutes on each side or until it flakes easily.

Makes 6 servings

1 serving = 3 proteins

1/2 teaspoon ground allspice
1 teaspoon cardamon (optional)
2 cloves garlic, minced
1/3 cup unsweetened lime juice
1-1/2 pounds salmon steak, about
   1-inch thick
4 lime slices

SALMON LOAF

1 medium onion, chopped
3/4 cup old-fashioned oats, uncooked
1/2 cup unprocessed wheat bran
1 can (15-1/2 ounces) salmon, drained
1 cup buttermilk
1/4 teaspoon garlic powder
2 eggs, lightly beaten
1 tablespoon dried parsley
1/2 teaspoon dill weed
1/2 teaspoon salt (optional)
1/4 teaspoon black pepper
6 lemon wedges to garnish
fresh parsley to garnish
nonstick cooking spray

Preheat oven to 350 degrees.

Combine all ingredients, mixing well.

Coat an 8-1/2 x 4-1/2-inch loaf pan with nonstick cooking spray. Pack salmon loaf mixture into pan.

Bake for 40 minutes or until firm. Garnish with lemon wedges and parsley if desired.

Makes 6 servings

1 serving = 3 proteins and 1/2 complex carbohydrate

MACARONI AND TUNA DELITE

1 cup whole grain macaroni,
    uncooked
1 medium onion, chopped
1/2 green pepper, chopped
2 teaspoons canola oil
1/4 cup water
1-1/2 cups fresh mushrooms, sliced
1 zucchini, diced
1 clove garlic, minced
1 teaspoon dried basil
1/4 teaspoon black pepper
1/2 teaspoon dried oregano
1/2 teaspoon salt
1 teaspoon dried marjoram
2 cans (6-1/2 ounces each)
    water-packed tuna
Parmesan cheese, grated

Cook pasta as directed.

In a large nonstick skillet sauté the onion and pepper. Reduce heat and add water. Add mushrooms and zucchini and cook until tender. Add garlic, basil, pepper, oregano, salt and marjoram during the last minute of cooking. Stir in tuna and heat through.

Toss with cooked macaroni and sprinkle with Parmesan cheese.

Makes 4 servings

1 serving = 2 proteins, 1 complex carbohydrate, 1/2 simple carbohydrate and 1/2 added fat

Easy and good!

EASY SHRIMP MARINARA

Sauté onion in oil in a nonstick skillet for 1 to 2 minutes. Add green pepper, carrot, mushrooms and garlic; sauté until tender. Add peas, wine or stock, tomato paste, basil, oregano, salt and pepper; stir well. Thin mixture with water until it reaches desired consistency. Bring sauce to a boil; reduce heat and simmer for 5 minutes. Add shrimp and cook for 3 to 5 minutes or until done.

Serve over hot linguine or spaghetti. May sprinkle with Parmesan cheese to serve.

Makes 4 servings

1 serving (10 shrimp, 1/4 of sauce mixture and 1/2 cup pasta) = 2 proteins, 1 complex carbohydrate and 1 simple carbohydrate

1 medium onion, chopped
2 teaspoons olive oil
1 medium green pepper, chopped
1 carrot, finely chopped
1 cup fresh mushrooms, sliced
2 cloves garlic, minced
1/3 cup frozen peas, thawed
1/2 cup red wine or chicken stock
1 can (6 ounces) tomato paste
1-1/2 teaspoons dried basil
1 teaspoon dried oregano
1/2 teaspoon salt
1/2 teaspoon black pepper
1/2 to 1 cup water
1 pound shrimp, rinsed and peeled
2 cups whole wheat pasta noodles
 (preferably linguine), cooked and
 drained
Parmesan cheese, grated (optional)

GRILLED SCALLOP KABOBS

Drain pineapple, reserving 1/4 cup plus 2 tablespoons juice. Combine pineapple juice, lemon juice, pepper, wine, soy sauce, parsley and garlic powder in a large shallow dish, mixing well. Add pineapple, scallops, green peppers, mushrooms and tomatoes; toss well to coat. Marinate in the refrigerator for 1 to 1-1/2 hours.

Place pineapple chunks, scallops, green peppers, mushrooms and tomatoes alternately on skewers. Place kabobs 4 to 5 inches from hot coals; grill for 10 to 12 minutes, turning kabobs and basting them frequently with marinade.

Makes 4 servings

1 serving = 3 proteins

1 can (15 ounces) unsweetened
 pineapple chunks
2 tablespoons lemon juice
1/2 teaspoon black pepper
1/4 cup Chablis or other dry white
 wine or chicken stock
1/4 cup low-sodium soy sauce
2 tablespoons fresh parsley, chopped
1/4 teaspoon garlic powder
1 pound fresh scallops
2 green peppers, cut into squares
18 medium-sized fresh mushrooms
18 cherry tomatoes

DANIELLE'S BEST SCALLOPS

1 medium onion, chopped
1/2 bunch broccoli, trimmed and
   sliced
3 carrots, scraped and sliced
2 zucchini, diced
1 tablespoon olive oil
1 clove garlic, minced
1/4 teaspoon cayenne pepper
1/2 teaspoon dried basil
1/4 teaspoon salt
1/4 teaspoon black pepper
1 pound fresh scallops, rinsed
2 cups whole wheat spaghetti noodles,
   cooked and hot

Sauté onions, broccoli, carrots and zucchini in a nonstick skillet with oil until just tender, about 5 minutes. Add garlic, cayenne pepper, basil, salt and pepper during last minute of cooking. Add scallops; let cook until white, about 4 minutes. Toss with spaghetti.

Makes 4 servings

1 serving = 3 proteins, 1 complex carbohydrate, 1 simple carbohydrate and 1 added fat

BEEF

CELEBRATION ROAST

Preheat oven to 325 degrees.

Brown roast in a nonstick skillet. Transfer to a rack in a roasting pan. Season with salt, pepper and ginger.

Add crushed garlic and onions to tomato purée and spread over the top. Slowly pour wine or stock over the top.

Cover tightly and bake for 2-1/2 to 3 hours or until meat is tender, basting several times during cooking.

Makes 16 servings (3 ounces each)

1 serving = 3 proteins

1 boneless round roast
   (approximately 4 pounds), trimmed
   of all fat
1 teaspoon salt
1 teaspoon black pepper
1 teaspoon ground ginger
2 cloves garlic, crushed
2 medium onions, chopped
1 cup dry red wine or beef stock
1 cup tomato purée

ROYAL FLANK STEAK

Preheat oven to broil.

Combine soy sauce, garlic and wine or stock in a shallow dish. Marinate steak for 1 hour or longer in mixture, turning occasionally.

For medium rare, broil for 5 minutes on each side, basting once with marinade. Let rest for a few minutes. Slice in thin slices across the grain.

Makes 6 servings

1/4 cup low-sodium soy sauce
2 cloves garlic, minced
1/4 cup red wine or beef stock
1-1/2 pounds flank steak, trimmed of
   all fat

Beef Bourguignon

5 medium onions, sliced
1/2 pound fresh mushrooms, sliced
2 teaspoons olive oil
2 pounds round steak, trimmed of all
    visible fat and cut into cubes
1/4 teaspoon dried marjoram
1/4 teaspoon garlic powder
1/2 teaspoon dried basil
1/2 teaspoon salt (optional)
1/8 teaspoon pepper
2 tablespoons cornstarch
2 tablespoons cold water
1-1/2 cups red burgundy wine or beef
    stock
3/4 cup beef stock or low-sodium beef
    bouillon

Brown onions and mushrooms in oil; cook and stir until tender. Remove from skillet and set aside. Brown meat in the same skillet. Sprinkle marjoram, garlic powder, basil, salt and pepper over meat.

In a small bowl mix cornstarch and water to form a paste. Stir cornstarch paste into skillet. Bring to a boil, stirring constantly; cook and stir 1 additional minute. Stir in wine or stock. Add beef broth.

Cover and simmer for 1-1/2 to 2 hours until meat is tender. Stir in onions and mushrooms; heat through.

Makes 8 servings

1 serving = 3 proteins and 1 simple carbohydrate

Pepper Steak

1-1/2 pounds round steak, trimmed of
    all fat and cut across grain into thin
    cubes
1/2 teaspoon salt
1/4 teaspoon black pepper
1 small onion, chopped
1 clove garlic, minced
1 cup beef broth
3 tablespoons low-sodium soy sauce
2 green peppers, cut into 1-inch pieces
2 tablespoons cornstarch
1/4 cup cold water
2 tomatoes, cut into 8 wedges each
3 cups brown rice, cooked and hot

Brown meat in a nonstick skillet; season with salt and pepper. Push meat to one side of skillet. Add onion; cook and stir until tender. Stir in garlic, broth and soy sauce. Cover and simmer for 15 minutes. Add green peppers; cover and simmer for 5 minutes.

Mix cornstarch with water. Gradually add cornstarch mixture to meat, stirring constantly until thickened and boiling. Boil and stir for 1 minute. Add tomatoes and heat through.

Serve over rice.

Makes 6 servings

1 serving = 3 proteins, 1 complex carbohydrate and 1 simple carbohydrate

ITALIAN SWISS STEAK

Preheat oven to 350 degrees.

Brown steak in a nonstick skillet; add water.

Place steak and water in a roasting pan. Top with onion, green pepper, tomatoes and mushrooms. Sprinkle basil, oregano, parsley, salt and pepper over the top.

Cover and bake for 1-1/2 hours. Serve over whole wheat pasta noodles.

Makes 4 servings

1 serving = 3 proteins and 1 complex carbohydrate

1 pound lean round steak, trimmed of all fat
1/2 cup water
1 medium onion, thinly sliced
1 green pepper, thinly sliced
2 small tomatoes, cut into wedges
1/4 pound fresh mushrooms
1/2 teaspoon dried basil
1/2 teaspoon dried oregano
1 tablespoon dried parsley
1/2 teaspoon garlic powder
1/2 teaspoon salt (optional)
1/2 teaspoon black pepper
2 cups whole wheat pasta noodles, cooked and hot

MARVELOUS MEAT LOAF

Preheat oven to 400 degrees.

In a large bowl combine all ingredients except 1/2 cup tomato sauce; mix well.

Shape meat into 2 loaves and place on rack to allow fat to drain. Spread half of remaining tomato sauce on top of each loaf.

Bake for 40 minutes.

Makes 8 servings

1 serving = 3 proteins and 1/2 complex carbohydrate

*If desired, you may substitute ground turkey for ground round.

2 pounds ground round*
2 cups old-fashioned oats, uncooked
3/4 cup onions, minced
1/4 green pepper, minced
2 eggs, slightly beaten
1/2 teaspoon salt
1/2 teaspoon black pepper
1 tablespoon Worcestershire sauce
1 teaspoon dry mustard
1/4 cup skim milk
3/4 cup tomato sauce

HERBED CHILI SPAGHETTI

2 pounds ground round or ground
   turkey
2 medium onions, chopped
2 cloves garlic, minced
1 green pepper, chopped
4 large tomatoes, chopped
1 cup water
1 package (12 ounces) whole wheat
   spaghetti noodles, uncooked
2 to 3 tablespoons chili powder
1 teaspoon cayenne pepper
1 teaspoon salt (optional)
1 teaspoon ground cumin
1 teaspoon dried oregano
1 can (20 ounces) tomato purée
2 cups kidney beans, cooked
1/4 cup fresh parsley, chopped
1 teaspoon dried marjoram

Cook ground round, onions, garlic and green pepper in a large skillet until browned, stirring to crumble meat; drain well.

Transfer to a pot and add remaining ingredients, mixing well. Cover, reduce heat and simmer for 2 hours, stirring occasionally.

Makes 12 servings

1 serving = 2 proteins and 1 complex carbohydrate

LAMB

ROSEMARY ROAST LAMB

Preheat oven to 400 degrees.

With a sharp knife make 6 small incisions in the thickest part of the meat and insert garlic slivers. Rub meat with oil; sprinkle with rosemary, 1/2 teaspoon salt and 1 teaspoon pepper; press seasonings into the meat. Put meat in a large roasting pan and roast for 1 hour and 15 minutes.

Then surround meat with potatoes, eggplant and green beans, making two piles of each. Pour chicken broth over vegetables and sprinkle with onions, tomatoes, remaining salt, remaining pepper and garlic powder. Cover the pan with aluminum foil and bake for an additional 1 hour and 10 minutes. Meat will be medium-rare to medium, and internal temperature will register at 150 degrees on a meat thermometer.

Carve and arrange meat on a platter surrounded with vegetables.

Makes 8 servings

1 serving = 3 proteins, 1 complex carbohydrate and 1 simple carbohydrate

1 leg of lamb (6 to 7 pounds), trimmed
  of all fat and oven-ready
2 cloves garlic, cut into 3 slivers each
1 teaspoon olive oil
2 teaspoons dried rosemary
1 teaspoon salt
1-1/2 teaspoons black pepper
1 pound Idaho potatoes, cut into
  1-inch chunks
1 pound eggplant, halved crosswise
  and cut into 1-inch squares
1 pound green beans, boiled for 5
  minutes and drained
1 cup chicken broth or low-sodium
  chicken bouillon
2-1/2 cups onions, sliced
1 can (16 ounces) tomatoes, drained
1/2 teaspoon garlic powder

GARDEN LAMB CHOP SKILLET

4 lamb leg sirloin chops (1-1/2
    pounds), cut 1-inch thick and
    trimmed of all fat
2 teaspoons canola oil
1 cup onions, sliced
1/2 cup carrots, cut in strips
1 medium green pepper, cut in strips
1/2 cup beer or beef broth
2 teaspoons low-sodium beef bouillon
    granules
1/2 teaspoon dried basil
1/4 teaspoon black pepper
1/2 cup tomatoes, chopped

Trim fat from chops. In a skillet cook chops in hot oil over medium-high heat for 8 to 10 minutes, turning once. Remove meat to platter; keep warm.

Drain fat from skillet and add onions, carrots, green pepper, beer or beef broth, bouillon, basil and pepper. Cover and cook for 3 minutes. Add tomato and cook uncovered for 2 additional minutes. Serve over chops.

Makes 4 servings

1 serving = 3 proteins and 1 simple carbohydrate

ORANGE LAMB CHOPS

1/2 cup unsweetened orange juice
1 tablespoon fresh orange peel, grated
1/2 teaspoon dried thyme
1/8 teaspoon black pepper, freshly
    ground
4 lamb leg sirloin chops (1-1/2
    pounds), cut 1/2-inch thick and
    trimmed of all fat
2 teaspoons canola oil
1 cup fresh mushrooms, sliced
1/2 cup Chablis or other white wine or
    chicken stock
1/2 teaspoon dried basil
nonstick cooking spray

Combine orange juice, orange peel, thyme and pepper in a shallow baking dish. Place chops in dish and cover with orange juice mixture. Cover and refrigerate for 3 hours. Remove lamb chops from marinade, saving liquid.

Coat a large skillet with nonstick cooking spray. Brown chops on both sides over medium heat; remove from skillet.

Heat oil in skillet; add mushrooms and sauté just until tender. Stir in reserved marinade and wine or stock. Bring to a boil.

Return lamb chops to skillet; cover, reduce heat and simmer for 10 minutes. Uncover and simmer for 10 additional minutes or until sauce reduces to 1/2 cup.

Makes 4 servings

1 serving = 3 proteins and 1 simple carbohydrate

Combine tomatoes, lentils, chicken stock, onion, garlic, parsley, bay leaf, salt and hot pepper sauce; bring to a boil over medium-high heat. Add lamb; reduce heat to medium low. Simmer covered for 1-1/2 hours until lamb and lentils are tender.

Remove bay leaf; garnish with parsley sprigs.

Makes 6 servings

1 serving = 3 proteins and 1 complex carbohydrate

32 ounces tomatoes, crushed
1 cup lentils, uncooked
16 ounces chicken stock
1 small onion, chopped
2 cloves garlic, crushed
1 tablespoon fresh parsley
1 bay leaf
1/2 teaspoon salt
1 teaspoon hot pepper sauce
1 pound boneless lamb shoulder, trimmed of all fat and cubed
fresh parsley sprigs

VEAL

SAVORY VEAL CUTLETS

1 pound veal, trimmed of all fat
1/4 teaspoon black pepper, freshly
   ground
1 clove garlic, crushed
2 teaspoons olive oil
1/2 cup dry white wine or beef stock
1/2 cup water
1 teaspoon low-sodium beef bouillon
   granules
2 small onions, cut into strips
2 green peppers, cut into strips
1/2 teaspoon dried basil
1/4 teaspoon dried oregano
1 tablespoon cornstarch
2 tablespoons water
12 cherry tomatoes, halved
3 cups whole wheat pasta, cooked and
   hot

Cut veal into 1-inch-thick pieces; sprinkle with pepper.

In a large skillet, sauté garlic in oil over medium-high heat until tender. Add veal and cook until browned. Stir in wine or stock, 1/2 cup water, bouillon, onions, green peppers, basil and oregano; bring to a boil. Cover, reduce heat and simmer for 5 minutes until vegetables are crisp-tender.

Blend cornstarch and 2 tablespoons water; stir into veal mixture. Bring to a boil and cook for 1 minute or until slightly thickened. Stir in tomatoes and serve over pasta.

Makes 6 servings

1 serving = 3 proteins, 1 complex carbohydrate and 1 simple carbohydrate

Note: Extra portions freeze well.

VEAL STEW

In a Dutch oven or large saucepan cook the meat, onion and garlic in hot oil until meat is brown; drain fat.

Add vegetable juice cocktail, lentils, lemon juice, bay leaf and basil. Bring to a boil. Add celery, mushrooms, carrot, potatoes and cabbage. Reduce heat.

Cover and simmer over low heat for 50 to 60 minutes or until vegetables are tender; remove bay leaf.

Makes 6 servings

1 serving = 2 proteins, 1 complex carbohydrate and 1 simple carbohydrate

3/4 pound sirloin cut veal, cut in
   3/4-inch cubes
1 cup onion, chopped
1 clove garlic, minced
1 tablespoon olive oil
2 cans (12 ounces each) vegetable
   cocktail juice
1/4 cup lentils, uncooked
2 teaspoons lemon juice
1 bay leaf
1/2 teaspoon dried basil
1 large stalk celery, sliced
1 cup fresh mushrooms, sliced
1 carrot, sliced
2 small potatoes, cut into 1-inch cubes
1 cup cabbage, coarsely chopped

LEMON VEAL WEDGES

Preheat oven to 350 degrees.

Combine egg, carrot, lemon peel, lemon juice, pimento, water, salt and pepper. Stir in bread crumbs. Add veal; mix well. Press mixture evenly into an 8-inch round baking dish. Bake for 35 minutes. Drain fat and let stand for 10 minutes.

Cut into 6 wedges. Serve on lettuce-lined plates; garnish with red pepper rings.

Makes 6 servings

1 serving = 3 proteins and 1/2 complex carbohydrate

*Make crumbs by toasting bread and crumbling in a blender.

1 egg, beaten
1/2 cup carrots, shredded
1/4 teaspoon fresh lemon peel, grated
2 tablespoons lemon juice
1 tablespoon pimento, chopped
1 tablespoon water
1/2 teaspoon salt
dash of black pepper
1/3 cup whole wheat bread crumbs*
1 pound ground veal
lettuce leaves
6 red pepper rings

VEGETARIAN MEALS

EGGPLANT IN DISGUISE

1/2 teaspoon salt
1/4 teaspoon black pepper
3 medium eggplants, sliced in rounds
3/4 cup wheat germ
1-1/2 cups onion, finely chopped
2 cloves garlic, minced
2 teaspoons olive oil
1 pound part-skim or nonfat ricotta
   cheese
1 cup (packed) part-skim or nonfat
   mozzarella cheese, shredded
1 teaspoon dried basil
1 teaspoon dried oregano
2 large tomatoes, sliced
nonstick cooking spray

Preheat oven to 350 degrees.

Salt and pepper the eggplant lightly. Bake for 15 minutes on a tray coated with nonstick cooking spray. When cooked sprinkle with wheat germ.

Sauté onions and garlic in oil until soft; combine with ricotta cheese, mozzarella cheese, basil and oregano.

Coat an oblong pan lightly with nonstick cooking spray. Layer as follows: half of eggplant, all of cheese mixture, half of tomatoes, remaining half of eggplant and remaining half of tomatoes.

Cover and bake for 35 minutes. Uncover and bake for an additional 5 minutes.

Makes 6 servings

1 serving= 2 proteins and 1 simple carbohydrate

EGGPLANT-SQUASH CASSEROLE

Preheat oven to 350 degrees.

Layer half the eggplant, zucchini slices and yellow squash slices in a 9 x 13-inch baking dish. Sprinkle with half the onion, parsley, basil, oregano and garlic powder. Salt and pepper to taste. Pour half of tomato juice over this first layer. Top with half of grated cheese. Repeat layers.

Bake for 45 minutes.

Makes 6 servings

1 serving = 2 proteins and 1 simple carbohydrate

To make a complete meal add 1 cup bulgur to layering procedure (1/2 cup before the cheese addition each time).

1 serving = 2 proteins, 1 complex carbohydrate and 1 simple carbohydrate

1 large eggplant, peeled and sliced
2 zucchini, sliced
2 yellow crookneck squash, sliced
1 large onion, chopped
1 tablespoon dried parsley
1 teaspoon dried basil
1/2 teaspoon dried oregano
1/2 teaspoon garlic powder
1/2 teaspoon salt
1/4 teaspoon black pepper
2 cups tomato juice
12 ounces part-skim or low-fat cheddar cheese, shredded

SQUASH THAT'S STUFFED AND NUTTY

Preheat oven to 350 degrees.

Bake squash face down on a baking sheet coated with nonstick cooking spray for 30 minutes or until tender.

Sauté walnuts, apples and onions in canola oil until onion is clear. Combine with cottage cheese, lemon juice, cinnamon and cheddar cheese; stuff squash halves with mixture.

Bake for 15 to 20 minutes.

Makes 4 servings

1 serving = 3 proteins, 1 complex carbohydrate and 1 added fat

2 acorn squash, halved
1/4 cup walnuts, chopped
2 medium apples, chopped
1/2 cup onion, chopped
2 teaspoons canola oil
2 cups part-skim or nonfat cottage cheese
juice of 1 lemon
dash of ground cinnamon
1 cup part-skim or low-fat cheddar cheese, shredded
nonstick cooking spray

Winter Squash Quiche

2 tablespoons onion, chopped
2 teaspoons canola oil
2 cups Swiss cheese, shredded
1 cup winter squash, cooked and
    mashed
1/8 teaspoon ground nutmeg
1/8 teaspoon black pepper
3/4 cup egg substitute
1-1/2 cups skim milk
1/4 teaspoon salt
nonstick cooking spray

Preheat oven to 325 degrees.

In a skillet cook onion in oil until tender. Coat a pie pan with non-stick cooking spray. Sprinkle cheese and onion in the pie pan.

In a bowl combine the squash, nutmeg, pepper, egg substitute, milk and salt; pour into the pie pan.

Bake for 40 to 50 minutes or until knife inserted near center comes out clean. Let stand for 10 minutes.

Makes 4 servings

1 serving = 2 proteins, 1 complex carbohydrate and 1 added fat

Stuffed Zucchini

3 zucchini
1/2 pound fresh mushrooms, chopped
1 large onion, chopped
1 clove garlic, crushed
2 tablespoons sunflower kernels
2 teaspoons canola oil
1/4 teaspoon dried rosemary
1/4 teaspoon dried basil
3 eggs, beaten
1-1/4 cups part-skim or nonfat cottage
    cheese
1/4 cup wheat germ or whole wheat
    bread crumbs
3 tablespoons low-sodium soy sauce
dash of White Wine Worcestershire
    sauce
dash of hot pepper sauce
1 cup brown rice, cooked
paprika
1/4 cup part-skim or nonfat
    mozzarella cheese, shredded

Preheat oven to 350 degrees.

Slice each zucchini in half lengthwise and scoop out the insides, leaving a 1/4-inch rim.

Chop the zucchini insides and sauté with mushrooms, onion, garlic and sunflower kernels in oil. Add rosemary and basil; set aside.

Mix eggs with cottage cheese, wheat germ or bread crumbs, soy sauce, Worcestershire sauce, hot pepper sauce and rice. Add the sautéed vegetables.

Stuff the zucchini generously with mixture. Sprinkle with paprika.

Bake for 40 minutes. Sprinkle tops with shredded cheese.

Makes 6 servings

1 serving = 2 proteins, 1 complex carbohydrate and 1 added fat

ZUCCHINI ITALIAN-STYLE

Preheat oven to 375 degrees.

In a 10-inch skillet cook zucchini, onions, garlic, salt, basil, pepper and cayenne pepper in oil for 8 minutes over medium heat, stirring frequently until zucchini is tender but still firm; remove from heat. Remove 1-1/2 cups of the zucchini mixture from the skillet and set aside. Stir cottage cheese into remaining vegetables in the skillet.

Spread half of the tomato purée in the bottom of an oblong 2-quart baking dish. Heap zucchini-cheese mixture in center. Top with remaining tomato purée and sprinkle with Parmesan cheese. Sprinkle reserved zucchini mixture around the edge of the dish.

Bake for 15 to 20 minutes until hot and bubbly.

Makes 4 servings

1 serving = 2 proteins and 1 simple carbohydrate

2 pounds zucchini, diced (2 cups)
1 cup onions, chopped
1-1/2 teaspoons fresh garlic, minced
1/2 teaspoon salt
1/2 teaspoon dried basil
1/8 teaspoon black pepper
dash of cayenne pepper
2 teaspoons olive oil
1-3/4 cups part-skim or nonfat cottage cheese
1 cup tomato purée
1/4 cup Parmesan cheese, grated

ZUCCHINI PIE

Preheat oven to 375 degrees.

In a large nonstick skillet, sauté zucchini and onion in oil until tender, about 10 minutes. Stir in salt, garlic powder, oregano, parsley, pepper and basil; continue to cook for 1 minute. Add tomatoes.

In a large bowl, blend eggs and cheese. Stir in vegetable mixture.

Coat a pie pan with nonstick cooking spray. Pour vegetable mixture into pie pan.

Bake for 18 to 20 minutes or until knife inserted into center comes out clean. Let stand for 10 minutes before serving. Cut into 6 wedges to serve.

Makes 6 servings

1 serving = 2 proteins, 1 complex carbohydrate, 1 simple carbohydrate and 2 added fats

4 cups zucchini, thinly sliced
1 cup onions, coarsely chopped
2 teaspoons olive oil
1/2 teaspoon salt
1/4 teaspoon garlic powder
1/2 teaspoon dried oregano
2 tablespoons fresh parsley, chopped, or 1 tablespoon dried
1/2 teaspoon black pepper
1/2 teaspoon dried basil
2 tomatoes, chopped
2 eggs, well beaten, or 1/2 cup egg substitute
10 ounces (2-1/2 cups) part-skim or nonfat mozzarella cheese, shredded
nonstick cooking spray

SPINACH-RICE AND YOU!

1 cup onion, chopped
2 cloves garlic, minced
2 teaspoons canola oil
2 pounds fresh spinach or 2 packages
   (10 ounces each) frozen spinach,
   chopped
1 cup skim milk
2 cups part-skim or low-fat cheddar
   cheese, shredded
4 cups brown rice, cooked
2 tablespoons fresh parsley, chopped,
   or 1 tablespoon dried
2 tablespoons low-sodium soy sauce
4 eggs, beaten, or 1 cup egg substitute
dash of ground nutmeg
dash of cayenne pepper
1/2 teaspoon salt
nonstick cooking spray

Preheat oven to 350 degrees.

Sauté onion and garlic in oil until soft. Add spinach and cook for 2 minutes.

Remove from heat and add remaining ingredients; spread into a casserole dish coated with nonstick cooking spray. Sprinkle with paprika.

Bake covered for 35 minutes.

Makes 8 servings

1 serving = 2 proteins and 1 complex carbohydrate

SPINACH SOUFFLÉ

2 eggs
1 cup evaporated skim milk
1/4 teaspoon ground nutmeg
2 ounces part-skim or nonfat
   mozzarella cheese, diced
1 package (10 ounces) frozen spinach,
   thawed
1/2 teaspoon dried minced onion
1/4 teaspoon salt
1/3 cup Parmesan cheese, grated

Preheat oven to 350 degrees.

Mix all ingredients except Parmesan cheese in a blender and process until smooth. Pour into a 1-quart baking dish. Sprinkle with Parmesan cheese.

Bake for 45 to 50 minutes.

Makes 4 servings

1 serving = 2 proteins and 1 simple carbohydrate

SCALLOPED SPINACH

Preheat oven to 350 degrees.

Cook spinach according to package directions. Press spinach through a coarse sieve into a bowl and add eggs, cheddar cheese, onion, milk, salt and pepper. Mix and pour into a 1-quart baking dish coated with nonstick cooking spray. Cover with cracker crumbs.

Bake for about 20 minutes.

Makes 2 servings

1 serving = 2 proteins, 1 complex carbohydrate and 1 simple carbohydrate

1 package (10 ounces) frozen spinach
2 eggs, beaten, or 1/2 cup egg substitute
1/4 cup part-skim or low-fat cheddar cheese, shredded
2 tablespoons onion, chopped
1/2 cup skim milk
1/8 teaspoon salt
1/8 teaspoon black pepper
1/2 cup whole wheat crackers, crushed
nonstick cooking spray

VEGETABLE GARDEN DINNER

In a 10-inch skillet cook onions and green pepper in heated oil until crisp-tender. Stir in remaining ingredients except 1 cup of cheese. Cook over low heat until heated through, stirring occasionally. Top with remaining cheese.

Makes 6 servings

1 serving = 2 proteins, 1 complex carbohydrate and 1 simple carbohydrate

1/2 cup onions, chopped
1/2 cup green peppers, chopped
2 teaspoons canola oil
1 can (14-1/2 ounces) tomatoes, crushed
3 cups brown rice, cooked and hot
1/2 teaspoon salt
1 teaspoon chili powder
1/8 teaspoon black pepper
1 bag (16 ounces) frozen cauliflower-broccoli-carrot mixture, thawed and drained
1/8 teaspoon garlic powder
3 cups part-skim or low-fat cheddar cheese, shredded

BROCCOLI-CHEESE FRITTATA

3 eggs or 3/4 cup egg substitute
3 tablespoons skim milk
1/4 teaspoon salt
dash of cayenne pepper
2 teaspoons canola oil
1 package (10 ounces) frozen chopped
    broccoli, thawed and well drained
1 small onion, finely chopped
1 small clove garlic, crushed
2 cups part-skim or low-fat cheddar
    cheese, shredded

Combine eggs, milk, salt and red pepper; beat well and set aside.

Heat oil in a 10-inch skillet. Add broccoli, onion and garlic; sauté until tender. Remove from heat. Stir in egg mixture. Sprinkle with shredded cheese.

Cover and cook over low heat for 10 minutes or until egg is set and cheese is melted.

Cut into 4 wedges and serve immediately.

Makes 4 servings

1 serving = 2 proteins and 1 simple carbohydrate

SWISS BAKED POTATO

4 baking potatoes (about 5 ounces
    each)
1/2 cup part-skim or nonfat ricotta
    cheese
1/4 teaspoon salt
1/4 teaspoon black pepper
6 ounces part-skim or nonfat
    mozzarella cheese, shredded
2 tablespoons pimentos, chopped
paprika

Preheat oven to 400 degrees.

Prick potatoes and bake for 1 hour. Cut in half lengthwise and scoop out most of the pulp, leaving a 1/4-inch shell.

In a bowl, mash pulp with ricotta cheese, salt and pepper. Stir in mozzarella cheese and pimentos. Spoon into potato shells. Sprinkle with paprika.

Increase oven temperature to broil; broil filled potato shells for 3 to 5 minutes or until heated through and lightly browned on top.

Makes 4 servings

1 serving = 2 proteins and 1 complex carbohydrate

LEGUMES

Beans, peas and lentils should first be washed by dumping them into a deep pot and covering them with cold water. Discard broken or cracked legumes that float to the top. Drain the water.

Beans must be soaked overnight to soften. They should be soaked in water in the refrigerator to prevent fermentation. A quick-soak method is to boil them for five minutes and then let them sit for one hour before cooking. Pour off this water. (Note: Lentils and split peas do not require soaking.)

The heavier and bigger the pot, the better it is for cooking beans and peas. Cover legumes completely with cold water. Allow them to come to a boil slowly and then simmer until tender, adding more boiling water if necessary. A well-cooked bean can be easily mashed against the roof of the mouth with the tongue. If this is not easily done, keep cooking.

During cooking, cover the pot only partially to prevent boiling over. When the beans become tender, add a pinch of salt (if desired), a bouquet garni, basil or bay leaf to the pot.

Crockpots are great for cooking beans because of their even, slow cooking. The slower the beans are cooked, the smoother and more concentrated their flavor. They must also be cooked thoroughly to prevent difficulty in digestion and gas production. Even when cooked properly, however, some beans are especially difficult to digest; kidney beans and soybeans are the toughest. Your body will adapt to the digestion of beans, as exposure encourages more specific intestinal bacteria to grow.

See Table 25 on page 162 for a guide to cooking various types of beans.

TABLE 25
How to Cook Beans

Type of Bean (1 cup uncooked)	Amount of Water	Time to Cook	Yield
Black beans	4 cups	1-1/2 hours	2 cups
Green or yellow split peas	2-1/2 to 3 cups	1 hour	2-1/4 cups
Garbanzo beans (chick-peas)	4 cups	3 hours	2 cups
Great Northern beans	3-1/2 cups	2 hours	2 cups
Kidney beans	3 cups	2 hours	2 cups
Lentils	3 cups	45 minutes	2-1/4 cups
Lima beans	2 cups	1-1/2 hours	1-1/4 cups
Navy beans	3 cups	1-1/2 hours	2 cups
Pinto beans	3 cups	2-1/2 hours	2 cups
Red and pink beans	3 cups	3 hours	2 cups
Soybeans	4 cups	3-1/2 hours	2 cups

FAVORITE LENTILS

In a large pot sauté oil, onions, carrots and garlic for 3 to 5 minutes. Add basil, salt and marjoram and sauté for an additional minute. Add stock and lentils.

Cover and cook until tender, about 45 minutes. Add wine, if used, and tomatoes and cook an additional 5 minutes. Serve.

Makes 6 servings

1 serving (1-1/2 cups) = 2 proteins

This will be a complete protein if served over brown rice (1/2 cup rice = 1 complex carbohydrate).

2 teaspoons olive oil
2 onions, chopped
2 carrots, thinly sliced
2 cloves garlic, minced
1/2 teaspoon dried basil
1/2 teaspoon salt
1/2 teaspoon dried marjoram
1 quart chicken or vegetable stock
2 cups lentils, uncooked
1/4 cup white wine (optional)
3 tomatoes, chopped

EASY SPLIT PEA SOUP

Preheat oven to 375 degrees.

Place the peas and stock in a large flameproof and ovenproof casserole dish. Add remaining ingredients. Bring the soup to a boil, stirring occasionally.

Cover and bake for 45 minutes or until the peas are tender.

Makes 6 servings

1 serving (1-1/2 cups) = 2 proteins

Serve with a corn muffin and salad for a complete meal.

2 cups split peas, uncooked
1 quart chicken or vegetable stock
2 stalks celery, chopped
2 carrots, diced
2 small onions, fincly chopped
1/2 cup fresh mushrooms, sliced
3 large ripe tomatoes, chopped
1 tablespoon low-sodium soy sauce
1/2 teaspoon ground cumin

BLACK BEAN SOUP

1 cup black beans, uncooked
7 cups chicken broth
1 tablespoon olive oil
1 large onion, minced
1 large clove garlic, minced
1/3 cup celery, diced
1/2 cup carrots, shredded
3/4 teaspoon ground cumin
1/4 teaspoon black pepper
1/2 teaspoon salt (optional)
8 tablespoons part-skim or low-fat
   cheddar cheese, shredded
8 tablespoons tomatoes, chopped

Soak beans overnight or by quick-soak method. Drain beans and add broth. Bring beans to a boil; reduce heat, cover and simmer for 2 to 3 hours or until tender.

Meanwhile, in a nonstick skillet, heat the oil and sauté the onion and garlic over low heat until transparent. Add the celery and carrots; stir and cook for a few additional minutes.

When the beans are done, add the vegetable mixture. Season with cumin, pepper and salt; simmer for an additional 30 minutes.

Serve hot; garnish each serving with 2 tablespoons chopped tomatoes and 2 tablespoons shredded cheese, if desired.

Makes 4 servings

1 serving (1 cup) = 2 proteins

SPICY CHILI SURPRISE

1 cup kidney beans, uncooked
1 cup pinto beans, uncooked
1/2 cup black beans, uncooked
water
1 large carrot, shredded
1 green pepper, chopped
1/2 cup raisins
2 bay leaves
2 tablespoons chili powder
1 teaspoon dried dill weed
1 teaspoon dried basil
1 teaspoon ground cumin
1/4 teaspoon cayenne pepper
1 teaspoon ground allspice
5 stalks celery with leaves, chopped
3 large tomatoes, peeled and cubed
1 medium onion, chopped
2 cloves garlic, minced
1/2 teaspoon salt
2 tablespoons fresh parsley, chopped,
   or 1 tablespoon dried
1/4 teaspoon black pepper
1 teaspoon dried oregano
1/4 cup unsalted, dry-roasted cashews
1/4 cup unsalted, dry-roasted
   sunflower kernels

Wash kidney, pinto and black beans; place in a large Dutch oven. Cover with water 2 inches above beans and let soak overnight.

Drain beans and cover with water again. Cover Dutch oven and bring to a boil; reduce heat and simmer for 1 hour. Add all remaining ingredients except cashews and sunflower kernels. Simmer for an additional 30 minutes or until beans are tender and chili is thickened. Add more water if necessary.

Remove from heat and discard bay leaves. Stir in cashews and sunflower kernels.

Makes 8 servings

1 serving (1 cup) = 1 protein, 1 complex carbohydrate and 1 added fat

NINE-BEAN SOUP MIX

Stir together and store in an airtight container. Use to make Nine-Bean Soup (recipe below).

Great for a Christmas gift basket!

1 pound barley, uncooked
1 pound red beans, uncooked
1 pound pinto beans, uncooked
1 pound lentils, uncooked
1 pound black-eyed peas, uncooked
1 pound black beans, uncooked
1 pound navy beans, uncooked
1 pound Great Northern beans, uncooked
1 pound split peas, uncooked

NINE-BEAN SOUP

Soak the soup mix; drain. Add water, garlic, chicken, onion and salt. Cover and simmer for 1-1/2 hours. Add no-salt tomatoes and tomatoes and green chilies; simmer for an additional 30 minutes.

Makes 10 servings

1 serving (1/2 cup) = 2 proteins

2 cups Nine-Bean Soup Mix (see recipe above)
2 quarts water
1 clove garlic, minced
1 pound chicken, cooked and diced
1 large onion, chopped
1/2 to 3/4 teaspoon salt
1 can (16 ounces) no-salt tomatoes
1 can (10 ounces) tomatoes and green chilies

WHOLE AND WONDERFUL GRAINS

Grains are truly the foundation of any healthy meal. While the rest of the world has *lived* on grains, Americans have closed their eyes to them. Many of these may sound and look strange to you and your family. Try them — it's time for something new. The names can be changed to protect the innocent! You may find that your family will accept "kasha" a lot better than "buckwheat groats" and "cracked wheat" better than "bulgur." Make up your own names as well.

The standard way to cook grains is to bring the water, stock or juice to a boil, add a pinch of salt, if desired, and then add the grains. Stir once, and when the water returns to a boil, turn down the heat to low; cover and let it cook until all the water is absorbed. Do not stir, play with the heat or continually check to see "how it's doing" — that makes it gummy!

See Table 26 on page 168 for a list of whole grains and their uses.

Pasta! Worth Its Weight in Gold — If It's Brown!

Pasta is a wonderful way to consume *whole* wheat and all its goodness. Although white pasta is familiar and convenient, whole grain pasta is more nutritious and satisfying than a pasta made from refined flour; you will be full with a much smaller portion. It also has a hearty, slightly nutty flavor. You may need to cook it 1 minute or so longer, but only to the *al*

dente (firm to the bite) stage. If you can mash the noodle against the roof of your mouth easily, it's overcooked!

Cooking Pasta

• Use one gallon of water to each pound of pasta to prevent clumping and uneven cooking.

• Water must be boiling rapidly before the pasta is added to it. You may add a touch of salt to the water if desired. A squeeze of lemon juice in the water produces far less clumping after cooking.

• Drop the pasta into rapidly boiling water without breaking it; it will immerse totally in the water as it softens.

• Stir pasta occasionally as it boils. Test for doneness by pulling out a strand and checking for a firm bite.

• When cooked, drain pasta in a colander, transfer to a bowl and toss with sauce, etc.

• When first attempting to use whole wheat pasta, use it hidden in lasagna or macaroni and cheese. Once approval is received, "brown spaghetti" will meet with much friendlier acceptance!

• Whole wheat pasta can be found in the dietetic or natural foods section of some supermarkets. It can always be found at a natural food store. It can be found in many shapes and sizes: as elbow macaroni, spaghetti, vermicelli, fettucine, linguine, lasagna noodles and more.

TABLE 26
WHOLE GRAINS

Grain	Description	How to Use
Barley	Usually pearled, barley is high in minerals and provides water-soluble fiber; it needs lots of water for expansion (3-1/2 cups water to 1 cup uncooked barley).	Add to soups and casseroles; use as a hot breakfast cereal; use as is or in combination with rice.
Bran	Bran is the outer covering of wheat; it richly increases the B vitamins and fiber in breads.	Add to granola (or any cereal); use in muffins, casseroles and breadings.
Buckwheat groats/ kasha	A high-fiber food, buckwheat groats or kasha is also high in protein and B vitamins; it has a strong flavor which requires a developed taste.	Use buckwheat flour in breads and pancakes; use groats/kasha as its own dish or in casseroles and sauces.
Bulgur/ cracked wheat	Bulgur is wheat that has been parboiled and cracked and is rich in minerals.	Add to cooked cereals, soups, casseroles and stews; use as a side dish; when soaked it is excellent as a base for salads.
Cornmeal	Cornmeal is high in nutrients, particularly phosphorus and niacin; look for *undegerminated* (unrefined).	Use in corn bread or polenta; use small amounts in bread making and pies.
Millet	A lightly flavored grain, millet makes a nutritious substitute for rice.	Use in any recipe calling for rice or in combination with rice; add to soups and casseroles.
Oats	High in iron, B vitamins and phosphorus, oats are water-soluble and are excellent for lowering LDL cholesterol.	Use as a hot cereal or in meat loaf, granola, breads or cookies; oats may also be blended into a flour.
Rice	Always choose a brown variety which is high in fiber and B vitamins; long grain is the lightest type.	Rice has extensive uses — in casseroles, soups, side dishes, puddings and with Chinese dishes; it's great with chicken. It takes much longer to cook brown rice than white. For convenience, cook large quantities and freeze or refrigerate extra in pint-sized containers. (Note: Any cooked whole grain can be substituted for rice.)
Rye	Usually ground into flour, rye must be used along with wheat flour for adequate gluten in baking bread.	Use flakes as a breakfast cereal, flour in making breads and grains as a side dish.
Wheat germ	Wheat germ is the heart of nutrients for the wheat kernel; very high in vitamins and iron, it should be bought fresh and kept in the freezer.	Use wheat germ in breads, casseroles and breading.
Whole wheat	Hard wheat flour is best in breads; soft or pastry flour in baking cakes or pastries. Always look for 100 percent whole wheat containing both the wheat germ and the bran layer.	Use whole wheat berries as a hot cereal with skim milk and fruit or in breads or casseroles; use flour in making bread or anywhere flour is used; it may be substituted for white flour in almost any recipe, producing a more full-textured, full-bodied product.

RICE

CURRIED RICE

Preheat oven to 400 degrees.

Heat oil in a large skillet. Add onion and sauté for 5 minutes until soft. Add rice and curry powder. Add stock. Bring to a boil. Cover and simmer for 45 to 50 minutes until rice has absorbed liquid.

Meanwhile toast almonds in oven for 3 minutes. Stir grapes into rice mixture; season with salt and pepper to taste. Stir in almonds just before serving.

Makes 6 servings

1 serving (1/2 cup) = 1 complex carbohydrate and 1 added fat

1 teaspoon canola oil
1 small onion, chopped
1 cup brown rice, uncooked
1 teaspoon curry powder
2 cups chicken stock or low-sodium chicken bouillon
1/3 cup slivered almonds
1/2 cup seedless grapes
1/2 teaspoon salt (optional)
1/4 teaspoon black pepper

WILD RICE AND MUSHROOMS

Combine broth, salt, pepper, onion and mushrooms in a medium saucepan; bring to a boil and add wild and brown rices. Boil for 1 minute; reduce heat and simmer for 45 minutes until the liquid is absorbed.

Garnish with parsley.

Makes 6 servings

1 serving (1/2 cup) = 1 complex carbohydrate

2-1/3 cups chicken broth or low-sodium chicken bouillon
1/2 teaspoon salt (optional)
1/4 teaspoon black pepper
1 medium onion, chopped
1 can (2-1/2 ounces) sliced mushrooms, drained
1/4 cup wild rice, uncooked
3/4 cup brown rice, uncooked
1 tablespoon fresh parsley, chopped

WALDORF RICE

1/2 cup onion, chopped
2 tablespoons canola oil
2 cups unsweetened apple juice
1/3 cup water
1/2 teaspoon salt
1 cup brown rice, uncooked
2 medium apples, chopped
1 cup celery, sliced
1/4 cup walnuts, chopped
1/2 teaspoon rum extract (optional)

Sauté onion in oil in a medium-sized pan until tender. Add apple juice, water and salt; bring to a boil.

Stir in rice; cover, reduce heat and simmer for 45 minutes.

Add apples, celery, walnuts and rum extract; remove from heat and let stand for 5 minutes.

Makes 6 servings

1 serving (1/2 cup) = 1 complex carbohydrate, 1 simple carbohydrate (from the fruit and juice) and 1 added fat

Great with baked chicken or sliced turkey.

WILD RICE PILAF MIX

3 cups brown rice, uncooked
1 cup wild rice, uncooked
1-1/2 cups barley, uncooked
3 tablespoons low-sodium chicken
    bouillon granules
3 tablespoons dried parsley
1 tablespoon dried basil
2 tablespoons dried minced onion
2 teaspoons dried minced garlic
1/4 teaspoon black pepper

In a large bowl combine all ingredients and mix well. Store in an airtight container (keeps forever!). Use to make Wild Rice Pilaf (recipe below). Makes a wonderful side or main dish.

Makes 10 cups

Make one large batch for your own "convenience food."

Great for gift baskets!

WILD RICE PILAF

1 cup Wild Rice Pilaf Mix, uncooked
    (see recipe above)
2-1/4 cups water

In a saucepan combine rice mix and water. Bring to a boil and reduce heat. Cover and simmer for 30 minutes or until rice and barley are tender.

Makes 6 servings

1 serving (1/2 cup) = 1 complex carbohydrate

PASTA

PAM'S PASTA PRIMAVERA

Sauté onion, carrots and broccoli in oil. When onion begins to soften, add zucchini and mushrooms; sauté until tender. Add tomatoes, garlic, basil, salt and pepper; let simmer for 5 minutes. Add peas and heat through.

Toss with hot pasta and Parmesan cheese.

Makes 6 servings

1 serving = 1 complex carbohydrate, 1 simple carbohydrate and 1/2 added fat

Variation: Add 3 cups of chicken, scallops or clams for a complete meal.

Makes 6 servings

1 serving = 2 proteins, 1 complex carbohydrate, 1 simple carbohydrate and 1/2 added fat

1 large onion, chopped
1 cup carrots, diced
1 cup broccoli florets
1 tablespoon olive oil
1/2 cup zucchini, diced
1 cup fresh mushrooms, sliced
1 large can (28 ounces) tomatoes, drained and crushed
1 to 2 cloves garlic, minced
1 tablespoon dried basil
1/2 teaspoon salt
1/4 teaspoon black pepper
1 cup frozen peas, thawed
2 cups whole wheat linguine or spaghetti noodles, cooked
1/4 cup Parmesan cheese, grated

LASAGNA

2 cups part-skim or nonfat ricotta
   cheese
2 eggs, beaten
2 teaspoons dried parsley
1 teaspoon dried basil
1 teaspoon dried oregano
1/2 teaspoon salt
1/4 teaspoon black pepper
4 cups Perfect Tomato Sauce (see
   recipe on page 78) or no-salt
   commercial spaghetti sauce
12 whole wheat lasagna noodles,
   cooked and drained
1 pound part-skim or nonfat
   mozzarella cheese, shredded
1/2 cup Parmesan cheese, grated
nonstick cooking spray

Preheat oven to 375 degrees.

Make filling by combining ricotta cheese, eggs, parsley, basil, oregano, salt and pepper.

Coat an oblong casserole dish with nonstick cooking spray.

Layer ingredients in casserole dish as follows: one fourth of sauce, one third of noodles, half of filling, one fourth of sauce, half of mozzarella cheese, one third of noodles, remaining half of filling, one fourth of sauce, remaining half of mozzarella cheese, remaining third of noodles and remaining fourth of sauce. Sprinkle the Parmesan cheese on top.

Bake covered for 35 minutes and uncovered for 10 minutes. Let stand for 10 minutes before serving.

Makes 10 servings

1 serving = 2 proteins, 1 complex carbohydrate and 1 simple carbohydrate

BAKED MACARONI AND CHEESE

1-1/4 cups whole wheat macaroni
water
2 eggs
1/2 cup part-skim or nonfat cottage
   cheese
1/2 cup skim milk
1/8 teaspoon paprika
1/4 teaspoon black pepper
1/2 teaspoon salt (optional)
1 cup part-skim or low-fat cheddar
   cheese, shredded
paprika for garnish
nonstick cooking spray

Preheat oven to 350 degrees.

Bring saucepan of water to a boil; add macaroni and boil until tender.

Combine eggs, cottage cheese, milk, paprika, pepper and salt in a blender and process until smooth.

Drain macaroni; place one-third of maraconi in the bottom of a 1-quart baking dish coated with nonstick cooking spray. Sprinkle with one third of cheddar cheese. Repeat layers of pasta and cheese two more times. Pour blended mixture on top. Sprinkle with additional paprika to garnish.

Bake for 40 minutes.

Makes 6 servings

1 serving (1/2 cup) = 1 protein and 1 complex carbohydrate

Preheat oven to 350 degrees.

Gently cook lasagna noodles to *al dente* (slightly firm) stage; cool in a bowl of cold water.

Sauté onions in oil until tender (3 minutes); set aside.

Beat cottage cheese in small mixing bowl until smooth. Mix all but 1/4 cup of cheddar cheese into the cottage cheese. Mix in broccoli, salt, garlic powder, basil, oregano, pepper and onion.

In a separate bowl mix flour and Parmesan cheese; set aside.

Spread a small amount of spaghetti sauce in the bottom of a rectangular baking dish.

Remove lasagna noodles from water one at a time. Pat dry with a paper towel; spread 1/4 cup cottage cheese mixture on each noodle and sprinkle with Parmesan cheese mixture. Roll up jelly-roll fashion. Arrange lasagna roll-ups in the baking dish and cover with remaining sauce.

Bake for 30 minutes. Remove from oven and sprinkle with reserved cheddar cheese. Return to oven for 3 minutes or until cheese is melted.

Makes 6 servings

1 serving (2 roll-ups) = 2 proteins, 1 complex carbohydrate and 1 simple carbohydrate

12 whole wheat lasagna noodles
3/4 cup onions, chopped
2 teaspoons olive oil
1-1/4 cups part-skim or nonfat cottage cheese
1-1/2 cups part-skim or low-fat cheddar cheese, shredded
1 package (10 ounces) frozen chopped broccoli, cooked and well drained
1/4 teaspoon salt
1/8 teaspoon garlic powder
1/4 teaspoon dried basil
1/4 teaspoon dried oregano
1/8 teaspoon black pepper
1 tablespoon whole wheat flour
1/2 cup Parmesan cheese, grated
2 cups Perfect Tomato Sauce (see recipe on page 78) or no-salt commercial spaghetti sauce

VEGETABLE-SPAGHETTI PIE

8 ounces whole wheat spaghetti
　　noodles, uncooked
1 teaspoon olive oil
2 eggs, beaten
1 cup part-skim or nonfat mozzarella
　　cheese, shredded
1/2 cup onion, chopped
1/4 cup green pepper, chopped
1 clove garlic, minced
1 cup fresh tomatoes, chopped
1/2 cup water
1 can (6 ounces) tomato paste
1-1/2 teaspoons dried basil
1 teaspoon dried oregano
1/4 teaspoon salt
1/8 teaspoon ground nutmeg
1 cup part-skim or nonfat ricotta
　　cheese
8 ounces part-skim or nonfat
　　mozzarella cheese, sliced into 8
　　pieces (1 ounce each)
1 package (10 ounces) frozen chopped
　　spinach, thawed and well drained
nonstick cooking spray

Preheat oven to 400 degrees.

Cook spaghetti in boiling water according to package directions; drain. Add oil, eggs and 1/4 cup of the mozzarella cheese.

Press mixture onto the bottom of a 14-inch pizza pan coated with nonstick cooking spray. Build the edges high to form a crust. Bake for 10 minutes.

In a nonstick skillet cook the onion, green pepper and garlic until tender. Stir in the tomatoes, water, tomato paste, basil, oregano, salt and nutmeg; set aside.

Spread ricotta cheese over top of spaghetti crust. Layer mozzarella cheese slices on top. Layer the spinach on top of this and then the tomato mixture.

Cover the pie with foil and bake for 12 to 15 minutes. Uncover and sprinkle with remaining shredded mozzarella cheese. Bake for an additional 2 minutes.

Makes 8 servings

1 serving = 2 proteins, 1 complex carbohydrate and 1 simple carbohydrate

SPECIAL BREADS AND MUFFINS

WHOLE WHEAT BREAD

Preheat oven to 375 degrees.

Dissolve yeast and a drop of honey in the water; let sit for a few minutes while it "comes alive."

Mix together milk, 3 tablespoons honey, oil, eggs and salt in a large bowl; add yeast mixture and 2 cups flour, mixing well. Continue mixing in flour until mixture becomes too difficult to stir.

Turn the dough out onto a lightly floured board and continue to knead in more flour until the dough is smooth and elastic (indentation from a finger poking will bounce back).

Form into a ball and put in a large bowl coated with nonstick cooking spray, turning dough over once to coat both sides lightly with oil; cover bowl with a damp towel and leave in a warm place to double in size for about 1-1/2 to 2 hours.

Punch down the dough and let it rise again for another hour. Punch down the dough once more and divide it in half; form each half into a loaf.

Place each loaf, seam down, in a loaf pan which has been coated with nonstick cooking spray. Cover the loaf pans with a towel and let the dough rise again until it has almost doubled in size, about 1 hour.

Bake for 45 to 50 minutes.

Makes 2 loaves with 20 slices (3/8-inch) per loaf

1 serving (1 slice) = 1 complex carbohydrate

2 tablespoons yeast (2 packages)
drop of honey
1/2 cup lukewarm water
2 cups skim milk, scalded and cooled
   to lukewarm
3 tablespoons honey
1/4 cup canola oil
2 eggs, slightly beaten
1 teaspoon salt
5 to 6 cups whole wheat flour
nonstick cooking spray

RAISIN BREAD

2 tablespoons yeast (2 packages)
drop of honey
3-1/2 cups lukewarm water
1-1/2 teaspoons salt
1 tablespoon ground cinnamon
1/2 teaspoon ground ginger
2 tablespoons canola oil
2 tablespoons honey
1-1/2 cups raisins
9 cups whole wheat flour
nonstick cooking spray

Preheat oven to 350 degrees.

In a large bowl dissolve the yeast and a drop of honey in 1/2 cup of the warm water until it "comes alive."

Add salt, cinnamon and ginger; stir well. Stir in the remaining 3 cups water, oil, 2 tablespoons honey and raisins. Add 4 cups of flour and stir until well blended. Add the remaining flour 1 cup at a time until too thick to stir.

Turn dough out onto a lightly floured board and continue to knead in more flour until dough is smooth and elastic (indentation from a finger poking will bounce back).

Divide dough into 3 portions; form each portion into a loaf. Place each loaf in a small (7-7/8 x 3-7/8 inch) loaf pan coated with nonstick cooking spray. Allow dough to rise in uncovered pans until doubled in bulk. This bread will only rise once.

Bake for 50 minutes until brown and hollow-sounding when tapped.

Makes 3 loaves with 16 slices per loaf

1 serving (1 slice) = 1 complex carbohydrate

DATE NUT BREAD

2 cups whole wheat pastry flour
1/2 teaspoon salt
2 teaspoons baking powder
1 teaspoon ground cinnamon
1 cup unsweetened pitted dates, chopped
1/2 cup walnuts, chopped
1 egg, beaten
1 cup skim milk
1-1/2 tablespoons canola oil
2 tablespoons honey
nonstick cooking spray

Preheat oven to 400 degrees.

Combine flour, salt, baking powder and cinnamon; stir with a fork to mix. Add dates and walnuts.

In a separate bowl combine egg, milk, oil and honey. Add dry ingredients to egg mixture and stir briefly. Pour into a loaf pan coated with nonstick cooking spray. Bake for 45 to 50 minutes. Cut into 24 slices.

Makes 24 servings

1 serving (1 slice) = 1 complex carbohydrate and 1 added fat

APRICOT PECAN BREAD

Preheat oven to 350 degrees.

Combine flour, baking soda, baking powder and salt in a small bowl; set aside.

Mix together oil and honey; add eggs one at a time, beating well after each addition; set aside.

Combine banana and milk. Add to creamed mixture alternately with the dry mixture. Fold in apricots and pecans.

Coat a loaf pan with nonstick cooking spray and pour in batter. Bake for 1 hour. Cool in pan for 10 minutes. Remove from pan and continue to cool on a wire rack to room temperature. Cut into 24 slices.

Makes 24 servings

1 serving (1 slice) = 1 complex carbohydrate and 1 added fat

2 cups whole wheat pastry flour
1/2 teaspoon baking soda
2 teaspoons baking powder
1/2 teaspoon salt
1/2 cup canola oil
2 tablespoons honey
2 eggs
1-1/2 cups banana, mashed
1/4 cup skim milk
1 cup dried apricots, chopped
1/2 cup pecans, chopped
nonstick cooking spray

BANANA BLUEBERRY BREAD

Preheat oven to 350 degrees.

Combine oil, honey and eggs in a food processor. Beat in bananas; set aside.

In a small bowl mix flour, baking soda and salt. Add oats. Carefully stir in blueberries (or raisins) and walnuts. Add to banana mixture, stirring just until moistened.

For bread: pour batter into a glass loaf pan that has been coated with nonstick cooking spray. Bake for 55 to 60 minutes. Cut into 18 slices.

For muffins: line muffin cups with paper baking cups and fill 2/3 full with batter. Bake for 20 to 25 minutes or until golden brown.

Makes 18 servings of bread or 18 muffins

1 serving (1 slice of bread) = 1 complex carbohydrate and 2 added fats

1 serving (1 muffin) = 1 complex carbohydrate and 2 added fats

1/4 cup canola oil
2 tablespoons honey
2 eggs
3 very ripe bananas, mashed
1-1/2 cups whole wheat pastry flour
1 teaspoon baking soda
1/4 teaspoon salt
1/2 cup old-fashioned oats, uncooked
1 cup blueberries (or raisins)
3/4 cup walnuts, broken into pieces (optional)
nonstick cooking spray

APPLE DATE MUFFINS

1-1/2 cups Shredded Wheat 'N Bran
   cereal
1-1/2 cups whole wheat pastry flour
1 tablespoon baking powder
1/2 teaspoon salt
1/2 teaspoon ground cinnamon
1/2 teaspoon apple pie spice
3 tablespoons canola oil
1/4 cup honey
1 egg
1 cup skim milk
1 cup unsweetened pitted dates,
   chopped
3 cups apples, peeled and chopped
dash of ground cinnamon
nonstick cooking spray

Finely process cereal in a blender or food processor. Mix with flour, baking powder, salt, cinnamon and apple pie spice; set aside.

In a separate bowl beat oil, honey and egg until well blended. Add milk. Add flour mixture and stir until well blended; fold in dates and apples.

Coat a muffin pan with nonstick cooking spray or line with paper muffin cups; fill each cup 2/3 full. Sprinkle top with dash of cinnamon.

Bake for 25 minutes or until toothpick inserted in center comes out clean. Cool in pan on wire rack for 10 minutes; remove from pan and cool completely.

Makes 16 muffins

1 serving (1 muffin) = 1 complex carbohydrate, 1 simple carbohydrate and 1 added fat

Delicious!

SPICED BRAN MUFFINS

1-1/2 cups whole wheat pastry flour
3/4 cup unprocessed wheat bran
2 teaspoons baking powder
1/2 teaspoon salt
3/4 teaspoon ground cinnamon
1/8 teaspoon ground nutmeg
2 eggs, slightly beaten
1-1/4 cups skim milk
1/4 cup canola oil
2 tablespoons honey
1/2 cup raisins
nonstick cooking spray

Preheat oven to 350 degrees.

Combine flour, wheat bran, baking powder, salt, cinnamon and nutmeg in a large bowl; make a well in the center of the dry mixture.

In a separate bowl combine eggs, milk, oil and honey; add to dry ingredients, stirring just until moistened. Stir in raisins.

Spoon into muffin pans coated with nonstick cooking spray or lined with paper baking cups, filling each cup 2/3 full.

Bake for 25 minutes.

Makes 12 muffins

1 serving (1 muffin) = 1 complex carbohydrate and 1 added fat

Preheat oven to 425 degrees.

Process oat bran with the large blade in a food processor while mixing the other ingredients (this will lighten up the muffins).

In a bowl, mix milk, egg whites, honey and oil together.

Add baking powder, cinnamon, pie spice and salt to the bran in the processor and blend. Add the liquid mixture to the processor and process just until blended. Add raisins.

Line muffin pans with paper baking cups and fill 2/3 full with batter.

Bake for 15 to 17 minutes. Test for doneness with a toothpick at 15 minutes; toothpick should come out moist but not wet.

Store muffins in a plastic bag to retain moisture. If you will not use muffins within 3 days, store in freezer and thaw 1 at a time.

Makes 12 muffins

1 serving (1 muffin) = 1 complex carbohydrate and 1 added fat

Variation: Omit pie spice, 1/2 cup skim milk and raisins. Add 1 small can (8 ounces) unsweetened crushed pineapple and 1 small mashed banana.

Makes 12 muffins

1 serving (1 muffin) = 1 complex carbohydrate and 1 added fat

2-1/4 cups oat bran
1-1/4 cups skim milk
2 egg whites
1/4 cup honey
2 tablespoons canola oil
1 tablespoon baking powder
3/4 teaspoon ground cinnamon
1/2 teaspoon pumpkin pie spice or
   apple pie spice
1/4 teaspoon salt
1/4 cup raisins

ORIGINAL BRAN MUFFINS

1 egg, slightly beaten
2 tablespoons canola oil
1/4 cup honey
3/4 cup nonfat plain yogurt
1 teaspoon baking soda
1/2 teaspoon salt
1 cup bran
3/4 cup whole wheat pastry flour
1/4 cup cold water
1/2 cup raisins

Preheat oven to 350 degrees.

Mix egg, oil, honey and yogurt together; set aside.

Combine baking soda, salt, bran and flour.

Add dry mixture to liquid mixture. Add water; mix only until moistened. Stir in raisins.

Fill paper-lined muffin cups half full with batter.

Bake for 30 minutes or microwave on high for 4 minutes (turning pan 180 degrees once during cooking).

Makes 12 muffins

1 serving (1 muffin) = 1 complex carbohydrate and 1 added fat

Variation: Add 1/4 teaspoon ground nutmeg, 1/2 teaspoon ground cinnamon and 1/2 cup chopped apple to the above recipe.

Makes 12 muffins

1 serving (1 muffin) = 1 complex carbohydrate and 1 added fat

MAGNIFICENT CORN BREAD — NORTHERN-STYLE

2 tablespoons canola oil
1/2 cup onion, finely chopped
1 egg, lightly beaten
1 tablespoon honey
1 cup skim milk
1 cup whole wheat pastry flour
1 cup yellow cornmeal
1 tablespoon baking powder
1/2 teaspoon salt
1 cup fresh or frozen corn
1/2 cup part-skim or low-fat cheddar
   cheese, shredded
nonstick cooking spray

Preheat oven to 375 degrees.

Heat oil in a small skillet. Add onion and sauté for 5 to 8 minutes or until onion is soft.

In a separate bowl beat together egg, honey and milk; set aside.

Combine flour, cornmeal, baking powder and salt. Add to liquid mixture. Add corn, shredded cheese and onions with all excess oil. Mix well. Spread into an 8-inch square pan coated with nonstick cooking spray.

Bake for 25 to 35 minutes or until brown and firm on top. Cut into 16 pieces.

Makes 16 servings

1 serving = 1 complex carbohydrate and 1 added fat

SOUTHERN-STYLE CORN MIX

In a blender or food processor fitted with a mixing blade, combine flour, cornmeal, milk powder, baking powder and salt, mixing well. Add oil slowly, mixing until oil is completely absorbed. Store in an airtight container in the refrigerator, mixing well before each use. Use to make Southern-Style Corn Muffins (recipe below).

Makes 5 cups

A tasty mix to have on hand for extra-quick muffins!

2 cups whole wheat pastry flour
2 cups yellow cornmeal
1 cup nonfat dry milk powder
2-1/2 tablespoons baking powder
1 teaspoon salt
1/4 cup canola oil

SOUTHERN-STYLE CORN MUFFINS

Preheat oven to 400 degrees.

Place corn mix in a bowl; add egg, honey and milk, mixing gently until mix is completely moistened.

Spoon batter into a muffin pan coated with nonstick cooking spray or lined with paper muffin cups, filling each cup 2/3 full. Bake for 15 to 20 minutes or until lightly browned.

Makes 12 muffins

1 serving (1 muffin) = 1 complex carbohydrate and 1 added fat

2-3/4 cups Southern-Style Corn Mix
  (see recipe above)
2 egg whites, beaten
1 tablespoon honey
1 cup skim milk
nonstick cooking spray

VEGETABLES WITH NEW ZEST

Vegetables cooked to the point of mushiness require a lot of seasoning to give them any taste at all, thereby creating the "need" some people have for bacon grease and lard. But cooking vegetables to a crisp-tender stage allows the full flavor to be present in the vegetable, and the use of herbs and spices will complement the fresh taste.

After vegetables have been cooked just right, sprinkle lightly with complementary spices or a seasoning blend (try mine on page 82). Spices are meant to flavor, not overpower, so always start out light!

See Table 27 on pages 184-185 for a guide to preparing vegetables.

Steaming

Steaming is an ideal method of cooking vegetables since it provides good retention of vitamins as well as taste. Vegetables will be more flavorful and nutritious if they are not cooked in a big pot of boiling water until limp and mushy. Steaming provides a healthy and tasty alternative. Place vegetables in a steaming basket (inexpensive and easily purchased at any grocery store) above a small amount of water (keep 1/4 inch below the bottom of the steamer) and cover. Bring to a boil and continue to boil on medium heat until vegetables are crisp-tender. Placing a garlic clove or a sliced onion in the steaming water will help to flavor vegetables without fat or calories.

BE CAREFUL: Steam burns! Remove the cover slowly, with the opening away from you.

Microwaving

Microwaving is a great way to cook vegetables to retain nutrients and flavor, but you must be sure not to overcook.

TABLE 27
VEGETABLE EXTRAVAGANZA GUIDE

Vegetable	Preparation	Minutes to Steam	Yield	Complementary Seasonings
Asparagus	remove tough ends before cooking; stand in boiling water	uncovered 5 minutes; covered 7 to 10 additional minutes	1 pound raw = 2 cups cooked	chives, garlic, lemon juice, parsley
Green beans	wash and snap ends off	15 to 25 minutes until crisp-tender	1 pound raw = 3 cups cooked	basil, dill, garlic, lemon, parsley, rosemary
Beets	scrub well; do not peel	20 to 30 minutes until crisp-tender	1 pound raw = 3 cups cooked	basil, cloves, mint, tarragon
Broccoli	pare stalk of tough skin before cooking	8 to 20 minutes until crisp-tender	1 bunch (2 pounds) raw = 2 cups cooked	garlic, lemon juice, pimento, vinegar
Brussels sprouts	cut off stems and slash stem ends for quicker cooking	12 minutes	1 pound raw = 3 cups cooked	chives, nutmeg
Cabbage	core and cut into wedges or quarters or shred	wedges 12 to 15 minutes; shredded 5 minutes	1 pound raw = 2 cups cooked	basil, caraway seeds, dill, poppy seeds, sage
Carrots	scrub thoroughly or pare; leave whole or slice	10 minutes	7 to 8 raw = 2 cups cooked	basil, ginger, mint, nutmeg, parsley
Cauliflower	core and remove outer leaves; leave whole or cut in florets	12 to 15 minutes	1 head (2 pounds) raw = 3 cups cooked	basil, chives, nutmeg, rosemary, tarragon
Corn	remove husks; wash; remove silks	boil or steam for 8 minutes	1 small ear per person	celery seeds, chives, green pepper, pimento
Eggplant	peel and slice; salt slices and let stand 15 minutes; rinse well before use	best used in soups or casseroles	11 slices (1/2-inch thick) raw = 2 cups cooked	basil, oregano, parsley, tarragon, thyme
Greens	wash well; discard discolored leaves	8 to 9 minutes or until wilted	1 pound raw = 1-1/2 to 2 cups cooked	basil, dill, oregano, onion, black pepper, vinegar
Mushrooms	wash gently or wipe with damp cloth; trim stem ends	sauté for 5 to 7 minutes or use raw or cooked in other dishes	10 mushrooms raw = 1 cup cooked	basil, chives, marjoram, parsley, thyme

Vegetable	Preparation	Minutes to Steam	Yield	Complementary Seasonings
Okra	wash and remove stem ends	use in mixtures for soups and stews	1 pound raw = 2 cups cooked	basil, bay leaf, onion, parsley, thyme
Onions	remove outer, loosest layer of skin	sauté 3 to 4 minutes or bake at 400 degrees for 40 minutes	1 medium onion raw = 1/2 cup chopped raw	dill, cloves, mint, parsley, tarragon
Parsnips	scrub well or pare; leave whole or slice	10 minutes	4 medium raw = 2-1/2 cups cooked	dill, parsley, sage
Peas	fresh: shell and wash frozen: be aware of salt content	6 to 7 minutes	1 pound raw = 1 cup cooked	basil, dill, mint, parsley, rosemary
Potatoes, white and sweet	scrub and remove any brown spots; do not peel	bake 1 hour; steam 15 to 20 minutes	3 medium raw = 2-1/2 cups cooked	white: dill, chives, parsley, rosemary sweet: chives, cinnamon, nutmeg
Spinach	wash thoroughly and remove stems	steam 4 to 5 minutes until wilted; serve raw in salads	1 pound raw = 1-1/2 to 2 cups cooked	basil, chives, dill, garlic, lemon, vinegar
Squash, spaghetti	cut in half; remove seeds	bake at 350 degrees, cut side down in small amount of water for 45 minutes, until strands pull free with a fork	1 squash (2 pounds) = 2 cups cooked	basil, oregano, parsley
Squash, summer	wash; trim off ends	steam or boil for 6 to 8 minutes	2 pounds raw = 2 cups cooked	basil, oregano, parsley
Squash, winter	wash; cut in half and place cut side down on baking sheet or peel and cut into small pieces to steam	bake 1 hour at 350 degrees or steam pieces for 20 to 30 minutes	2 pounds raw = 2 cups cooked	cinnamon, nutmeg, orange peel

VEGETABLES WITH STYLE

GREEN BEANS WITH MUSHROOMS

1 clove garlic, minced
1/2 pound fresh mushrooms, washed
2 tablespoons olive oil
1/2 teaspoon dried rosemary
1 teaspoon dried basil
1 tablespoon dried parsley
1/2 teaspoon salt
1/4 teaspoon black pepper
2 pounds fresh green beans, steamed

Sauté garlic and mushrooms in oil for 5 minutes. Add rosemary, basil, parsley, salt and pepper; simmer covered for an additional 3 to 4 minutes.

Toss well with green beans.

Makes 6 servings

1 serving = 1 simple carbohydrate and 1 added fat

COLORFUL GREEN BEANS

1 pound fresh green beans
2 teaspoons olive oil
1/2 cup onion, chopped
1/2 cup celery, chopped
1/2 teaspoon salt
1/4 teaspoon black pepper
2 medium tomatoes, peeled and cut
   into 8 wedges

Remove strings from beans; wash and cut diagonally into 2-inch pieces.

Heat oil in skillet; add onion and celery to skillet and sauté until tender. Add beans, salt and pepper. Cover and simmer for 10 minutes, stirring occasionally. Add tomatoes; cover and cook an additional 5 minutes.

Makes 4 servings

1 serving = 1 simple carbohydrate and 1 added fat

STEAMED BROCCOLI WITH TANGY CHIVE SAUCE

Trim large leaves off broccoli and remove tough ends of lower stalks. Wash broccoli thoroughly and separate into spears. Arrange broccoli on a steaming rack with stalks to the center of the rack. Place steaming rack over boiling water; cover and steam for 10 to 15 minutes or to desired degree of doneness.

Arrange broccoli spears in serving dish and keep warm.

Combine flour, salt and cayenne pepper in a small saucepan; gradually add chicken broth and milk, stirring with a wire whisk until smooth. Cook over medium heat, stirring constantly until the mixture thickens. Add chives, lemon juice and mustard, mixing well. Cook 2 additional minutes, stirring constantly.

Spoon sauce over steamed broccoli to serve.

Makes 4 servings

1 serving = 1 simple carbohydrate (1 tablespoon sauce = "free")

1 pound fresh broccoli
2 tablespoons whole wheat flour
1/8 teaspoon salt
dash of cayenne pepper
2/3 cup chicken broth
1/3 cup skim milk
2 teaspoons chopped chives
1 teaspoon lemon juice
1 teaspoon prepared mustard

BROCCOLI WITH ORANGE AND SWEET RED PEPPER

Wash orange; finely shred 1/4 teaspoon peel. Peel and section orange over 1-cup glass measure to catch juice. Stir orange peel into juice. Set juice mixture and orange sections aside.

In a 1-1/2-quart glass casserole dish combine broccoli, red pepper and water. Microwave covered on high for 6 to 8 minutes or until broccoli is crisp-tender; drain and set aside.

For sauce, add sesame oil to reserved juice mixture. Microwave uncovered on high for 1 minute or until bubbly.

Gently stir reserved orange sections into broccoli and red peppers. Microwave uncovered on high for 30 seconds.

To serve, drizzle sauce over broccoli mixture.

Makes 4 servings

1 serving = 1 simple carbohydrate

1 large orange
1/2 pound broccoli spears
1 large sweet red pepper, cut into thin strips
2 tablespoons water
1 teaspoon sesame oil

CAULIFLOWER WITH HAPPY-DAISE SAUCE

1 head cauliflower
1/2 cup nonfat plain yogurt
2 tablespoons prepared brown
   mustard
1 tablespoon lemon or lime juice
1/4 teaspoon salt
1/8 teaspoon black pepper
1/2 cup part-skim or low-fat cheddar
   cheese, shredded

Steam cauliflower until crisp-tender.

Mix yogurt, mustard, lemon or lime juice, salt and pepper. Pour over the cauliflower and top with shredded cheese.

Heat or microwave until the cheese is melted.

Makes 6 servings

1 serving = 1 simple carbohydrate and 1 added fat

OKRA AND TOMATOES

2 small onions, chopped
1 clove garlic, minced
2 teaspoons canola oil
1 pound fresh or 1 package (10
   ounces) frozen okra
3 small tomatoes, cut into small
   wedges
1/4 teaspoon salt
1/8 teaspoon black pepper
1/2 teaspoon dried basil
2 small bay leaves

Sauté onions and garlic in oil until slightly tender. Add okra; reduce heat to low and cook for 5 minutes, stirring constantly. Add tomatoes, salt, pepper, basil and bay leaves. Cook until okra is crisp-tender, about 10 to 15 minutes. Remove bay leaves.

Makes 4 servings

1 serving = 1 complex carbohydrate and 1 added fat

TANGY BRUSSELS SPROUTS WITH TOMATO SAUCE

10 ounces Brussels sprouts, fresh or
   frozen
1 teaspoon olive oil
1 large onion, coarsely chopped
1 clove garlic, minced, or 1/2 teaspoon
   fresh garlic, minced
1 cup tomato purée
1/2 teaspoon salt (optional)
1/4 teaspoon black pepper, freshly
   ground

Bring hot water to a boil in steamer. Wash and trim Brussels sprouts; steam for 10 minutes.

Heat oil in a skillet. Sauté onion until tender. Add garlic and sauté quickly. Stir in tomato purée. Add cooked Brussels sprouts. Season with salt and pepper.

Makes 4 servings

1 serving = 1 simple carbohydrate and 1 added fat

SPINACH WITH A TWIST

Heat oil in a skillet; add garlic and sauté for 1 minute.

If using frozen spinach, cook according to package directions; drain. If using fresh spinach, wash and trim then combine with water in a saucepan; cover and simmer for 2 to 3 minutes or until tender; drain.

Add spinach to garlic in skillet and heat through for 2 to 3 minutes.

Turn spinach onto serving plate; sprinkle with lemon juice.

Makes 4 servings

1 serving = 1 simple carbohydrate

1 teaspoon olive oil
2 cloves garlic, minced
1/4 cup water
2 pounds fresh or 2 packages (10 ounces each) frozen chopped spinach
juice of 1 lemon

CARROTS HAWAIIAN

Combine carrots and water in a small saucepan; cover and cook until carrots are crisp-tender.

Combine pineapple, cornstarch and ginger in a small bowl; mix well.

Add pineapple mixture to carrots; cook over low heat, stirring constantly until thickened.

Makes 4 servings

1 serving = 1 simple carbohydrate

4 medium carrots, cut into 3 x 1/4-inch strips (about 2 cups)
1/2 cup water
3/4 cup unsweetened pineapple tidbits, undrained
2 teaspoons cornstarch
1/4 teaspoon ground ginger

ORANGE AND NUTTY CARROTS

Slice carrots and boil covered in orange juice until crisp-tender.

In a separate bowl combine the water and cornstarch to make a paste. Add the paste to the carrots and stir until clear and thickened. Stir in walnuts.

Makes 6 servings

1 serving (1/2 cup) = 1 simple carbohydrate and 1 added fat

1 pound carrots, scrubbed, with tops and bottoms trimmed
1 cup unsweetened orange juice
2 tablespoons cold water
1 tablespoon cornstarch
1/2 cup walnuts, chopped

Peas Rosemary

1 package (10 ounces) frozen peas,
   cooked and drained
1/4 cup chopped onion
2 cloves garlic, minced
1 teaspoon olive oil
1 teaspoon dried rosemary
1/4 teaspoon salt
1/8 teaspoon black pepper

Sauté onion and garlic in oil until tender. Add rosemary, salt and pepper; continue to sauté for 1 additional minute. Toss with peas.

Makes 4 servings

1 serving (1/2 cup) = 1 complex carbohydrate and 1 added fat

New Year's Black-eyed Peas

4 strips turkey bacon
1/4 cup onion, chopped
2 packages (10 ounces each) frozen
   black-eyed peas
1/2 cup brown rice, uncooked
2-1/2 cups water
1/2 teaspoon salt (optional)
1/2 teaspoon black pepper

Dice turkey bacon into deep saucepan; add onion and sauté over medium heat until onion is tender. Add peas and rice, then water and seasonings.

Cover and simmer over low heat about 45 minutes.

Makes 8 servings

1 serving (1/2 cup) = 1 complex carbohydrate and 1 added fat

Potato-Tomato Wonder

4 cups potatoes, thinly sliced
2 cups onions, thinly sliced
2 cups tomatoes, sliced
1/2 teaspoon salt
1/4 teaspoon black pepper
1/2 cup part-skim cheddar cheese,
   shredded

Preheat oven to 350 degrees.

Alternate layers of potatoes, onions and tomatoes. Lightly season each layer with salt and pepper.

Bake for 30 minutes or microwave on high for 12 minutes. Top with cheese at the end of the cooking period.

Makes 8 servings

1 serving (1/2 cup) = 1 complex carbohydrate

Variation: Substitute zucchini for the potatoes.

Makes 8 servings

1 serving (1/2 cup) = 1 simple carbohydrate

Preheat oven to 350 degrees.

Mash potatoes. Add cornstarch, salt, pineapple juice, nutmeg, milk powder, eggs, cinnamon and oil; beat. Add pineapple and pour into a casserole dish coated with nonstick cooking spray. Sprinkle with a small amount of coconut and walnuts to garnish, if desired.

Bake for 30 minutes.

Makes 12 servings

1 serving (1/3 cup) = 1 complex carbohydrate

4 pounds sweet potatoes, boiled and peeled
2 tablespoons cornstarch
1/2 teaspoon salt
1-1/3 cups unsweetened pineapple juice
2 teaspoons ground nutmeg
2 tablespoons nonfat dry milk powder
3 eggs
1/2 teaspoon ground cinnamon
1 tablespoon canola oil
1 small can (8 ounces) unsweetened crushed pineapple
unsweetened flaked coconut
walnuts, chopped
nonstick cooking spray

SALADS

CAESAR SALAD

2 cloves garlic, minced
2 teaspoons olive oil
1/2 teaspoon dry mustard
1 teaspoon White Wine
   Worcestershire sauce
1/8 teaspoon salt (optional)
1/8 teaspoon coarse black pepper
4 cups romaine lettuce, washed and
   torn into pieces
1 egg, coddled*
juice of one lemon
1/4 cup Parmesan cheese, grated

Rub bottom and sides of large salad bowl with garlic; leave in bowl.

Add oil, mustard, Worcestershire sauce, salt and pepper; beat together with a fork. Add chilled romaine lettuce and toss well. Add coddled egg and lemon juice. Toss until lettuce is well covered. Top with Parmesan cheese.

Makes 4 servings

1 serving = 1/2 added fat

*Coddle an egg by immersing the whole egg (in its shell) into boiling water for 30 seconds. This destroys the bacteria found in raw eggs.

ANTIPASTO

1 large head romaine lettuce, washed
4 small tomatoes, quartered
2 cups frozen Italian-mix vegetables,
   steamed
4 ounces part-skim or nonfat
   mozzarella cheese, cubed
1 small jar (6 ounces) marinated
   artichoke hearts, drained
1 small Bermuda onion, sliced very
   thinly
no-oil Italian salad dressing, as needed

Chop and scatter lettuce over a large platter. Spread tomatoes, Italian-mix vegetables, mozzarella cheese, artichoke hearts and onion on top. Drizzle salad dressing lightly over the entire platter.

Makes 4 servings

1 serving (1 cup) = 1 protein and 1 simple carbohydrate

Cook green beans according to package directions, omitting salt; drain well. Combine green beans with onions, basil, pepper, mushrooms, salad dressing and salt in a medium bowl. Cover and chill for 3 to 4 hours.

Cut top off each tomato; scoop out the pulp, leaving the tomato shells intact; reserve the pulp for use in other recipes. Invert tomato shells on paper towels to drain. Fill tomato shells with bean mixture immediately before serving.

Makes 6 servings

1 serving = 1 simple carbohydrate

2 packages (10 ounces each) frozen French-cut green beans
1/4 cup green onions, sliced
1/8 teaspoon dried basil
1/8 teaspoon black pepper
1/2 cup fresh mushrooms, sliced
1/3 cup no-oil Italian salad dressing
1/2 teaspoon salt (optional)
6 medium tomatoes

SPINACH AND APPLE SALAD

In a large bowl combine spinach, apples and orange sections. Toss with dressing. Serve immediately.

Makes 6 servings

1 serving = 1/2 simple carbohydrate and 1 added fat

4 cups fresh spinach, torn in bite-size pieces
2 cups apples, thinly sliced
1/2 cup orange segments (optional)
3/4 cup Tasty Apple Juice Dressing (recipe on page 81)

WALDORF IN DISGUISE

Combine apples, pineapple chunks, celery, carrots, green pepper, orange and raisins. Add dressing, mixing well. Chill. Top with chopped nuts before serving.

Makes 6 servings

1 serving (1/2 cup) = 1 simple carbohydrate

2 large apples, cut into chunks
1/2 cup unsweetened pineapple chunks
1/2 stalk celery, chopped
1/2 cup carrots, sliced
1 green pepper, sliced
1 small orange, peeled and sectioned
1/4 cup raisins
1-1/4 cups Orange Yogurt Dressing (recipe on page 81)
1/4 cup walnuts, chopped

FRESH CARROT SALAD

1 pound carrots, coarsely grated
2 medium apples, grated
1 cup nonfat plain yogurt
1/2 cup unsweetened crushed
   pineapple
1/2 cup raisins

Combine all ingredients, mixing well. Chill.

Makes 4 servings

1 serving (1/2 cup) = 1 simple carbohydrate

COLE SLAW WITH A DIFFERENCE

1/4 head red cabbage
1/4 head green cabbage
2 large carrots
8 ounces unsweetened crushed
   pineapple
1/2 cup nonfat plain yogurt
1/2 cup raisins

Grate cabbage and carrots in a food processor or by hand.

Mix pineapple, yogurt and raisins together. Pour over cabbage mixture and stir until well blended.

This may be made far in advance; the flavors will blend together.

Makes 6 servings

1 serving = 1 simple carbohydrate

MARINATED VEGETABLES

zucchini
broccoli
cauliflower
fresh mushrooms
carrots
no-oil Italian salad dressing
Parmesan cheese, grated (optional)

Cut vegetables into bite-size pieces. Marinate in salad dressing for at least an hour. Drain.

May sprinkle with Parmesan cheese before serving.

1 serving (2 cups) = 1 simple carbohydrate

CHILLED BROCCOLI SALAD

Blanch broccoli for 5 minutes in boiling water. Toss with parsley and onions.

Make dressing by blending cottage cheese, mayonnaise, milk, garlic and dill until smooth. Toss with vegetables and chill well.

Makes 8 servings

1 serving = 1 simple carbohydrate and 1 added fat

2 bunches fresh broccoli, trimmed and cut into pieces
1 cup fresh parsley, chopped
2 to 3 green onions, sliced
1/2 cup part-skim or nonfat cottage cheese
1/4 cup light mayonnaise
1/2 cup skim milk
1 clove garlic, minced
3/4 teaspoon dill weed

CRANBERRY SALAD MOLD

Combine orange juice and apple juice in a small bowl. Sprinkle gelatin over juices and let soften for 5 minutes.

While gelatin is softening, combine cranberries and water in a large saucepan. Bring to a boil. Lower the heat and simmer for 5 minutes.

Add gelatin-juice mixture to cranberries. Stir until gelatin is dissolved, about 2 minutes.

Let cool in refrigerator until thickened to consistency of egg whites. Add celery, carrots, raisins and apples; gently mix.

Pour into a 6-cup mold that has been coated with nonstick cooking spray. Refrigerate overnight or until salad is firm.

Makes 12 servings

1 serving = 2 simple carbohydrates

2 envelopes unflavored gelatin
1 cup unsweetened orange juice
1 can (6 ounces) unsweetened apple juice concentrate, undiluted
1 bag (12 ounces) unsweetened cranberries, fresh or frozen
1 cup water
1 cup celery, diced
1 cup carrots, shredded
1/2 cup raisins
1 cup apples, chopped (2 apples)
nonstick cooking spray

DESSERTS:
A NEW WAY

Simply knowing the importance of reducing your daily sugar intake is not enough; you need to know how to do so and still enjoy life! Many dessert recipes that do not need sugar for texture will actually taste better with the amount of sugar reduced. Using honey instead of sugar is not necessarily a healthy substitution; but because of its sweeter taste honey can be used in much smaller amounts without sacrificing sweetness. Concentrated fruit juices, applesauce, crushed pineapple and mashed bananas are excellent substitutes for sugars, and the addition of cinnamon or vanilla will enhance the sweetness of the dessert even more. Given below are recipe modifications that will allow you to omit sugar completely.

Some recipes cannot be modified. But this phase of culinary change begins with knowing when and how to reduce or replace sugar. Keep your eyes open for recipes that call for a low amount of sweetening or omit sugar altogether. Although much information is available for baking with artificial sweeteners, such as aspartame, lean toward desserts that use no sugar or sugar substitutes and are sweetened only with fruit and spices.

Learning to enjoy foods with a lighter touch of sweetness and letting your taste buds change will transform your eating habits. Taste buds *do* change, but it takes time (about eight weeks). Keeping concentrated sweets in your daily, or even weekly, eating pattern will prevent this needed adjustment. It's not easy, but the results are well worth it!

Beware of many recipes that proclaim to be sugar-free. They may be loaded with artificial sweeteners instead, preventing the needed change in your taste buds. Or they might be sugar-free but loaded with saturated fats and calories. Sugar is only *one* of the unhealthy problem ingredients in many desserts; calories and health risks can be just as high, if not higher, without it. For example, you might be able to sweeten a brownie with dates and bananas, but what about the chocolate? Or you might use carob, but what about the white flour? Or you might use whole wheat pastry flour, but what about the fat content of all the nuts and butter? *Many* foods are not worth changing; there's no way to make them healthy. Let your taste buds change and learn what wellness is all about!

No-Sugar Recipe Modification

If your recipe calls for 1 cup of sugar, you can use instead:

• 1/4 to 1/3 cup honey (reduce liquid by 3 tablespoons or add 3 tablespoons flour); reduce baking temperature by 25 degrees;

• 3 mashed bananas plus 1 teaspoon ground cinnamon;

• 1 cup apple juice plus 1/3 cup nonfat dry milk powder as substitute for 1 cup milk in recipe;

• "sweet milk" instead of milk in recipe; sweet milk is 1/4 cup raisins to 1 cup skim or low-fat milk, placed in the refrigerator for 48 hours; drain off and use raisins in another recipe;

• 1/2 cup dried fruit purée (puréed apricots, unsweetened pitted dates, prunes); or

• 1 cup unsweetened applesauce or crushed pineapple with 1 teaspoon ground cinnamon.

Cookies and More

Peanutsy Surprise Cupcakes

1/2 cup old-fashioned oats, uncooked
3/4 cup water, boiling
1/4 cup canola oil
1/4 cup honey
2 egg whites
1/2 teaspoon vanilla
2 ripe bananas
1 cup whole wheat pastry flour
1/2 teaspoon baking soda
1 teaspoon ground cinnamon
1/2 teaspoon ground allspice
1/8 teaspoon salt
2 ounces light cream cheese
3 tablespoons natural peanut butter
1 tablespoon honey

Preheat oven to 375 degrees.

Combine oats and boiling water in a small bowl, stirring well; set aside and let cool.

Cream together oil and honey, beating well on medium speed of an electric mixer. Add egg whites and vanilla, beating well. Add bananas and beat until smooth; set mixture aside.

In a separate bowl combine flour, baking soda, cinnamon, allspice and salt.

Add half of the flour mixture to the creamed mixture and stir until well mixed. Add half of the oatmeal mixture, stirring until well mixed. Add the remaining flour mixture, mixing well. Add the remaining oatmeal mixture, mixing well; set aside.

Combine the cream cheese, peanut butter and honey in a small bowl.

Spoon 1 tablespoon of the cupcake batter into each of 12 paper-lined muffin cups. Spoon 2 teaspoons of the peanut butter mixture into each muffin cup. Fill each cup two-thirds full with remaining batter.

Bake for 20 minutes. Remove cupcakes from pans and let cool on wire racks.

Makes 1 dozen cupcakes

1 cupcake = 1 complex carbohydrate and 1 added fat

Preheat oven to 350 degrees.

Combine flour, raisins, rice, walnuts, baking soda, cinnamon, ginger, nutmeg and allspice in a large mixing bowl; set aside.

In a small bowl beat the eggs; set aside.

In a saucepan heat together oil and honey. Add eggs, buttermilk and orange juice.

Stir liquid mixture into the dry ingredients until thoroughly combined.

Place the batter in an 8 x 8-inch baking dish coated with nonstick cooking spray.

Bake for 30 to 35 minutes or until a knife inserted in the center comes out clean. Cut into 24 bars.

Makes 24 bars

1 serving (2 bars) = 1 complex carbohydrate and 1 added fat

1-1/2 cups whole wheat pastry flour
1 cup raisins
1/2 cup brown rice, cooked
1/2 cup walnuts, chopped
1-1/2 teaspoons baking soda
1-1/2 teaspoons ground cinnamon
1/2 teaspoon ground ginger
1/4 teaspoon ground nutmeg
1/8 teaspoon ground allspice
2 eggs
1/4 cup canola oil
1/3 cup honey
1 cup buttermilk
1 tablespoon orange juice
nonstick cooking spray

APPLE DATE COOKIES

Preheat oven to 350 degrees.

Cream together oil and honey in a medium-sized bowl. Add egg whites and vanilla; beat well on medium speed of electric mixer.

In a separate bowl combine flour, baking soda and allspice.

Gradually add dry mixture to honey mixture, beating well. Stir in oats, apples and dates.

Drop dough by rounded 2-teaspoonful measures 2 inches apart on a cookie sheet coated with nonstick cooking spray.

Bake for 12 to 14 minutes. Remove from cookie sheets and cool completely on wire racks.

Makes 3 dozen cookies

1 serving (two cookies) = 1/2 complex carbohydrate, 1 simple carbohydrate and 1 added fat

1/4 cup canola oil
1/4 cup honey
2 egg whites
1 teaspoon vanilla
1-1/4 cups whole wheat pastry flour
1/2 teaspoon baking soda
1/2 teaspoon ground allspice
3/4 cup old-fashioned oats, uncooked
1/2 cup Golden Delicious apples, grated
1/4 cup unsweetened pitted dates, chopped
nonstick cooking spray

DATE BARS

1 cup whole wheat pastry flour
1/2 cup wheat germ
1 teaspoon baking powder
2 teaspoons ground cinnamon
1/4 teaspoon ground allspice
1 cup unsweetened pitted dates,
    chopped
1/2 cup walnuts, chopped
3 eggs, beaten
1/3 cup honey
1 cup skim milk
1 teaspoon vanilla
nonstick cooking spray

Preheat oven to 350 degrees.

Combine flour, wheat germ, baking powder, cinnamon, allspice, dates and walnuts in a medium-sized bowl; set aside.

Mix the eggs, honey, milk and vanilla in a medium-sized bowl. Fold in the dry ingredients.

Spread the batter in a 9 x 13-inch baking pan coated with nonstick cooking spray.

Bake for about 20 minutes until golden brown.

Makes 24 bars

1 serving (1 bar) = 1 complex carbohydrate, 1 simple carbohydrate and 1 added fat

DRIED FRUIT BALLS

1 cup dried apricots
1/2 cup raisins
1/2 cup prunes
1/2 cup unsweetened pitted dates
1/2 cup unsweetened flaked coconut
1/2 cup pecans or walnuts, chopped
1/2 teaspoon fresh orange peel, grated
juice from 1 orange
1/2 cup additional pecans or walnuts,
    finely chopped

In a blender or food processor grind the apricots, raisins, prunes and dates. Add the coconut, nuts, orange peel and orange juice. Mix well and form into balls. Roll in finely chopped nuts.

Makes 4 dozen balls

1 serving (2 balls) = 1 simple carbohydrate and 1 added fat

Oatmeal Raisin Cookies

Preheat oven to 350 degrees.

Combine all ingredients except 1 cup oats. Mix well. Form into teaspoon-sized balls and roll in reserved oats. Place on a cookie sheet coated with nonstick cooking spray.

Bake for 9 to 11 minutes.

Makes 2 dozen cookies

1 serving (2 cookies) = 1 complex carbohydrate, 1 simple carbohydrate and 1 added fat

3-1/2 cups old-fashioned oats, uncooked
1 teaspoon ground cinnamon
1/2 teaspoon salt (optional)
4 bananas, mashed
1 teaspoon vanilla
1-1/2 cups whole wheat pastry flour
1/2 teaspoon baking soda
1/3 cup honey
1/3 cup canola oil
1 egg
1/2 cup raisins
1/2 cup walnuts, chopped
nonstick cooking spray

Cake Alternative

Prepare a fruit bread. Pour into paper liners in a muffin pan or bake in flat-bottomed ice cream cones. Frost with Icing With Style. This is perfect for children's — or adults' — birthday parties!

fruit bread (recipes on pages 176-177)
flat-bottomed ice cream cones (optional)
Icing With Style (recipe below)

Icing With Style

Blend cream cheese, dates and walnuts. Thin with milk to proper consistency.

Makes 3/4 cup

3 ounces light cream cheese
1/2 cup unsweetened pitted dates, chopped
1/4 cup walnuts chopped
skim milk

Icing Alternative

Place a doily on a loaf of fruit bread. Sprinkle with dry milk powder. Lift doily for a safe and pretty pattern design.

nonfat dry milk powder
doily

PIES AND PUDDINGS

OATMEAL COOKIE CRUST

2 tablespoons butter
1/4 cup honey
1-1/2 cups old-fashioned oats,
   uncooked
1/4 cup sesame seeds
1/2 cup whole wheat pastry flour
1/2 teaspoon salt
1 teaspoon ground cinnamon
1/4 cup walnuts, finely minced
1/2 teaspoon vanilla

In a small saucepan melt butter and honey together; set aside.

In a bowl combine oats, sesame seeds, whole wheat flour, salt, cinnamon, nuts and vanilla. Add butter-honey mixture, stirring until well mixed.

Press crust firmly and evenly into the bottom and around the sides of a 9- or 10-inch pie pan.

Makes 1 pie crust.

1 serving (1/8 pie crust) = 1 complex carbohydrate and 1 added fat

RAISIN PIE

Preheat oven to 350 degrees.

Make Oatmeal Cookie Crust.

Boil raisins in 2 cups of water for 5 minutes.

Combine cornstarch and cold water; add to raisins and boil for 1 additional minute until thick. Add orange peel, orange juice, walnuts and salt.

Pour into pie shell. Bake for 30 minutes.

Makes 8 servings

1 serving = 1 complex carbohydrate, 2 simple carbohydrated and 1 added fat

Oatmeal Cookie Crust (recipe on page 202)
1 box (15-1/2 ounces) raisins
2 cups water
2 tablespoons cornstarch
1/2 cup cold water
2 teaspoons fresh orange peel, grated
2 tablespoons orange juice
1/4 cup walnuts, chopped
1/4 teaspoon salt

FRESH FRUIT PIE

Preheat oven to 325 degrees.

Toss coconut and egg whites together and press into a pie pan. Bake for 10 minutes; cool.

In a saucepan mix the pineapple and cornstarch and cook over medium heat until thickened.

Layer the bananas, strawberries and pineapple mixture into the pie shell. Sprinkle with coconut and strawberries to garnish. Chill for 3 hours.

Makes 8 servings

1 serving = 1 simple carbohydrate and 1 added fat

1-1/2 cups unsweetened flaked coconut
2 egg whites, lightly beaten
1 can (20 ounces) unsweetened crushed pineapple with juice
1 tablespoon cornstarch
2 bananas, sliced in orange juice and drained
1 pint fresh strawberries, sliced (or kiwi or papaya)
unsweetened flaked coconut to garnish
additional strawberry slices to garnish

CHILLED PEACH PIE

10 ounces fruit-juice sweetened
    graham crackers, crumbed
1 tablespoon canola oil
6 ounces peach nectar
1 envelope unflavored gelatin
1/3 cup frozen unsweetened orange
    juice concentrate, undiluted
1/4 teaspoon vanilla
drop of almond extract
8 ounces nonfat plain yogurt
1 pound peaches, peeled, pitted and
    sliced

Combine graham cracker crumbs and oil; press mixture into a 9-inch pie pan. Place in freezer while preparing filling.

Place peach nectar in a small saucepan, sprinkling the gelatin over the top; let mixture stand a few minutes to soften the gelatin. Heat and stir the mixture until gelatin is dissolved. Stir in the orange juice concentrate, vanilla and almond extract; set the mixture in the refrigerator until it has chilled to the consistency of raw egg whites.

Whip the mixture until it is fluffy. Stir in the yogurt; whip the mixture again.

Arrange half the peach slices on the bottom of the chilled crust. Pour in two-thirds of the yogurt mixture. Arrange another layer of peach slices on top of this and top with the remainder of the yogurt mixture.

Chill the pie until firm; garnish with additional fresh peach slices if desired.

Makes 8 servings

1 serving = 1/2 complex carbohydrate and 1 simple carbohydrate

APPLE-DATE BREAD PUDDING

3 slices whole wheat bread, cubed
6 unsweetened pitted dates, chopped
3 small apples, peeled and chopped
1/4 cup unsweetened apple juice
2 large eggs
3/4 cup skim milk
1/4 teaspoon ground cinnamon
1 teaspoon vanilla
nonstick cooking spray

Preheat oven to 350 degrees.

Sprinkle bread cubes and dates into a square pan coated with non-stick cooking spray. Sprinkle with chopped apples; set aside.

Beat together apple juice, eggs, milk, cinnamon and vanilla until smooth; pour over bread and fruit mixture in pan.

Bake for 30 minutes. Press apples down into custard with spatula and bake an additional 20 minutes until custard is set.

Serve warm or cold with fresh fruit or applesauce.

Makes 6 servings

1 serving = 1 complex carbohydrate and 1 simple carbohydrate

STRAWBERRY-PINEAPPLE YOGURT PIE

Preheat oven to 325 degrees.

In a mixing bowl toss coconut with egg whites. Press on the bottom and up the sides of a 9-inch pie plate.

Bake for 10 to 15 minutes until golden; cool.

Drain the pineapple, reserving the juice; set pineapple aside.

Add water, if necessary, to reserved juice to make 3/4 cup liquid. In a saucepan sprinkle the gelatin over the juice mixture. Heat and stir until the gelatin dissolves; chill until partially set (should be the consistency of unbeaten egg whites). Whip partially set gelatin with electric mixer until fluffy.

Set aside 1/3 cup of drained pineapple.

Fold yogurt, remaining pineapple, strawberries, banana and honey into gelatin mixture.

Pour into cooled crust. Chill until firm. Top with reserved pineapple just before serving.

Makes 8 servings

1 serving = 1/2 complex carbohydrate, 1 simple carbohydrate and 2 added fats

1-1/3 cups unsweetened flaked coconut
2 egg whites, lightly beaten
1 can (20 ounces) unsweetened crushed pineapple
1 envelope unflavored gelatin
1-1/2 cups nonfat plain yogurt
1 cup fresh strawberries, sliced
1 cup ripe banana, mashed
3 tablespoons honey

APPLESAUCE PUDDING

Preheat oven to 350 degrees.

In a medium-sized bowl beat applesauce, eggs, cinnamon, nutmeg and milk powder. Stir in raisins.

Pour into a baking dish coated with nonstick cooking spray.

Place baking dish on a baking sheet and bake for 45 to 50 minutes until knife inserted in center comes out clean.

Makes 8 servings

1 serving = 1 simple carbohydrate

3 cups unsweetened applesauce
2 large eggs
1/2 teaspoon ground cinnamon
1/4 teaspoon ground nutmeg
1/3 cup nonfat dry milk powder
3 tablespoons golden raisins
nonstick cooking spray

CHILLED DELIGHTS

FRESHLY FRUITED DESSERTS

natural serving containers:
    1/2 of pineapple, including top
      leaves, or
    1/2 of cantaloupe, with seeds and
      some melon scooped out, or
    large orange, with top sliced off and
      pulp scooped out, or
    bibb lettuce leaves
variety of fresh fruit

Any combination of fruit will do to fill fruit containers. Cut fruit into distinct pieces to allow distinct flavor of each piece. Remember that a variety of colors and textures makes a more interesting salad. Melon and citrus always make a good backdrop; add peaches, nectarines or plums for sweetness; add apples or pears for texture; add berries or cherries for a splash of color; add bananas for a garnish.

1/2 cup fruit salad = 1 simple carbohydrate

SPICY APPLESAUCE

10 large cooking apples (4 ounces
    each)
1 cup unsweetened apple juice
1/4 teaspoon ground cloves
1/4 teaspoon ground nutmeg
1-1/2 teaspoons ground cinnamon
1/4 teaspoon ground allspice

Peel, core and quarter apples. Combine with apple juice, cloves, nutmeg, cinnamon and allspice in a large pan.

Cook over low heat for 25 to 30 minutes until apples are tender, stirring frequently.

Process in a blender or food processor at high speed for 10 seconds until smooth.

Spoon into jars. Refrigerate.

Makes 3 pints

1 serving (1/2 cup) = 1 simple carbohydrate

VANILLA POACHED PEARS

Combine apple juice, vanilla and water.

Peel pears, leaving stem if desired. Insert apple corer in blossom end of each pear and carefully remove core.

Place pears in juice mixture; turn to coat. Bring to a boil; reduce heat. Cover and simmer for 5 to 10 minutes, turning often. Reserve 2 tablespoons of liquid. Cover and chill pears in remaining liquid.

Make topping by combining cottage cheese, yogurt and reserved fruit liquid in a blender. Cover and blend until smooth. Place in a storage container, cover and chill until cool.

Serve each pear with 1 tablespoon of topping.

Makes 4 servings

1 serving = 1 simple carbohydrate

2/3 cup unsweetened apple juice
2 teaspoons vanilla
1/3 cup water
4 pears
1/4 cup part-skim or nonfat cottage cheese
1 tablespoon nonfat plain yogurt

RASPBERRY PRUNES

Combine prunes and wine or grape juice; cover and let stand at room temperature for 8 hours.

Process raspberries in a food processor or blender; strain, discarding the seeds.

Add raspberry pulp and orange slices to prune mixture. Stir gently. Cover and chill for 2 to 3 hours.

Serve in stemmed glasses.

Makes 8 servings

1 serving = 1/2 complex carbohydrate and 1 simple carbohydrate

1 package (12 ounces) pitted prunes
1 cup Chablis or other white wine or unsweetened white grape juice
1 package (10 ounces) frozen unsweetened raspberries, thawed
1 medium orange, peeled and thinly sliced

APPLE CHUNK-N-FLUFF

1 envelope unflavored gelatin
3/4 cup water
1/2 teaspoon ground cinnamon
1 teaspoon ground nutmeg
1-1/4 cup unsweetened apple juice
1 medium apple, chopped

Sprinkle gelatin over water in a saucepan. Heat over medium heat, stirring until gelatin dissolves, about 3 minutes. Remove from heat; stir in cinnamon and nutmeg; set aside.

Pour apple juice into a large bowl; add gelatin mixture. Chill in refrigerator until slightly thickened, about 40 to 45 minutes.

Beat until light and fluffy. Stir in apple. Chill again until thickened.

Makes 6 servings

1 serving = 1 simple carbohydrate

Great for children!

APRICOT-BANANA SURPRISE

1 can (16 ounces) unsweetened apricot
  halves, drained
3 small ripe bananas, 2 cut into 1-inch
  chunks and 1 mashed
2 tablespoons honey
2 tablespoons lemon juice
2 large egg whites
dash of salt

Process apricots, chunked bananas, honey and lemon juice in a blender or food processor until smooth.

In the small bowl of an electric mixer, beat egg whites and salt at high speed until soft peaks form when beaters are lifted. Add mashed banana and beat 1 to 2 minutes longer until stiff peaks form. Gently fold into puréed fruit.

Pour into 6 parfait glasses or dessert dishes. Chill for 1 hour or overnight.

Makes 6 servings

1 serving = 1 simple carbohydrate

RICOTTA CHERRY MOUSSE

1 pound part-skim or nonfat ricotta
  cheese
2 tablespoons honey
2 teaspoons fresh orange peel, grated
few drops of almond extract
1/2 teaspoon vanilla
2 cups fresh dark cherries, pitted
2 ounces slivered almonds, toasted

Whip the ricotta cheese at high speed for about 5 minutes. Gradually add the honey and keep beating until it is well-blended. Mix in the orange peel, almond extract and vanilla. Fold in the cherries.

Pour into parfait glasses and chill. Top with slivered almonds.

Makes 6 servings

1 serving = 1 protein and 1 simple carbohydrate

In a saucepan sprinkle gelatin over milk; cook over medium heat, stirring until gelatin is dissolved; set aside.

Separate egg whites from egg yolks; gently beat yolks. Slowly stir half of the hot mixture into the beaten yolks; return all to saucepan. Cook and stir over medium heat for 1 to 2 minutes or until slightly thickened.

Remove from heat. Blend in honey and peanut butter. Stir in the dates and vanilla. Chill until partially set.

Beat egg whites until stiff peaks form; fold in the gelatin mixture.

Spoon into 6 dessert glasses or custard cups. Chill until firm. Garnish each with additional snipped dates, if desired.

Makes 6 servings

1 serving = 1 protein, 1 simple carbohydrate and 1/2 added fat

1/2 envelope unflavored gelatin
1-1/2 cups skim milk
2 eggs
3 tablespoons honey
1 tablespoon natural peanut butter
1/3 cup unsweetened pitted dates, snipped
1 teaspoon vanilla
additional dates, snipped

In a saucepan sprinkle gelatin over water. Cook over medium heat and stir until dissolved. Stir in milk, honey and orange juice concentrate until blended.

Pour into a square baking pan that has been coated with nonstick cooking spray. Chill until firm, about 1-1/2 hours.

Cut into 1-inch cubes. Serve stacked in sherbet dishes.

Makes 6 dozen cubes

1 serving (4 cubes) = 1 simple carbohydrate

Great for kids!

3 envelopes unflavored gelatin
1 cup water
1 cup evaporated skim milk
1/4 cup honey
1 can (6 ounces) frozen unsweetened orange juice concentrate, undiluted
nonstick cooking spray

FROZEN TREATS

FROZEN FRUIT SALAD

1 can (8 ounces) unsweetened crushed pineapple
3/4 cup part-skim or nonfat cottage cheese
4 tablespoons frozen unsweetened orange juice concentrate, undiluted
1 cup ripe banana, mashed
1/2 teaspoon vanilla
1-1/4 cups nonfat plain yogurt
1 tablespoon lemon juice
2 fresh peaches, peeled and sliced
1 cup fresh strawberries, sliced
1/2 cup fresh blueberries

Drain pineapple, reserving juice.

In a blender combine cottage cheese, orange juice concentrate, mashed banana, vanilla, yogurt, lemon juice and reserved pineapple juice; blend well.

Layer peaches, pineapple, strawberries and blueberries in a 2-quart dish. Pour yogurt mixture over fruits. Freeze until firm. Allow to thaw slightly before serving.

Slice into small wedges and place on a serving platter.

Makes 12 servings

1 serving (1 wedge) = 1 simple carbohydrate

May use frozen unsweetened fruit for a quick dessert.

STRAWBERRY-BANANA SHERBET

Cut bananas into chunks. Combine bananas, milk, honey and vanilla in a blender or food processor. Process until smooth.

Add strawberries to mixture one at a time while processor is still running. Blend until smooth.

Serve immediately, garnished with sliced strawberries and a few banana slices, if desired.

Makes 4 servings

1 serving = 2 simple carbohydrates

2 small ripe bananas, peeled and
   frozen
1/2 cup evaporated skim milk
1/2 teaspoon vanilla
2 tablespoons honey
1 cup frozen unsweetened whole
   strawberries
additional strawberry and banana
   slices to garnish

RASPBERRY FREEZE

In a blender or food processor combine all ingredients. Cover and blend until fluffy.

Pour into a 9 x 9 x 2-inch pan. Freeze until firm.

Break up mixture with a fork and place in a chilled mixing bowl. Beat with electric mixer until fluffy and return to pan. Cover and freeze for 2 hours.

Serve scoops in dessert bowls.

Makes 8 servings

1 serving = 1/2 complex carbohydrate and 1 simple carbohydrate

1 package (10 ounces) frozen
   unsweetened red raspberries
2 cups buttermilk
1/2 teaspoon vanilla
1/3 cup honey
1 teaspoon fresh lemon peel, grated
2 tablespoons frozen unsweetened
   apple juice concentrate, undiluted

WARM DESSERTS

BAKED AMBROSIA

3 large seedless oranges
1/4 cup unsweetened pitted dates,
   chopped
1/4 cup walnuts or pecans, chopped
3 tablespoons unsweetened flaked
   coconut
1/2 cup nonfat plain yogurt
1/2 teaspoon vanilla extract

Preheat oven to 350 degrees.

Cut oranges in half crosswise. Clip membranes and carefully remove pulp (do not puncture bottom); set orange shells aside.

Chop orange pulp. Combine orange pulp, dates, chopped nuts and 2 tablespoons of coconut. Spoon orange mixture into orange shells and place in a 12 x 8 x 2-inch baking dish.

Bake for 25 minutes.

Combine yogurt and vanilla; divide mixture over tops of oranges. Sprinkle tops with remaining 1 tablespoon of coconut. Serve immediately.

Makes 6 servings

1 serving = 1 simple carbohydrate and 1 added fat

Drain peaches, reserving juice; set aside.

Combine cornstarch, nutmeg, whole cloves, ground cloves, cinnamon and orange juice in a medium saucepan; stir in reserved peach juice, mixing well. Add peaches and bring to a boil, stirring constantly. Reduce heat and simmer for 2 minutes.

Serve warm.

Makes 2 servings

1 serving = 1 simple carbohydrate

1 can (16 ounces) peach halves in unsweetened juice
1/2 teaspoon cornstarch
dash of ground nutmeg
1/4 teaspoon whole cloves
dash of ground cloves
1/8 teaspoon ground cinnamon
1 tablespoon frozen orange juice concentrate, undiluted

POACHED PEARS IN ORANGE SAUCE

Peel and core pears from bottom, leaving stem end intact.

Combine orange juice, lemon peel, lemon juice, cinnamon and cloves in a large pan; bring to a boil. Place pears in juice mixture, stem end up, spooning juices over pears. Reduce heat; cover and simmer for 10 to 15 minutes until pears are tender.

Make a paste from the arrowroot (or cornstarch) and cold water.

Remove pears from pan and add paste to juice mixture, stirring constantly until thickened.

Pour orange sauce over pears. Garnish with lemon peel strips and fresh mint leaves.

Makes 8 servings

1 serving = 1 simple carbohydrate

8 pears
10 ounces unsweetened orange juice
1/2 teaspoon fresh lemon peel, grated
1 ounce lemon juice
1/2 teaspoon ground cinnamon
3 whole cloves
1 teaspoon arrowroot (or 2 teaspoons cornstarch)
2 ounces cold water
lemon peel strips
fresh mint leaves

APPLE CRISPY

10 medium cooking apples
juice of 1 lemon
3/4 cup raisins
3 tablespoons canola oil
3 tablespoons honey
1 cup old-fashioned oats, uncooked
1/2 teaspoon ground allspice
1 teaspoon ground cinnamon
1/4 teaspoon salt
2 tablespoons walnuts, chopped
2 tablespoons sunflower kernels
1/3 cup whole wheat pastry flour
1/2 cup unsweetened apple juice

Preheat oven to 375 degrees.

Pare and slice apples; drizzle with fresh lemon juice. Spread half into a large rectangular pan. Top with raisins; set aside.

Heat together the oil and honey. Add oats, allspice, cinnamon, salt, walnuts, sunflower kernels and flour.

Crumble half of this mixture onto the apples in the pan. Cover with remaining apples and the rest of the topping. Pour apple juice over the top.

Bake uncovered for 40 to 45 minutes.

Makes 10 servings

1 serving = 1/2 complex carbohydrate, 1 simple carbohydrate and 1 added fat

Also good with peaches and pears; reduce baking time to 25 minutes.

PEAR-ALMOND TORTILLA TART

1 large flour tortilla (10-inch
    diameter), preferably whole wheat,
    brushed lightly with honey
2 ounces almonds, minced
1 tablespoon honey
2 egg whites, lightly beaten
3 medium fresh pears, peeled, cored
    and sliced
lemon juice
1 ounce slivered almonds, blanched
3 ounces all-fruit apricot preserves

Preheat oven to 375 degrees.

Bake flour tortilla about 5 to 6 minutes until brown and crispy. Remove tortilla and increase oven temperature to 400 degrees.

Combine almonds, honey and egg whites, stirring well. Spread almond mixture over tortilla.

Dip sliced pears in lemon juice to prevent darkening. Arrange pear slices over almond mixture, letting slices fan out slightly. Sprinkle with slivered almonds.

Bake until golden brown.

Melt apricot preserves over low heat. Carefully brush jam over tart.

Makes 4 servings

1 serving = 1/2 complex carbohydrate and 1 simple carbohydrate

RECIPE INDEX

Other Books and Tapes by Pamela M. Smith, R.D.

Alive and Well in the Fast Lane!

A lighthearted and informative nutrition guidebook for the whole family. This book presents the Ten Commandments of Good Nutrition in a fun, handwritten, illustrated format. Includes menus for perfect breakfasts, lunches and dinners for the busy family, as well as meal plans. Coauthored with Carolyn Coats.

Perfectly Pregnant

This handbook for expectant mothers gives the latest information to nourish mother and baby properly. Included is a wonderful, proven solution for morning sickness. Handwritten. Tasty recipes too! Coauthored with Carolyn Coats.

Come Cook With Me

The cookbook for kids! A wonderful way to teach children nutrition by teaching them how to cook. Great for picky eaters. Includes kid-proven recipes, how to set a table and some great manners. Featured nationally on network and cable television. Handwritten and fun. Coauthored with Carolyn Coats.

The Food Trap

As she explores our relationship with food, Pamela Smith asks: Is the refrigerator light the light of your life? Informative and enlightening, this book reveals case studies and personal insights into the physical, emotional and spiritual aspects of food dependencies. Learn how to break free in all areas.

The Food Trap Seminar

In this audio tape album from a live seminar, Pamela Smith discusses our physical, emotional and spiritual needs and how to meet and nourish these needs properly. She also presents a nutritional strategy for dealing with stress. Very practical and informative.

Audio tapes are also available on numerous nutrition and health topics.

For more information on books, tapes and seminars, please write or call:

Pamela M. Smith, R.D.		Creation House
P.O. Box 541009	or	600 Rinehart Road
Orlando, FL 32854		Lake Mary, FL 32746
(407) 896-1179		1-800-451-4598

Special Offer

by Pamela M. Smith, R.D.

"Nutrition Principles"
Audio Cassette Tape

Free!!

For a free copy of Pamela Smith's audio cassette tape
on nutrition principles, please complete and mail the following
coupon (plus $2.00 to cover postage and handling).

Please send me a free copy of "Nutrition Principles" by Pamela Smith.
I have enclosed $2.00 to cover postage and handling.

Name:_____

Address:_____

City: _____ State:_____ ZIP Code: _____

Send coupon and money to:
Pamela M. Smith, R.D. • P.O. Box 541009 • Orlando, FL 32854